797,885 Books

are available to read at

Forgotten Books

www.ForgottenBooks.com

Forgotten Books' App
Available for mobile, tablet & eReader

ISBN 978-1-331-99707-8
PIBN 10265265

This book is a reproduction of an important historical work. Forgotten Books uses state-of-the-art technology to digitally reconstruct the work, preserving the original format whilst repairing imperfections present in the aged copy. In rare cases, an imperfection in the original, such as a blemish or missing page, may be replicated in our edition. We do, however, repair the vast majority of imperfections successfully; any imperfections that remain are intentionally left to preserve the state of such historical works.

Forgotten Books is a registered trademark of FB &c Ltd.
Copyright © 2015 FB &c Ltd.
FB &c Ltd, Dalton House, 60 Windsor Avenue, London, SW19 2RR.
Company number 08720141. Registered in England and Wales.

For support please visit www.forgottenbooks.com

1 MONTH OF FREE READING

at

www.ForgottenBooks.com

By purchasing this book you are eligible for one month membership to ForgottenBooks.com, giving you unlimited access to our entire collection of over 700,000 titles via our web site and mobile apps.

To claim your free month visit:
www.forgottenbooks.com/free265265

* Offer is valid for 45 days from date of purchase. Terms and conditions apply.

Similar Books Are Available from
www.forgottenbooks.com

Beautiful Joe
An Autobiography, by Marshall Saunders

Theodore Roosevelt, an Autobiography
by Theodore Roosevelt

Napoleon
A Biographical Study, by Max Lenz

Up from Slavery
An Autobiography, by Booker T. Washington

Gotama Buddha
A Biography, Based on the Canonical Books of the Theravādin, by Kenneth J. Saunders

Plato's Biography of Socrates
by A. E. Taylor

Cicero
A Biography, by Torsten Petersson

Madam Guyon
An Autobiography, by Jeanne Marie Bouvier De La Motte Guyon

The Writings of Thomas Jefferson
by Thomas Jefferson

Thomas Skinner, M.D.
A Biographical Sketch, by John H. Clarke

Saint Thomas Aquinas of the Order of Preachers (1225-1274)
A Biographical Study of the Angelic Doctor, by Placid Conway

Recollections of the Rev. John Johnson and His Home
An Autobiography, by Susannah Johnson

Biographical Sketches in Cornwall, Vol. 1 of 3
by R. Polwhele

Autobiography of John Francis Hylan, Mayor of New York
by John Francis Hylan

The Autobiography of Benjamin Franklin
The Unmutilated and Correct Version, by Benjamin Franklin

James Mill
A Biography, by Alexander Bain

George Washington
An Historical Biography, by Horace E. Scudder

Florence Nightingale
A Biography, by Irene Cooper Willis

Marse Henry
An Autobiography, by Henry Watterson

Autobiography and Poems
by Charlotte E. Linden

The Annals

OF

COGGESHALL,

OTHERWISE SUNNEDON,

IN THE COUNTY OF ESSEX.

BY

BRYAN DALE, M.A.

"THINGS ARE NOT TO BE VALUED ON ACCOUNT OF PLACES, BUT PLACES FOR THE GOOD THINGS THEY CONTAIN."

BEDE.

COGGESHALL:
A. H. COVENTRY, MARKET END.

LONDON:
JOHN RUSSELL SMITH, 36 SOHO SQUARE.

1863.

Gift of William Endicott, Jr.

" There be of them that have left a name behind them;
That their praises might be reported:
And some there be which have no memorial;
Who are perished as though they had never been;
And are become as though they had never been born;
And their children after them."

ECCL. XLIV. 8, 9.

A. H. COVENTRY, PRINTER, MARKET END, COGGESHALL.

PREFACE.

I HAVE arranged in the following pages such materials as have been collected during a short period of investigation, and added only a few connecting links. The result in every work of the kind bears little proportion to the labor bestowed upon it; and in order to write a complete parish history one should understand all mysteries and all knowledge. Much more remains to be obtained from sources which I have partially, or not at all examined; and the reader will doubtless observe inaccuracies in statements of fact and modes of expression: but I prefer to issue now what is here collected, however imperfect, to delay with the chance of its being altogether laid aside. Some things will probably be new to most readers, and afford a glimpse of men who lived long ago, and 'the times that went over them.' If space permitted, I should have extended considerably the particulars relating to religious and ecclesiastical matters, which are frequently ignored in parish histories; but I have refrained from unnecessarily obtruding my opinions to the offence of others. Adopting the language of one of my predecessors, a silenced Nonconformist, "I row but in a small boat, and liking the valleys hope to escape the blasts of proud envy. Nevertheless, 'tis man's duty *sui sæculi felicitatem et infelicitatem sapere*—to take some cognizance of the good or evil of the days he lives in:" nor will it be doubtful, even from these pages, who are likely to speak without hesitancy, when freedom of inquiry, the individuality of religious conviction, and union for the attainment of the great aims of Christianity, are subjects discussed afresh.

I have to thank Mr. A. J. Dunkin of Dartford, for his kind assistance in several ways; and only regret the loss of his copy of documents relating to Coggeshall made a few years ago, which would have rendered most of my labor unnecessary. Robert Hills, Esq., of Colne Park, courteously allowed me to make use of a manuscript written by Mr. Holman, from among his valuable collections. To several other gentlemen also my thanks are due: chiefly to the Rev. T. W. Davids of Colchester, whose History of Evangelical Nonconformity in Essex, now in the press, will be a noble contribution to the History of the County.

COGGESHALL, 31*st December*, 1862.

CONTENTS.

CHAPTER I.
NAME AND DESCRIPTION OF THE TOWN.
Page 1

CHAPTER II.
TRACES OF ROMAN OCCUPATION.
Queen Boadicea—Roman Dominion—Opinions of Antiquaries—Canonium—Existing Remains ... ...

CHAPTER III.
SAXON AND NORMAN POSSESSORS.
The Saxons—Godwin's Gift of Coggeshael to the monks of Canterbury—Colo—Eustace, earl of Boulogne—Domesday Book—The Priest... 15

CHAPTER IV.
THE ABBEY.
Foundation by Queen Matilda—Cistercian Order of Monks—The Abbots: William, Simon de Toni, Odo, Peter, Thomas, Ralph and his Chronicles, (John Godard), Benedict, Geoffry, William Joldayn, John Taseler, Simon Pabenham, John Sampford, William Love, Henry More—Patrons and Possessions: Henry II. confirmation, William Fillol, Robert Hovel—Richard I. freedom from toll—King John, licence to enclose wood—Henry III., free warren, a fair, market, enclosure of woods and heaths—Ralph de Coggeshall—Herbert de Markshall—Edward I., licence and confirmation, Taxation—Edward II., confirmation—Edward III., chantry and pipe of red wine, William de Humberstane—Richard II., Roger Ketterich and Adam Cook—Henry IV., Countess of Hereford and others, Tiptree Heath, Henry Bourchier, earl of Essex, John de Vere, earl of Oxford, Extracts from the Manor Rolls—The Dissolution—Condition of the Abbey—Surrender and Seal ... 23

CHAPTER V.
ABBEY LANDS, ETC.

Grant to Sir Thomas Seymour—Site of the Monastery and Abbey Farm—St. Nicholas' Chapel and the Parish of Little Coggeshall—Rectory of Great and Little Coggeshall and Vicarage of Little Coggeshall—Manors of Great and Little Coggeshall—Home Grange, Curdhall and Capons—Manor of Little Coggeshall Hall—Bourchier's Grange—Holfield Grange—Hovels—Monkdowns—Other Lands and Tenements—Bridges 65

CHAPTER VI.
THE PARISH CHURCH.

Endowment of the Vicarage of Sunnedon—General Description of the Church—Funeral Monuments—Chantries: Countess of Hereford, Thomas Paycocke—Certificate of Lands—The Parish Register ... 92

CHAPTER VII.
ROMAN CATHOLICS AND THE REFORMATION.

Roman Catholic Vicars—Times of Reformation—Image of the Crucifix destroyed—Court of the Archdeacon—The Martyrs: Thomas Haukes; Thomas Osmond, William Butler, Nicholas Chamberlain and others: William Flower, Christian Pepper and Cicely Warren—Mrs. Honywood 121

CHAPTER VIII.
ANGLICANS AND PURITANS.

Early Puritanism, &c.—Laurence Newman and William Dyke suspended—Lord Rich—John Jegon, Thomas Jegon, Thomas Stoughton, Ralph Cudworth, John Heyley, John Dodd—Brownists—Presbyterians and Independents: Obadiah Sedgwick—Sir Thomas Honywood, Jeremy Aylett, Robert Crane, William Tanner—John Owen—Constantine Jessop—John Sames—James Parnell the Quaker 145

CHAPTER IX.
CONFORMITY.

Thomas Jessop—James Boys—Gilbert Burnet—Joseph Gulliver—Henry du Cane—John Duddell—John Bull—Richard Mant—E. W. Mathew—H. Stephens—Percy Smith—A. C. J. Wallace—H. Eley—W. J. Dampier (John Carter) 176

CHAPTER X.

NONCONFORMITY.

Ejected and silenced Ministers; John Sames, Thomas Lowry, Matthew Ellistone, William Grove, Thomas Millaway, Thomas Browning, Robert Gouge (Isaac Hubbard)—Independent Chapel: Edward Bentley, (Isaac Buxton), John Farmer, N. Humphrey, H. Peyto, (Registers), M. Andrews, (Sunday Schools), J. Fielding, A. Wells, J. Kay, B. Dale —The Society of Friends—Baptists—Wesleyans 187

CHAPTER XI.

THE CLOTHING TRADE.

Early History—Edward III. tax on wool—Act of Parliament—Coggeshall Whites—Tradesmen's Tokens—The Guild 229

CHAPTER XII.

PUBLIC CHARITIES.

Paycocke—Hitcham—Guyon—Smith—Gooday—Crane—Hibben—Market Hill—Alms Houses—Land—Richardson—Benevolent Society 238

CHAPTER XIII.

BUFTON'S DIARY.

Page 256

APPENDIX.

Local and Family Name of Coggeshall—Holman's and other Collections for Essex—Records of the Abbey—King Stephen's Charter—King John at Coggeshall—Public Records—John Sewale, Sheriff—Chief Stewards of the Abbey—Ecclesiastical Surveys—Will of John Fabyan —Subsidies—Manor of Coggeshall, &c.—Markshall 277

STEEL-PLATE ILLUSTRATIONS.*

1. The Town of Coggeshall . . . . . *Frontispiece.*

                                                                                            To face page

2. Abbey Farm & Remains of Coggeshall Abbey   22

3. St. Nicholas' Chapel (Coggeshall Abbey) .   72

4. Holfield Grange   86

5. Coggeshall Bridge   90

6. Coggeshall Church   96

7. Markshall and Church   144

8. Independent Chapel   204

9. Hitcham School   244

* For most of these I am indebted to Mr. A. W. Tanner. No. 3, (incorrectly named Coggeshall Abbey), No. 6, (the Church before its restoration) and No. 8, (before the building of enlarged Schoolroom) were taken in 1851.

NAME AND DESCRIPTION OF THE TOWN.

THE town of Coggeshall is about forty-four miles from London. It lies on the ancient line of road which leads direct from Colchester to Braintree, Dunmow, Bishop's Stortford, and St. Alban's, and is situated on the north side of the river Blackwater, Freshwell or Pant, which rises near Wimbish, about four miles from Saffron Walden, flows by Radwinter, Great Bardfield and Bocking, on reaching Coggeshall makes a considerable bend in the direction of Kelvedon, and at Maldon joins the Chelmer and enters the sea. It is built principally on a gentle slope with a southern aspect, a circumstance from which it probably derived its former name of SUNNEDON or SUNNY-BANK, although its present seems to have been likewise its most ancient name.* On its highest elevation stands

---

* "Coggeshall."—It has been ingeniously conjectured that this name was compounded of two Celtic words, Cor or Cau (enclosure,) and Gafael (hold); or otherwise was derived from Coed (wood) and Caer or Gaer (camp) —Coed-Gaer, Cogger=camp in a wood. "The Saxon thane might have occupied the Caer with the house and out-houses, and the rustics would call it Coed-Gaer's Hall, or Coggeshall." *(Monumenta Anglicana.— Coggeshall.—By A. J. Dunkin)* The name is variously spelt in old

the parish church, dedicated to St. Peter, and commanding a pleasant prospect of rich gardens, fields and meadows, adorned with lofty poplars and spreading elms. The projecting beams and carved wood-work of several houses of considerable antiquity appear in the streets, which are placed somewhat irregularly. Church street leads to the Market Hill, an open space in the centre of the town, from which Stoneham (Stanham) or Meeting street leads to Tilkey (or Tile-kiln,) where many cottages have been recently built. East and West streets are on the great level road already mentioned. Bridge-street joins Little Coggeshall or "the Hamlet" by means of the " Short Bridge" over the watercourse forming the division between the parishes of Great and Little Coggeshall, and marking the ancient direction of the river, which flows in an artificial bed, cut for it from a place called "the upper osiers," for the purpose of getting a head of water for the Abbey mill. The river is crossed by a bridge called " Long Bridge," formed of three arches of brick, originally built by King Stephen, whose arms were carved in stone on the middle arch; but the upper works are quite modern. At the top of the hill beyond, a lane on the left-hand passes by an ancient Chapel, and terminates at some farm-buildings which were once part of a Cistercian Abbey.

---

documents:—Gogshall, Goggeshall, Hoggeshall, Cogeshal, Cogeshale, Coggashael, Cogshal, Coxhall, Coxall. Morant thinks the true and original name to have been Cocks-hall, and this seems to be confirmed by the seal of the Abbey. The name of Coggashael occurs as early as 1046; that of Sunnendon or Sunnedon not until two centuries later.

The parish of Great Coggeshall is in the Hundred of Lexden, and contains 2639 acres of land, of which 1730 are arable, 462 meadow and pasture, and 403 wood. Little Coggeshall is in Witham Hundred, and contains 1002 acres, of which 821 are arable and 163 pasture. The number of inhabitants in the former, according to the census of 1861, is 3680; and in the latter, 429. The clothing trade, which formerly flourished here, has vanished long ago; but a silk factory exists; many persons are occupied in velvet-weaving, and several females in working tambour, a kind of lace work. A gelatine factory also employs some hands; others cultivate the garden-fields, in which are produced a variety of garden seeds for the London market, or work on the large farms in these or the adjacent parishes of Markshall, Tey, Feering, Kelvedon, Bradwell and Pattiswick.

In ecclesiastical matters Little Coggeshall is regarded as a peculiar of the see of Canterbury, and subject to the Archbishop's Commissary, the Dean of Bocking. Great Coggeshall was in the diocese of London until 1845, when it was transferred to that of Rochester; and is in the Deanery of Lexden and Archdeaconry of Colchester.

There are in the town, an Independent Chapel, Friends' Meeting-house, Baptist Chapel and Wesleyan Chapel, and three public schools—Sir Robert Hitcham's Charity School, the National and the Congregational. There is also a Mechanics' Institute and a Parochial Library.

4   NAME AND DESCRIPTION OF THE TOWN.

Both the annual fair and weekly market have ceased to be of any importance. The line of railway runs along not far from the old coach-road from Colchester to London, and its nearest station is Kelvedon, distant about two miles and a half. The prosperity of the town does not at present much increase: the following Annals, however, will show that in past time it had its full share of interest and importance.

II.

TRACES OF ROMAN OCCUPATION.

Queen Boadicea.

ABOUT two thousand years ago this neighbourhood, like the greater part of the county of Essex, was covered with forest, and occupied by the old Celtic tribe of the Trinobantes, whose sustenance was principally derived from their numerous flocks and herds, and whose dwellings were wicker or clay huts, enclosed in the midst of woods. It is not unlikely that on some eminence overlooking the river one of their camps existed, and that many of them flocked to the standard of *Queen Boadicea,* when she swept along this road in her war chariot, taking vengeance on the Romans. She was the widow of Prasutagus, king of the Iceni, the tribe inhabiting the district afterwards called Suffolk and Norfolk, who by his will left the emperor Nero co-heir with his daughters, in the hope of procuring protection for his family and people. But this was to leave the sheep in the care of the wolf; and Catus, the governor of Camalodunum (Colchester) the first Roman colony in Britain, immediately seized their possessions and committed outrages which roused the spirit of the people to attempt to cast off the Roman yoke altogether. Under the leadership of the royal widow they marched direct for the colony, from which Catus had fled in terror, and inflicted upon it a terrible retribution. From Camalodunum they came along the ancient road to Verulamium (St. Alban's,) their numbers being continually increased by the accession of the oppressed and enslaved native populations. Having destroyed this city they proceeded to Trinobantum or Londinium (London,) then a place of lesser note, and put its inhabitants to the sword. Suetonius Paulinus, the Roman General, who had abandoned the city to its fate, awaited them at a place called Battle Bridge,* whither they followed and were speedily defeated and slain by thousands. The Queen ended her days by poison.

Roman Dominion.

The whole country was gradually reduced beneath the Roman sway: but, though subject to the imperial authority, several of the native princes retained something of their former dignity, and sometimes attempted to regain their independency. Such was the case at Colchester where Coel II had fixed his seat of government, and was besieged by Constantius Chlorus, who betrothed his daughter Helena, and became father of Constantine the Great, the honor of whose nativity is claimed by that town. Constantius appears to have afforded protection to many of the adherents of the Christian religion, which had been introduced to

---

* Cromwell's History of Colchester, p. 36.

Britain some time before, (about A.D. 160,) when a furious persecution raged against them, in which St. Alban was put to death at Verulamium; nor is it at all improbable that many Christians in this immediate neighbourhood experienced the benefit of this governor's tolerant sway.

During the Roman dominion, large numbers of soldiers occupied the colonies; and great roads over the old British trackways, or newly-made, traversed the country in all directions, on which were fixed numerous military stations. Of these an account is handed down to us in the Itinerary of Antoninus; but it is difficult in all cases either to trace the exact line of the roads, or identify the places situated upon them. In the 9th iter, which is from Norfolk to London, the following are mentioned:—

Ad Ansam to Camalodunum.	vi	thousand paces.
Thence to Canonium	ix	,,
Thence to Cæsaromagus	xii	
Thence to Durolitum .	xvi	,,
Thence to Londinium	xv*	

Opinions of Antiquaries.

Camden (Brittania, translated by Holland, p. 449,) says in reference to the first of these stations—"But in

---

* Richard of Cirencester gives them in a reversed order. Iter iii. From London to Lincoln.

From Durositum to Cæsaromagus	xii.
Thence to Canonium	xv.
Thence to the colony of Camalodunum, where there was the temple of Claudius, a triumphal arch, and an image of the Goddess of Victory	viii.

whatsoever place this AD ANSAM was, I betake myself again to my former opinion for the signification of this word, viz.—that Ad Ansam was either a bound mark or only a resting place, or some inn by the highway side under such a sign, and that I collect by the distance to have been near to Coggeshall. I will here impart what I accidentally happened upon in a private note, while I was inquisitive here about for Ad Ansam. In a place called West Field, three quarters of a mile from Coggeshall, and belonging to the Abbey, there was found, by touching with a plough, a great brazen pot. The ploughman, supposing it to have been hid treasure, sent for the Abbot to see it taken up, and he going thither met with Sir Clement Harleston, and desired him to accompany him thither. The mouth of the pot was closed with a white substance like paste or clay, as hard as burnt brick, and when that was removed another pot enclosed a third, which would hold about a gallon, and this covered with a velvet-like substance fastened with a silken lace: within this were found whole bones and many pieces of small bones wrapped up in fine silk of fresh colour which the abbot took for the relics of some saint and laid up in his vestiary."

Weever, (in his "Funeral Monuments," p. 618,) quoting the above, adds that "more probably it was a Roman urn," and then gives the following account of the finding of other remains:—

"Adjoyning to the Rode called Coccill-way, which to this towne leadeth, was lately found an arched vault of bricke, and therein a burning lampe of glasse covered with a Romane tyle some 14 inches square, and one urne with ashes and bones, besides two sacrificing dishes of smooth and pollished red earth, [paterae of Samian ware,] having the bottome of one of them with faire Romane letters inscribed COCCILIM. I may probably conjecture this to have beene the sepulchrall monument of the Lord of this towne, who lived about the time of Antoninus Pius, (as by the coyne there likewise found appeareth,) the affinitie betweene his and the now townes name being almost one and the same. These remaine in the custody of that judicious great statesman, Sir Richard Weston, knight, Baron Weston of Nealand, Lord Treasurer of England, and of the most honourable Order of the Garter, companion."

Burton, (in his "Commentary on Antoninus," p. 230) agrees with Camden, and refers to the above account of Weever as proof, adding "truly the distance may seem to persuade it, for that the Romans sometime possessed these parts—an Hypogœum or grot with arched work opened not long since by the Road-side is a sufficient argument. There was a lamp yet burning still in a glass vial covered with a Roman tile whose diameter was 14 inches. There were also some urns or crocks which contained in them ashes and bones; amongst them there was one of a polite and most fine substance resembling rather coral than red earth, and had the cover thereof inscribed, COCCILIM, perhaps for *Coccilli M* i. e. *Coccilli Manibus*, (to the manes or shades of Coccilus,) from whom the old town may seem to have received its name, remainders of which seem visibly to continue yet in the present one at this day. Meric Casaubon, son of Isaac, in his most learned notes upon Marcus Antoninus, the Emperor, his books that Sireno-Phœnix of better philosophy procured it to be set forth in this manner, which argues that he had a sight of it." A print of the above mentioned urn is given by Burton.

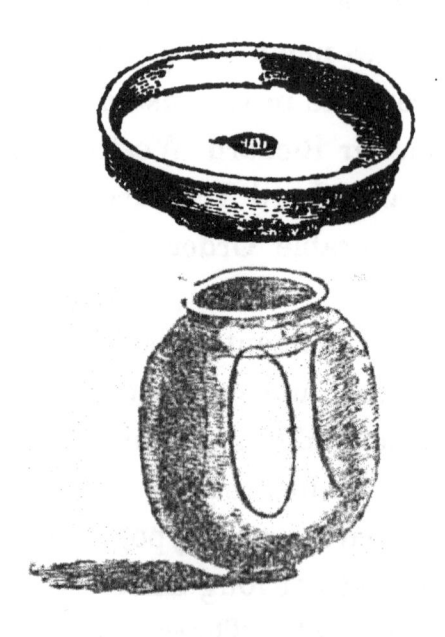

These statements are quoted fully as little other than matters of curiosity. The inscription is only the potter's mark and occurs on many urns of a similar kind found in England and elsewhere;* the so-called lamp of glass was probably a glass vase, into which a lighted lamp may have been placed at first; but an

* Camden by Gough.

ever-burning lamp under such conditions is of course a mere imagination. There can, however, be little doubt that, although we must dismiss the conjecture concerning the derivation of the name of the town, this was the sepulchre of some Roman of importance.

Coggeshall was fixed upon as the site of Ad Ansam on the supposition that Camalodunum was elsewhere than at Colchester; but since it has been generally admitted to have been there, the only station of the itinerary which could have been in this town is CANONIUM. It is 9 miles from Colchester (Camalodunum,) 12 to Dunmow (Cæsaromagus,) thence to Romford (Durolitum) is 16, and thence to London 15 miles. The name of Canonium has been derived by *Baxter* "from Caün or Caünon—reeds, and Iü—a wave or river. The milliaria of Antoninus show this to be Coggeshall among the East Saxons or Gueppones. I think, moreover, that it may have come by another name, the villa of Cocciliüs, whence also it may have been called by the Anglo-Saxons, Coggleshall. This the inscription, adduced in this place by the learned Camden, Gibson's edition, Coccil I M, to wit, to the manes of Coccilius, seems to hint." *Drake* (Archæologia, vol. v., p. 137) has also thus placed Canonium, and argues, from the appearance of the road through Coggeshall, that it was a military way. More recent antiquaries have fixed this station nearer Kelvedon, and Cæsaromagus at Chelmsford, and have supposed that the road through Coggeshall was rather a commercial than a military one.

Existing Remains.

But whether Canonium was at Coggeshall or not, there was certainly here a large Roman village, as the following particulars, in addition to those already enumerated, will show.

In a couple of fields, called Crow Barn and Garden Fields, on the north of the road from Coggeshall to Braintree, at a little distance to the west of the town, several Roman urns have been found deposited, as is usual in sepulchral deposits, on the top of the gravel, about two feet beneath the surface of the soil. Human bones have also been found here; and there occur two plots of soil of some yards square, in each of which was a layer of black ashes, perhaps the traces of funeral pyres. Such remains, scattered over a space of about three acres, seem to indicate that there was here a cemetery of considerable extent.

Roman bricks, fragments of scored and flanged tiles, querns, or stones of hand-mills, and other remains of various kinds, have likewise been found; and in one place there are traces of what might possibly have been a Roman encampment.*

---

* "To the east of this cemetery, with one field intervening, is the park-like field in the front of Highfield-house; an avenue of fine elms extends from Highfield-house to the road, running from north to south; the easternmost row of trees is planted on the edge of an artificial dyke, in the hollow of which runs the drive up to the house. This bank and hollow way have very much the appearance of the agger and ditch of a Roman camp. From the southern extremity of this another very similar ditch runs westward in the direction of the Roman cemetery. There are faint indications of a continuation of this along the western side; and the line of the hedge along the north side would complete a square enclosure of about an acre-and-half in extent. My attention was first called to the eastern and most conspicious of these lines of embankment by hearing it

ROMAN OCCUPATION. 13

But the most satisfactory evidence, perhaps, is the number of coins which have been found from time to time in the town itself, or in its immediate neighbourhood. There are about fifty, of which the following are the most noteworthy.

A *denarius* of Marcus Antoninus (31 B.C.) found at Curd Hall Farm—2nd bronze of Vespasian (A.D. 69-79)—a gold coin of same Emperor lately found at Bradwell, probably struck soon after the destruction of Jerusalem—2nd bronze of Domitian, (81-96)—*denarius* of Julia Domna, wife of Severus—3rd bronze of Victorinus, Claudius Gothicus, Tetricus, Diocletian, (284-305)—Carausius—and several of Constantine (327-337) —in the possession of Mr. Charles Smith.

2nd bronze of Nero (A.D. 54-68), Vespasian, Domitian, Trajan, were possessed by the late Miss Hunt.

3rd bronze of Hadrian (117-138), found in the field in front of Scripp's Farm—of Faustina, wife of Antoninus—in the possession of Rev. E. L. Cutts.

3rd bronze of Claudius Tacitus (275)—Mrs. R. M. White.

2nd bronze of Hadrian, Antoninus, M. Aurelius, Commodus, —3rd bronze of Gallienus, Claudius Gothicus, Magnentius, (350-353), Theodosius (379-395), and Head of Constantinopolis—in the possession of Mr. H. Doubleday.

The dates given above show that the occupation of this place by the Romans continued for several centuries, and ended only with their departure from Britain.

---

spoken of as Roman, but there does not appear to be any general tradition of this kind; and from the way in which the intimation came to me it may have been the echo of the opinion of some previous antiquary."— *Roman Remains at Coggeshall; by Rev. E L. Cutts, B.A.*, a paper read before the Essex Archæological Society, 1855.—From this several of the above particulars are taken.

It may be further added, that a place consisting of two or three cottages, a mile west of the town, is still called Stock *Street*, (Latin, *stratum—a paved way*,) and that when the Blackwater bridge, about a mile and a-half beyond, was repaired some years ago, there were several indications discovered, that a Roman road crossed the river at this point.

These particulars enable us to catch a glimpse of a period long past. Even if there was not here a military station, yet the Roman soldiers often marched along this road to and from the colony and castle at Camalodunum. Here Roman merchants often rested for the night, or tarried for a longer time. Near the river brink stood the villa of some man having authority; and not far off, numerous habitations of a lower class, "who came and tilled the earth and lay beneath." At length they were all gone, and have left as their memorial little more than a few coins or fragments of broken urns.

III.

SAXON AND NORMAN POSSESSORS.

The Saxons.

AFTER the Romans had left the country, the British tribes, enfeebled by long subjection and unable to resist the encroachments of their northern foes, obtained the aid of the Saxons, who, finding themselves the stronger party, and the land well prepared by its former occupants for permanent settlement, drove out the native populations or crushed them into bondage. Essex formed a part of the kingdom of the East Saxons, founded by Erchenwin, son of Offa. Whatever of Christianity existed among the native tribes shared their fate, and the idol-rites of the worshippers of Odin were established in its stead. About the year 596 Augustine was sent by Pope Gregory the Great to convert the Saxons, and came bringing along with him the secular aims, corruptions and intolerance, which had already appeared in the church of Rome. Mellitus was employed as a missionary among the East Saxons, over whom Saebyrht, nephew of Ethelbert, King of Kent, now reigned. He met at first with great success; and with as little change as might be, the temples and rites of Paganism were transformed into those of Christianity; but the sons of Saebyrht endeavoured to bring back the old order of things, and Mellitus fled to Canterbury, where he died Archbishop, in the year 624. Christianity was reintroduced under Sigebright the Good, and became the settled form of religion. The several Saxon kingdoms were also gradually reduced under one ruler: but the country was continually disturbed by the incursions of the Danes, against whom Brithnoth, earl of Essex, nobly fell; and they became more and more powerful, until Canute the Dane was king over all England.

Godwin, Earl of Kent.

One of Canute's favourites was Godwin, who long survived him, and lived to possess under Edward the Confessor, almost all the power. Among his possessions was the lordship of Coggeshall, which,—together with Stisted and Chich (St. Osyth), the latter of which he had as a gift of Canute,—he gave to the monks of Dorobernia or Canterbury. The grant is as follows:—

" I, Godwin and Wolfgith, with the permission and consent of my lord King Edward, give to the Church of Christ in Dorobernia part of the land of our right, called Stigestede and *Coggashael*, in East Sexia, exempt from all secular service, as I have held it up to this time from my aforesaid lord King Edward, and from his father (Ethelred.) If any one take them away from the right of the same Church may God take away from him his glory."[*]

[*] MSS. in Coll. Bened. Cantab. Also in the Chronicle of William Thorne. X. Script. Coll. 2224.

The following entry of this gift is also found in the "Antiquities of Canterbury."*

"A.D. 1046. Ulfgith, widow of Elfwine,† and Godwin, with the consent of Saint Edward the King, gave to the Church of Christ in Dorobernia, Stisted, Goggeshale, in Essex, for the sustenance of the monks, exempt like Adesham." [a lordship in Kent given to the monks by Ethelbald.]

The monks of Canterbury were of the Benedictine order: so called from St. Benedict, an Italian of great reputation, who established in his monastery on Monte Cassino a new rule, which spread rapidly throughout Europe. From the color of their habit they were generally called Black Monks. "Augustine the monk," says Fuller, "first brought them over into England and these blackbirds first nested in Canterbury, whence they have flown to all parts of the kingdom. For as one rightly observeth, all the Abbeys in England before the time of King William the Conqueror (and some while after) were filled with this order."

The Cathedral Church of Canterbury was first dedicated to the special patronage of our blessed Saviour, and therefore called Ecclesia Sancti Salvatoris; but on its being rebuilt after its destruction by fire, it was dedicated to the honor of the Holy Trinity, and hence called Ecclesia Sanctæ Trinitatis, as in the Domesday Book.

Of Godwin a few particulars may be further noted. He was the son of Wulfnoth, a Saxon herdsman; and the story is told of him, that when quite a youth, and once finding a Dane, who had been defeated in battle,

* Somner, Appendix p. 39, Ed. 1703.
† Probably a Saxon lord of some importance.

wandering out of his way in the enemy's district, he ventured to conduct him to his fleet at the risk of his own life: the Dane was not ungrateful: "He obtained for him from Canute military rank. Canute soon percieved the genius of the man, and Godwin was mainly instrumental in furthering the great work which Canute had at heart—the fusion of the two races. Godwin was the connecting link between the Saxon and the Dane; and as the leader of the united English people, became one of the greatest men this country has ever produced, although, as is the English custom, one of the most maligned."*

Editha, the daughter of Godwin, was married to Edward the Confessor; and his son Harold exercised viceregal authority over Essex. But the power of Godwin and his family was somewhat broken in Edward's time, chiefly by the influence of foreign ecclesiastics and nobles whom the King favored. On one occasion Eustace, Earl of Boulogne, who married Goda, sister of Edward, on his leaving England entered Dover at the head of an armed retinue, and took possession of it as if it had been a conquered town. The townspeople resented this insolence, and killed several of the Normans. Eustace fled to the king, who ordered Godwin to chastise the outbreak, but he declined, and a sentence of outlawry was passed upon him and his sons. They were however afterwards restored to their honors, and Godwin died of an apoplectic fit in 1053.

* Dr. Hook's Lives of the Archbishops of Canterbury. Vol. I. p. 509.

About this time the principal part of the soil of Coggeshall was possessed by COLO, a Saxon freeholder, who had under him numerous *ceorls* or peasants, (afterwards known as villani and bordarii;) and also slaves, who were either the descendants of the former occupants, or Saxons who had made themselves such.

In Saxon times probably arose several designations of particular localities, which continue to the present day: such as *Sunnedon*, *Stan-ham* or Stoney Street; *Ingring-downe* or Ingrydowns (meadows on a hill), at the end of the same street.

Count Eustace and Domesday Book.

Eustace, Count or Earl of Boulogne, fought under the banner of William the Norman at the battle of Hastings, and although severely wounded, lived to share the spoils of the conquest. He became the greatest landed proprietor in Essex, possessing no less than seventy-three manors in this county, among which was that of Coggeshall; and these he held of the King as feudal lord by military service. About a year afterwards, when William was in Normandy, and the Regents had filled the country with discontent and disorder, Eustace, who was now at variance with the King, was invited over to take possession of Dover, and came in the dead of night; but the garrison sallying out and driving most of his men down the precipices, he was obliged to retire to his ships. The date of his death is uncertain: his name and possessions are recorded in the Domesday Book about the year 1085.

This Record contains an account of the land and its occupants in the time of Edward the Confessor, when granted by William the Conqueror, and at the time of the Survey; by which it appears that whilst the chief ownership of the land was transferred to the Normans, the Saxon peasants still continued on it, under somewhat altered conditions.

"THE COUNT holds Cogheshal in demesne, which COLO a freeman [freeholder] held in the time of King Edward, for one manor, and for three hides [pasture land of about 100 acres each] and half, and 33 acres. Always 3 carucates [arable land of about 60 acres each] in demesne, and when he received it, one carucate. Then 16 carucates belonging to the men [tenants], since that, and lately 14. Then 11 villeins [husbandmen], since that, and lately 9. Then 22 borderers [cottagers on the outskirts of the manor], lately 31. Lately 4 servi [domestic slaves]. Then wood for 600 hogs, lately 500. 38 acres of meadow. Only so much meadow as is worth 10*d*. Always one mill. One working-horse. 15 hogs. 4 goats. 4 stocks of bees.

"To this manor belong 2 sochmen [inferior landowners, copyholders, yeomen], and one priest [presbyter], and one swineherd, and one mercenary. To this land are added 38 acres, which one free-man held of the King. Then this manor was worth 10£. Lately 14, but it now yields 20£, and the aforesaid 38 acres are worth 10*s*." [each equal in weight to rather more than three of ours.]—*Fol.* 26 *b. Witham Hund.*

These possessions include the greater part of what is now known as Great and Little Coggeshall, a distinction which is not found in any of the oldest documents. The following entry seems to refer to lands now included in the latter.

"In Coghessala THE HOLY TRINITY held 3 virgates [yard-lands of about 25 acres each], in the time of King Edward, and the same lately. Always 2 carucates. Then one borderer, lately 8. Then 3 slaves, lately 1. 8 acres of meadow. One mill, and worth 60s. in demesne. 4 working-horses. 3 head of cattle. 20 sheep. 7 hogs."—*Fol. 8. Witham.*

Lands were also held in Coggeshall by TEDRIC POINTELL. These included what is now known as Little Coggeshall Hall, or the adjacent Hamlet, mill and river, which are still called "*Pointell's.*"

"*Tedric* holds one hide and half in exchange for Cogheshal, which TISELINUS held. Then 2 carucates, lately none. Then 3 borderers, lately none. Wood for 3 hogs. 12 acres of meadow. Then worth 20s., lately but 10s."—*Fol. 134.*

"These two manors [Pakelesham and Canewdon] Tedricus Pointell held in exchange for Cogheshal."—*Fol. 99 b. Rochefort.* [*also Fol. 96. Witbrictesherna.*]

The number of inhabitants, according to the above enumeration did not exceed 60, and these were principally cottagers who cultivated each his little plot of ground, and handed over a portion of the produce to the lord. There were probably many more, for it was not the design of the Domesday Book to take a census of the people, so much as a survey of the land. The whole population of Essex according to it was only 16,000, of whom one half were borderers, and the rest chiefly husbandmen and slaves. With the exception of Colchester and Maldon, where there were several hundred burgesses, scarcely any other place was more thickly populated than this.

One of the most noteworthy particulars in the above extract, is that which refers to the "one priest" who dwelt here. His district or parish had now been marked out, and the laws had given him a claim to a tithe of the product of the land. There was probably some church in which he ministered, although not mentioned; but where it was is unknown. It has been conjectured that "the font in which the Saxon inhabitants were baptized, first by the missionary priest of Colchester, and afterwards by their common parish priest," was St. Peter's well, about a hundred yards westward from the present church yard.* Nor is it at all improbable that, the earliest building for religious purposes in this place, was on the site of the present church. But already great errors and evils had grown up in rank luxuriance; such as, the worship of images and superstitious veneration of relics, the doctrine of purgatory and prayers for the dead, unauthorised assumptions on the part of the priesthood, and blind dependence on external rites; and the only remedy for these things was hidden in an unknown tongue. Yet the influence of the clergy of those days was beneficial, in relieving the oppression of the weak by the powerful; for it was the aim of the Roman Catholic Church to humble both the lord and his slave at her own feet.

* It is a circular bricked well about 3 feet deep, which supplies the town with beautifully clear water. "Nearly 80 years ago it was opened and cleansed. Mr. Sprague states that he then witnessed the workmen discover, midway between the top and bottom, embedded in the steaning, a square stone, upon which was sculptured in relief the head of St. Peter with the keys." (*A. J. Dunkin.*) Mr. Joseph Denney, however, states that this was in another well, now closed up, in a cottage garden at the end of Church Lane, near Stoneham Street.

Abbey Farm & Remains of Leyyeshull Abm.

Foundation by Queen Matilda.

EUSTACE, Earl of Boulogne, left behind him three sons. Godfrey the eldest, was, at the close of the first crusade, elected king of Jerusalem, where his tomb is pointed out in the Church of the Holy Sepulchre at this day; and was succeeded by his brother Baldwin. Eustace, the third, married Mary, the daughter of Malcolm III. of Scotland, and their daughter Matilda became wife of Stephen, Earl of Blois, afterwards king of England. The manor of Coggeshall was a part of her inheritance, and was given for the purpose of founding an Abbey, according to the following charter:—

"MATILDA, by the grace of God Queen of the English to all the prelates and faithful of the Holy Church greeting. Be it known unto you all that my lord King Stephen, and I, and my son Eustace, give and grant in perpetual alms for the health of our souls, and the souls of our ancestors, and of our children, and of all our friends, as well living as dead, to God and the Holy Church of Mary, and to the abbot and convent of Coggeshal, all the same manor of Coggeshal, in land and men, in wood and plain, in water and out of water, in way and out of way, and in all things pertaining to the same, as free and peaceable as Earl Eustace and my father, and we afterwards more freely and peaceably held it: to wit freed and discharged from all pleas and complaints, from scots and aids, from shires and hundreds, from Danegelt and from all gelts and army of footmen and horse, from work of the park, and work and defence of the castle, and every other work and every kind of service, from murdur and all other matters, and all exactions with sacha and socha, and toll and team, and infangentheof [the right of taking and punishing thieves], and all customs, and their liberties. Wherefore I earnestly entreat your goodness, inasmuch as for the love of God to keep and maintain the same alms in the aforesaid liberties, so that you may be made partakers of the same benefaction, and receive from God your reward in eternal blessedness.

"Witnesses:—Count Walter de Mellent. C. Gilbert. C. Geoffrey de Mandeville. C. William de Guarrenne. C. Simon. William de Ipre. Ralph, my Chancellor. And Hubert, my Chamberlain at London. Given under our hand at St. Edmund's, 26 Decr."

This grant was confirmed by Stephen, at the request of Matilda and his son Eustace, in similar language.

"And that this my gift and confirmation may endure, I confirm it with the impression of my present seal, and corroborate it with the witness of the underwritten.

"Witnesses:—Matilda, Queen. Eustace, Count of Boulogne. Henry, Abbot of Colchester. Wm. de Ipre. Wm. de Warrenne, and Richard and Robert de Valenco, at Coggeshall."

It was further confirmed by William, son of Stephen, Earl of Boulogne, and Warren.

"Witnesses:—Reginald de Warren. Rob. de Wesevene. Simon de Cailli. Ralph de —. Torold de Boreham. Eustace, Chancellor. John, Abbot of Furnes. Geoffrey, Prior of Lanc."

The Queen also granted a charter to free the Abbot and monks from all toll and other customs, throughout all the lands of her patrimony in France and England.

"Witnesses:—Ralph Lucius. William filius Gant. Richard de Monteacuto, at Osensort."*

She died at Castle Hedingham, which belonged to Alberic De Vere, Earl of Oxford, and was soon followed by her son Eustace, who died of a fever at Bury St. Edmund's.

In the chronicle of Ralph, Abbot of Coggeshall, of whom more will be said, the foundation of the Abbey is thus mentioned:—

"1139. The Abbey of Coggeshal was founded by King Stephen and Queen Matilda, who also built the Abbey of Furnes, and the Abbey of Favresham, where also their bodies were interred. In the same year the convent came together at Coggeshale, III nones of August."

The monks who came to Coggeshall were of the Cistercian order, a branch or reformed order of the Benedictines already mentioned. Whilst the Cluniac or Black Monks abrogated the rule concerning manual labour, (which, in addition to the three vows of obedience, poverty and chastity, had been imposed by St. Benedict) the Cistercians or White Monks continued to adhere to it. Their name was derived from Cistercium or Citeaux, in Burgundy, where the first Abbey of this order was founded. Its third abbot, Stephen Harding, an Englishman, brought it into wide repute, but its most celebrated man was St. Bernard, whose influence was so great, that it was sometimes called after his

* The first Charter is given in Dugdale's Monasticon: the other three are found in Holman's MSS., probably copied from the collection of Nicholas Tekyll, of Castle Hedingham.

name. The chronicle notes, "1110, the blessed Bernard, being about 22 years old, entered Cistercium with more than 30 companions, and submitted his neck to the gentle yoke of Christ under abbot Stephen, in the 15th year from the foundation of the house of Cistercium. 1153, the blessed Bernard, first abbot of the convent of Cleirvaux, and the father of more than 160 other monasteries, in the hands of his children fell asleep in the Lord."

The first monks of Coggeshall came, in all probability, from Savigny in France * The site selected for their new abode was one of the best that could be found. It was the custom of monks of this order to

* See Furness Abbey. Jour. Brit. Arch. Assoc. Jan. 1851.

build their Abbeys in quiet and lowly valleys, as an indication of humility, but doubtless still more on account of the substantial advantages to be derived from fish ponds and fertile gardens. In their plan, the church occupied the chief place, and was generally very simple in its constuction; although the remains of Waverley, Rievaulx, Fountains, Furness and Tintern Abbeys, all of this order, show with what magnificence it was sometimes adorned. It was built in the form of a cross, and dedicated to the Virgin Mary; if there was a tower, it was always low. No image save that of the crucifix was permitted, and no prostration in the churches. A severe simplicity also marked most of their modes of life. On the south side of the church was the cloister, or quadrangular space, where the monks were accustomed to walk and talk, enclosed by various abbey-buildings; the principal of which were the Chapter House, where all important matters were transacted, and the Refectory or Dining Hall: over these respectively were the Library and Dormitory: and adjoining them the Frater house or great parlour of the brethren, and the Hospitium or Guest-house, a large hall with chambers for the reception of strangers. Other buildings, such as the Infirmary and the Abbot's house, were sometimes a little separated from the rest.

The Abbot was lord of the convent, and next to him in authority was the Prior. There were also a Cellarer, Chamberlain, Secretary, Porter and other officers.

The habit of the Cistercians " was a white robe in

the nature of a cassock, with a black scapular and hood: their garment was girt with a black girdle of wool; In the choir they had over it a white cowl, and over it a hood, with a rochet hanging down before to the waste, and in a point behind to the calf of the leg: when they went abroad they wore a cowl and a great hood all black: which was also their choir habit."[*] The monks devoted several hours each day to manual labor, and the wool trade was almost entirely in their hands. Fishponds, mills, vineyards and granges [granaries], surrounded the Abbey. Such lands as were in their own occupation were exempt from tithes.[†]

In this manner they enriched their order; but gave room for the severe portraiture of them by a satirical writer of the 13th century.—" The abbots and cellarers have ready money, eat large fish, drink good wine, and send the very worst to the Refectory for those who do the work. These monks I have seen put pig-sties in church yards, and stables for asses in chapels. They seize the cottages of the poor and reduce them to beggary."

The Abbots.

The first Abbot of Coggeshall was called WILLIAM, whose name has been rescued from oblivion by its being found as a witness to a deed in the chartulary

---

[*] Fosbroke's Brit. Monachism, p. 287.
[†] Pope Alexander and Paschal gave some monasteries this exemption, which was restrained by Pope Adrian IV. to the Cistercians, Hospitallers and Premonstratenses, and still further restrained by the Council of Lateran in 1215. On the dissolution of monasteries, (31 Hen. viii.) the above-mentioned privilege was continued to the lands which had belonged to them.

of Colne Priory,* in the year 1144. Under his eye the Abbey Church and other buildings were begun. The bricks used in their construction were probably made at Tilkey by the builders who accompanied him to this country.† A larger population than had previously existed began to gather around, to assist the monks in their various undertakings.

SIMON DE TONI was the next Abbot, and in his time the church was opened for divine worship, according to the following entry in the chronicle.

"1167. At Coggeshal the great altar was dedicated in honor of the glorious Virgin Mary and Saint John the Baptist, on the day of the assumption of the Blessed Virgin, by the Venerable Gilbert Foliot, Bishop of London, who on the same day solemnly celebrated Mass on that altar, the lord Simon de Toni being abbot of that place."

Simon afterwards retired to Melrose Monastery, and died Bishop of Moray, about 1184. His successor at Coggeshall was ODO.

"Lord Simon, 2nd Abbot, retired from Coggeshal, and returned to his Monastery at Milros, to whom succeed Lord Odo, third Abbot of this place. 1172. The ordination of Lord Simon, Bishop of Moray, X. Cal. Feb., formerly Abbot of Coggeshal."

PETER, monk of Vaudey, was next Abbot.

* Founded by Aubrey de Vere, first of the name, who became a monk and died there.

† "About a dozen years ago, in reopening the ground to obtain the brick earth which was found to exist there, an old kiln was discovered; it fell in and was destroyed: but it is described as having its fireplace arched with bricks like those in the Abbey; the fire grate was of long iron rods, and broken moulded bricks, like those of the Abbey, were found, and still are occasionally found in the neighbourhood."—*Architectural Account of the Remains of Coggeshall Abbey; by Rev. E. L. Cutts.* 1858.

"1176, died Lord Odo of revered memory, third Abbot of Coggeshal, to whom succeeded Lord Peter, monk of Valle-Dei, brother of Master Stephen, Chancellor of the Church of Lincoln."

The following story is told in Ralph's Chronicle:—

"In the time of the Lord Peter, the fourth Abbot of Coggeshall, it happened that Brother Robert, a convert of that house, who had the care of the guests, as his custom was, entered the Guest-house one day before the hour of refection, and, when he was entered, he found sitting in the hall certain persons reverend in countenance and dress, who wore mantles like those of Templars, and each had a hood on his head. They were nine or more in number, for the brother did not accurately notice how many they were. Then the foresaid brother, thinking that these men were Templars, politely saluted them; and one, who seemed to be the chief of them, said to him, 'When shall we dine?' and he said, 'You will dine in the chamber with the Lord Abbot;' but he answered, 'It is not our custom to dine in private chambers, but in the hall with the guests.' After this the brother left the hall, and hastened to the Abbot to announce to him the arrival of such guests as these; and he immediately bade to prepare what was necessary and to lay the table, and declared that they should dine with him in his chamber. So when the Abbot was about to go to table he bade the foresaid brother to introduce those guests. But when the brother went into the hall he could not find the guests whom he had left there a little before. He went into the chambers, and divers other places, but he could not find any of them. Then he went out and ran here and there about the court, enquiring of everybody he met if they had seen such-like men. One declared that he had seen men of that description going in the direction of the Church, and hastening to the Cemetery of the Brethren. But when he had sent a messenger thither in haste, the messenger found no one. Lastly, the porters were interrogated concerning guests of such a description, and they asserted that no such men had that day either entered or left by the gate. Who these men were, how they came, or whither they departed, remains unknown even to this day. But we, who knew his life and his conscientiousness, do not doubt the narration of the aforesaid brother, that he did thus see and speak with them; he often narrated these things to us, and also in his last sickness, by which he was removed from this world, he related these things plainly to the Convent. And he was an honest relator of things, using few words, and not given to ostentation either in words or deeds."

He was succeeded by THOMAS.

"1207, died Lord Thomas, fifth Abbot of Coggeshal, to whom succeeded Lord Ralph, monk of the same place, who wrote this Chronicle, from the taking of the Holy Cross to the [eleventh] year of King Henry III, son of King John, and undertook to note down certain visions, which he heard from worthy men, for the edification of many."

RALPH was a man of considerable learning, which was not a common thing among the monks of this order, and was the most eminent of the Abbots of this Abbey. "He was by birth an Englishman, and was carefully educated even from infancy in the study of polite learning. He was at one time Canon of Barnwell, nigh Cambridge, as John Stow relates; afterwards he learnt to bear the easy yoke and light burden of the Lord in the holy society of the Cistercians. He was a man adorned with many natural gifts, and well skilled in various branches of learning, of incredible moderation and abstinence, temperate, chaste, humble, modest, of blameless life in every respect, and of great learning, whence partly thro' the bounty of nature partly thro' his own unwearied industry he acquired a great reputation among all men: he was held in high estimation and shone among his fellows, so that at length, by the unanimous consent of his brethren he was chosen Abbot of the Monastery of Coggeshall, and when established in this dignity he cultivated the muses no less than before, and daily either read and meditated upon something in the Scriptures, or was diligently occupied in reading histories or in writing them."* "He made an appendix of Ralph Niger's Chronicle concerning the distinguished deeds of the Emperors and Kings of France and England, from the Capture of the Cross as is therein stated, or from the year of grace 1113 to the 11th year of Henry III, son of King John, which work he calls 'Additions to Ralph Niger.'—He also wrote a Chronicle of the Holy Land. Concerning Certain Visions. Certain Sermons."†

Before Ralph was chosen Abbot, he had gone with the Crusaders to the Holy Land. The second crusade which had been preached up by St. Bernard had effected little, and the Christian dominion was now threatened by the arms of Saladin. The Patriarch of

---

* Pits de Illus. Ang. Script. c. 325.
† Bale de Script. Britan. Cent. 3 c. 88. Mr Dunkin has printed all the existing works of Ralph in one vol., which contains Ralph's Chronicle of the Holy Land, (De Expugnatione Terræ Sanctæ per Saladinum), a Chronicle of English affairs, &c.: (the first few pages from A.D. 1066 to 1114: then followed by "Additions of a monk of Coggeshal" until the year 1224), and certain Stories. They are from MSS. in Brit. Museum Library. Cott. Vesp. D. X. (on parchment, illuminated). Cott. Cleopatra B. I. Both Chronicles are among the MSS. in Herald's College Norfolk II. Also in the Library of St. Victor, Paris, there is a MS. entitled "Libellus de Motibus Anglicanis sub Johan. R., auctore Rad. Abbate," some portions of which have been published by the Benedictine brothers Dom. Martene et Dom. Durand, and as reedited by Dom. Bouquet. See Dunkin—Mon. Angl. Coggeshall.

Jerusalem came into England in 1185, and on his return was probably accompanied by Ralph, amongst other "pious men, who were needed to comfort the weak, instruct the ignorant, and animate the brave in the battle of the Lord." The dissensions of the Christians led to their defeat at Nazareth, and at Tiberias, where the Holy Cross was taken; a calamity over which Ralph mourns in the genuine spirit of a Crusader:—

"Why should I prolong the tale? the Saracens prevailed against the Christians and did with them what they would. Woe is me! what shall I say? It is fitting rather to weep and complain than to say anything! Woe is me! shall I pollute my lips by telling how the sacred Wood of our redemption, was taken by the accursed hands of the accursed? Woe is me, miserable! that in the days of my miserable life I should be compelled to witness such things. But woe also to that wicked race! a people laden with iniquity, through whom the faith of all Christians is blasphemed; and by whom Christ is again compelled to be scourged and crucified. O sweet and beloved Wood bedewed and bathed with the blood of the Son of God! O sweet cross on which our salvation hung, and by which the handwriting of death was taken away, and life, lost in the first-created, was found again! Why should I live any longer, now that the tree of life is taken away? And verily, I believe it was taken away because the faith of the Sons of the Cross had vanished, and because without faith it is impossible to please God. Woe to us miserable, who have lost our defence, our sins requiring it. Therefore was the wood of our salvation, the worthy (wood), unworthily, by the unworthy, alas! alas! carried away! Nor was it wonderful, if, by the might of visible enemies, they lost the bodily substance of the Holy Cross, which, spiritually, they, being wanting in the good works of righteousness, had long since in mind and heart cast away. Mourn for this, all ye worshippers of the cross, and weep; and fix the true Cross in your hearts, by a right and unshaken faith; and be ye comforted in hope, since the Cross deserts not those who trust in it, unless it be first deserted. Why should I prolong the tale? The Cross was taken, and the king, and the master of the Temple, and the bishop of Lydda, and the King's brother, and the Templars and the Hospitallers, and the Marquis of Mont-Ferrat; and all the rest, were either killed or taken. And the army of the Christians was wasted away by slaughter, and captivity, and miserable flight, whilst their enemies carried off and divided their spoils. Therefore God humbled his people, bending down the cup from his hand, and making them drink the wine of bitterness, even to the dregs. But its dregs are not yet drunk out. The Saracens shall yet drink from the same cup, the dregs of damnation, even to the bottom. Over this the Prophet David mourned, saying, 'They have smitten down thy people, and troubled thine heritage, they have slain the widow and stranger, and put the fatherless to death.' 'How long, O Lord, shall they do this?' 'Until the pit be digged up for the ungodly, and righteousness be turned again unto judgment.' Then indeed 'He shall recompense them their wickedness; and destroy them in their own malice,' viz., the Saracens. O Prophet, what dost thou say to us, 'You who are planted in the House of the Lord, and flourish in His Courts,' 'O come let us sing unto the Lord,' &c. 'for the Lord is a great God; for He will not cast off His people, neither will He forsake His inheritance."

He then describes the advance of Saladin upon Jerusalem.

" And since the Saracens who were with Saladin invaded the territory of Jerusalem in different parts, it seemeth good to us to string together compendiously, in a short and unpolished narration, what we ourselves saw and heard, and to lay what was done before those who have not heard nor seen. . . . .

"On the twentieth day of the month of September, the holy city Jerusalem was besieged, and surrounded on every side by the unbelievers, with great clang of trumpets and din of arms, and yelling and howling of infidels, shouting Hai! Hai! the standards waving on every side. Therefore the city was moved by the roar and tumult of the barbarians, and they exclaimed every moment, 'O holy true cross, and sepulchre of the resurrection of Jesus Christ, protect the city of Jerusalem with its inhabitants.' The battle then was commenced, and they began to attack fiercely on every side. But since afflicted with the grief and sorrow of so great a misery, we are unable to enumerate all the movements and attacks of the Turks with which they harrassed the Christians for fifteen days; we shall omit the rest of the things which took place, which would only produce weariness, without serving any good purpose either to the writer or the reader. For who, forgetting all else in sympathy for so great grief, would not break forth into tears, when he saw here monks and priests, to wit priests and levites, ermites, and anchorites stricken with old age, wearing armour, and carrying arms; in another place, orphans and children with arms stretched towards the Lord, going through the churches and squares in crowds, with pale faces, and crying mournfully with their innocent mouths, and incessantly imploring the divine clemency, and the protection of the saints? But what tongue can tell how many of the Saracens, pierced by lances and arrows, lost life and found eternal death. And who can tell how that nephew of Saladin deceived by the arrogance of his pride, splendidly clad in silken robes even to his horse hoofs, trapped with mirrors set in gold, by reason of the exceeding pride of his heart, being struck by a certain soldier before the gate of St. Stephen, perished by a miserable death. Or, who can tell how many Christians wounded by the weapons of their adversaries, losing the temporal life for the sake of Christ, earned the life eternal. And so in those days in which God appeared to rule the city, who can tell how one was struck and died, another was wounded and escaped. But the arrows fell like drops of rain, so that no one could expose a finger at the barricades without being wounded; and there was so great a multitude of wounded, that scarcely all the surgeons of the city or the Hospital were sufficient to draw out the weapons fixed in their bodies. And the face also of him who relates these things was wounded by an arrow fixed through the middle of the nose, and though the shaft was extracted, yet the iron remains to this day. And the men of Jerusalem fought with sufficient courage throughout one week, the army being set down opposite the tower of David. . . . .

"The Chaldeans therefore fought a cruel battle for some days, and prevailed. For now the Christians were so reduced, that hardly twenty or thirty appeared at the defences of the city walls; nor was there found one man in all the city so bold that for the reward of one hundred besants he dared to keep guard at the defence for one night. So that I myself with my own ears heard it proclaimed by the voice of a herald on the part of the Lord Patriarch and the other magnates of the city, between the great wall and the ante wall, that if fifty able and bold soldiers could be found who would guard the breached angle, with what arms they would, for that night only, they should receive five thousand besants, and they could not be found. But now almost every one had the same desire, viz: to die in their innocence, and in the holy city, confessing Christ, so that each might obtain his portion of the promised land in which his body might lie trodden under foot of the Gentiles for the sake of Christ. Woe to me miserable sinner, and worse than all sinners, because I did not receive my portion of the holy land thus meted out me. Meantime the men, the inhabitants of Jerusalem, loving their land, full of their iniquities, more than Christ, moved with the recollection of beautiful wives, of sons and daughters, and of the mammon which they served, took counsel how, preserving all these things, but deserting the holy city and the sacred places, they might escape. . . .'

"And they sent beseeching Saladin; who, having taken counsel, appointed the following tribute to the men of Jerusalem, that every male should pay ten besants for his freedom, a woman five, a boy of seven years and under one, and so delivered from slavery they might depart in safety whither they would. .

"This speech therefore pleased the Lord Patriarch, and the rest who had money. . . . . But when these things were heard, the common people bewailed with a lamentable voice throughout the city, saying, woe to us wretched ones, what shall we do who have no gold.

"Who ever would have thought that such wickedness could be perpetrated by Christians? to betray voluntarily the noble sepulchre of the resurrection, and the noble temple, and the most holy mount Sion, and the other places of the holy city into the hands of the Gentiles. Perish those base traffickers who a second time have sold Christ and the holy city, like that malignant trafficker who being hanged burst asunder in the midst, and what is worse, all the bowels of his malignity gushed out upon them. So shall it be also to those who demand gifts for the imposition of hands, and for the Sacraments of the Church. . . . .

"Therefore in the year from the incarnation of our Lord Jesus Christ, 1187, in the month of October, the third day of the month,—whence a certain man made these verses:

'Twelve hundred after Christ, excepting thirteen years,
'While the 3rd day of the 10th month o'er Jerusalem appears,
'D was the Sunday letter, and 'twas on the Sabbath day,
'The Christians gave Jerusalem to the Infidels a prey.'

Jerusalem, alas! was betrayed into the hands of the wicked by wicked christians, and the gates were shut, and guards placed."

After this Ralph appears to have gone to Acre, which was besieged by the Crusaders, themselves surrounded by enemies. He tells us how they were wasted away by vice and pestilence, famine and war; and mentions, among others, one "Master Ralph de Hauterive, archdeacon of Colchester—a man who, after he had performed many distinguished deeds, made in that same siege a blessed end." Almost the last entry in his Chronicle of the Holy Land is the following:— "1191, after Easter, Philip King of France, landed at Acre, and not long afterwards, viz., about Pentecost, came Richard King of England." There is no allusion to his own journey homeward, or the time of his arrival in England; but there can be little doubt that, notwithstanding he could henceforth point to his Palm and Escalop, he was not slow to seek the retirement of monastic life, where he might recruit his broken health, cherish the memories and relics of the holy spots he had visited, and ponder the saying of St. Bernard: "It is better to struggle against the sinful lusts of the heart than to conquer Jerusalem."

It was not until nearly twenty years after the taking of Jerusalem, and after he had been for some time monk of the Abbey of Coggeshall, that he became Abbot (1207).

During this interval occurred many events of great interest, which are mentioned by Ralph in his Chronicle of English affairs, &c. After describing the exploits of Richard Cœur de Lion in the Holy Land, he tells of the storm which overtook the fleet on its departure thence "by the just judgment of God," and of his reaching Corfu with a few attendants "among whom were Baldwin de Bethune and Anselm chaplain of the

King, who related all these things to us as he saw and heard:"—at length, released from captivity the King landed in England, and "in the same hour there appeared a certain very bright and unusual splendour, not far distant from the sun," announcing his arrival! On the death of Cœur de Lion by a wound from an arrow in 1199, after enumerating his services for God and the church, Ralph says: "These, and works of piety of this kind, contending with his wrong-doings, will, as we hope, the Lord dealing mercifully with him, afford the greatest possible alleviation of his punishment, especially since at his latter end he confessed his sins and was penitent; for as water quenches fire, so alms-giving quenches sin."

Richard was succeeded by his brother, John (Lackland), of whom little good may be said by any one, least of all by an Abbot, the privileges of whose order he so often violated, and whose hospitality at Coggeshall it is probable that he shared more than once with a churl's recompense. In the year of Ralph's election to office came the struggle between the King and the Pope, and not long after, between him and his barons— England's deepest humiliation and the Great Charter of Rights: but the following brief extracts only can be given here from his Chronicle of these times.

"1207.—Master Stephen Langton, consecrated Archbishop of Canterbury by Lord Pope Innocent. The convent of Canterbury is expelled by King John, and all the possessions of the same church confiscated."

"1208.—All England and Wales are placed under a general

interdict. On the day before the annunciation of the Blessed Mary the lands, rents, and moveables of the clergy, and religious orders, are confiscated."

"1209.—On the first of June, very early in the morning, at the time of sunrise, a wonderful contest of the clouds with the sun appeared, and continued beyond the first hour of the day.

"King John commanded that the houses of those bishops who executed the interdict should be overturned, the woods cut down, and the fish destroyed."

"1210.—King John imposed a very heavy fine generally on all the houses of the religious of all England; but he oppressed the Cistercians most of all, and did not permit the Abbots of the Cistercian order to go to the annual Chapter."

"1213.—The King of England surrendered, in perpetual gift, all the kingdom of England, to the Lord Pope Innocent and his Catholic successors, and testified in his Charter that as feudatory, both himself and his heirs would do liege homage to the lord Pope, and pay in addition 1000 marks."

"1214.—The Interdict of all England is removed."

"1215.—The barons assemble between Windleshore and Stanes, in a meadow called *Runnemad*. . . . . A form of peace between King and barons was included in a CHARTER."

"1216.—And many of the knights and their attendants [part of the army of mercenaries whom John sent to ravage the eastern counties, and especially the estates of the barons who upheld the Charter which he now desired to annul], entered violently the church of the Abbey of Tiltey, [a Cistercian Abbey not far from Thaxted.] . . . . Also, on the day of the Circumcision of the Lord, at Coggeshall, while the third hour was said, they entered the church violently; and led away 22 horses, which belonged to the Bishop of London, and his brother the Treasurer, and others.

"The King died at the castle of Neuwerc. About the middle of the night, the hour that is of his decease, there was such roaring of wind and whirlwind that the citizens feared the overthrow of their houses, as lord John Saumiensis told us he heard from the citizens. . . . . To him succeeded Henry (III) his son."

Not very long after this, Ralph resigned the office which he had held during these miserable years.

"1218.—Lord Ralph, sixth Abbot of Coggeshall, having now administered for 11 years and 2 months, about the feast of St. John the Baptist, contrary to the wish of his convent, relinquished of his own accord the pastoral care, labouring under constant sickness."

On his retirement he lived in sickness and seclusion, occasionally noting events of several succeeding years, and ended his pilgrimage about the year 1228.

He was the patron of JOHN GODARD, a monk and mathematician. "John Godard," says Fuller, "wherever born, had his best being at Cogshall, where he became a Cistercian monk. (Bale, c. iv. n. 11, compared with Pits in 1550.) Great was his skill in arithmetic and mathematics, a science which had lain long asleep, and now first began to open its eyes again. He wrote many certain Treatises thereof, and dedicated them to Ralph, Abbot of Coggeshall."

At this time there prevailed generally the most entire ignorance of natural phenomena, and a credulity equally great, of which not a few instances appear in the Chronicle.

"In the time of King Richard there were found, at a villa called Edolfuesnesse [Foulness], on the sea shore in Essex, two teeth of a certain giant, of such a size, that two hundred teeth such as men now have, might be cut out of them. But we saw those teeth at Coggeshall, and examined them with great astonishment."*

"At the same time, at Daghewurthe, in Suthfolke, in the house of lord Osborn de Bradwelle, appeared a certain fantastic spirit, often and for a long time speaking with the family of the aforesaid knight, imitating the voice of an infant of a year old, and calling himself Malakin. He could be heard and felt, but not seen. But he spoke English according to the idiom of that region, and sometimes talked with the chaplain of the same knight, even in Latin and from the Scriptures, as he faithfully assured us."

After this, it will be no matter of surprise to hear, that at St. Mary de Wulpete's in Suthfolke there were found a boy and a girl, who had come from some dim subterranean region, "the whole surface of whose body was tinged with the color of green, and their only food beans."

"They were taken to the house of Richard de Calne, a certain knight at Wikes: the boy soon died, but the girl lived, and gradually recovered her natural color; and after being regenerated by the washing of Holy baptism, continuing for many years in the service of the aforesaid knight, as we have frequently heard from him and his family, became not a little wanton and pert."

A more than curious interest attaches to a story he

* "Cogshale.—Ther are to be seene 2 teeth of a monstrous man or gyant, of so great magnitude and weight, as 100 of anie men's teeth in this age cannot countervayle one of them."—*John Norden* in 1594. Similar giants have not unfrequently turned up of late. "In 1848, as the laborers employed on the Stour Valley Line were excavating in the parish of Lamarsh, they discovered, about 14 feet from the surface, embedded in gravel, the head and tusks of a mammoth or fossil elephant. The tusks broke when they attempted to remove them, but the teeth were taken out tolerably perfect, and are about ten inches long: the tusks when whole measured 11 feet in length. On two or three of the teeth the enamel is as fresh as if they had not lain in the earth a month, instead of at least 6000 years."

tells concerning the Publicani (or Paulicians,) a sect of Christians who ventured to deny the doctrines of the Roman Church, and were closely related to the Waldenses, Lollards, and other forerunners of the Protestants and Puritans. It shows in what light a monk regarded opinions now received in England, together with something of the spirit of his system, and the prevalence of principles by which it was overthrown.

"In the time of Louis, King of France, father of King Philip, when the error of certain heretics, vulgarly called Publicani, had crept into many provinces of Gaul, it happened that Lord Wm., Archbishop of Rheims, was taking exercise near the city with his clerks; one of whom, viz. Master Gervase, of Tilbury, seeing a beautiful damsel walking all alone in a vineyard, led by the curiosity of slippery youth, went to her, as from his own mouth we heard afterwards, when he was under canonical obedience. From her reply to his addresses, Master Gervase perceived that she was of that most impious sect of the Publicani, who at that time were searched out and suppressed everywhere, but especially by Philip, Count of Flanders, who punished them with just severity, and without mercy. But some of them came into England, and, at the command of Henry II., were seized at Oxford, branded in the brow with a red hot iron, and driven away. [1166.] Whilst he disputed with her on her error, the Archbishop came up with his attendants and commanded her to be taken and led into the city. In reply to their arguments, she said that she had not been sufficiently instructed to refute their objections, but confessed that she had a mistress in the city who could most easily refute the objections of all. This old woman was accordingly brought before the Archbishop, and when pressed on every side with many questions and authorities of divine scriptures, by him and his clerks, she turned aside every authority by a certain perverse interpretation, so that it now became plain to all that the spirit of all error spoke through her mouth. To all authorities and histories, as well of the Old as of the New Testament, which were objected to her, she replied with ease and from memory, as though she had the knowledge of all the Scriptures, and were always exercised in replies of this nature, mingling the false with the true, and on the true explanation of our faith putting a pernicious construction. When they persisted in error, it was decreed by the common council that they should be consumed in the flames. And now when the fire was kindled in the city, and they were about to be dragged to punishment, that mistress of malicious error exclaimed, 'O hard and unjust judges, do you think that you will now consume me with your fires? your judgment I do not fear, and your prepared fire I do not dread.'

"On saying this she suddenly drew from her bosom a ball of thread, and threw it out of a large window, holding the end of the thread in her hands, and in the hearing of all said with a loud voice, 'Recipe!' At this word she was immediately lifted from the earth, and followed the ball out of the window with rapid flight, drawn, as we believe, by the aid of evil spirits, who formerly bore up Simon Magus in the air. But whence that wicked creature came, or whither she was transported, could never be discovered.

"But the girl, who had not yet reached such a pitch of the madness of that sect, when she could be reclaimed neither by the persuasion of reasons, nor the offer of riches, was consumed in the fire, not without admiration on the part of many, since she bore the torment of the flame without any sighs, or weeping, or wailing, with constancy and joyfulness, like the martyrs of Christ, though from a different cause, who were of old slaughtered for the Christian religion by the pagans. The men of this most impious sect chose rather to die than to be converted from their error; but their constancy and endurance have nothing like that of the martyrs of Christ: because in the latter it is piety which produces contempt of death, but in them it is hardness of heart. They assert that infants ought not to be baptized until they come to an intelligent age; they add that we ought not to pray for the dead, nor seek the aid of the saints. They condemn nuptials. They do not believe that the fire of purgatory awaits men after death, but that straightway the soul is loosed from the body it passes either to rest or condemnation. They receive no sacred writings but the evangelists and canonical epistles. Those men are illiterate, and therefore are not convinced by reasons, nor corrected by authorities, nor changed by persuasions. They choose to die rather than be converted from that most impious sect. And some who have investigated their secret opinions, say that they believe other erroneous things, and practice the most diabolical crimes."

Ralph was succeeded by BENEDICT.

"To him [Ralph] immediately succeeded, by the election of the same Abbot and Convent, Lord Benedict, of Stratford, [another Cistercian Abbey in Essex], a man of great worth, and active in whatever he undertook; who had formerly presided with energy over the same Abbey at Stratford, and increased it in various ways with large returns and possessions, both ecclesiastical and in lands and marshes."

The condition in which he found the Abbey needed all his energy; and under his rule it became more prosperous than ever before. During his time a dispute arose with the Bishop of London, (Eustace de Falconberg—chosen 1221,) concerning the Church of Sunnedon, on the opposite side of the river from that of the Abbey, and it was referred to John, Bishop of Ely, (formerly Abbot de Fontibus—consecrated 1220,) as is further stated in the account of the Parish Church.

He continued Abbot only five years, and was succeeded by GEOFFREY.

"1223, died Lord Benedict, Abbot of Coggeshall, to whom succeeded Gaufridus, prior of the same place."

Here the Chronicle ends. There is no mention of an Abbot's name until upwards of a century afterwards, in the time of Edward III., when WILLIAM JOLDAYN was Abbot, (October 30, 1341.) Again there is a blank. In 1437, JOHN TASELER was Abbot.* He was succeeded in 1449 by SIMON PABENHAM. JOHN SAMPFORD resigned in 1527,† and WILLIAM LOVE was elected Abbot. The Abbey was surrendered by HENRY MORE, the last of the succession.

Patrons and Possessions.

The original grant of King Stephen was confirmed by the following charter of HENRY II. his successor.

"HENRY, King of England and Duke of Normandy and Guienne and Anjou, to the archbishops, bishops, abbots, earls, barons, justices, sheriffs, officers, and all his liege men, greeting. Know ye that we have taken into our hand, protection, and proper alms, the Abbey of Cokeshale, and all their goods and possessions, and for the health of my soul, and of my parents, ancestors and successors, and of my kingdom. Wherefore under the common seal of the present day, I do *confirm* to God, and to the holy mother of God, Mary, and to the Cistercian monks, all the manor of Cokeshale where the Abbey is situated, with their appurtenances in lands and men, in wood and plain, in water and out of water, and in all other things to the said

---

* Cole's MSS. Vol xxvi. p. 191. Vol. xl. p. 86.

† "John Samford, Abbas de Coggeshale, res. 1527, Wm. Love electus Abbat." Harleian. 6955, p. 86, from Bishop of London's Register.

manor anciently belonging. . . . . . I do also confirm to the same church what they have at *Toleshunt* of the fee of GEOFRY DE TREGOZ, of the fee of GEOFRY DE MAGNAVILLE at Neweshales, of the fee of BALDWIN DE ROUET, and what they possess in the lands of *Moldeburne* and in the marshes of Hely.

" Witnesses :—The Earl Wm. my brother. Thos. Chancellor. Hen. de Essex. Wm. Sorrof Ham, Maurice Biset, Butler—at Rouen."

About this time also WM. FILIOL (Filiol's or Felix Hall,) gave to the Abbot of Coggeshall, and the monks there serving God, one acre, one rood, and two perches, "lying near the rivulet from the spring of Stokewelle, on the east of the Abbey."

" Wit.—Gamaliel de Witham, Ralph my bro., Theobald de Ewelle."

In 1249 ROBERT HOVEL, and Margaret his wife, granted to them lands in Childerditch, and the advowson of the Church and Warley.

RICHARD CŒUR DE LION granted to this Abbey the following charter :—

" *Richard, &c.*

" We will and command that the brethren of the Abbey of Coggeshall, and all their men and things be quit at fairs and sea ports from *toll and passage*, and portage and pedage, and every other custom and secular exaction, for all things which they shall buy and sell, or cause to be carried away, throughout every place of our authority, by land and by water to their proper use. And we forbid any one to vex or disturb them or their men or things in any manner, for that we do hold in our hands, protection and custody, both them and theirs. Neither can we protect in any manner any one who shall vex, disturb or injure them, their goods or liberties, or interdict the same granted by us or our ancestors. We do also forbid that any of their tenants be impleaded, unless before us or our chief Justice.

"Witness. The Earl Wm. de Madville. 15 Sep. at Gaytingdon."

JOHN also granted the following license, for which the Abbot paid 40 marks.*

"John, &c. Know ye that we for the love of God, and for the health of our soul, and for the souls of our ancestors and successors have granted, and by this our present charter confirmed, to the monks of Coggeshall, license *to enclose their wood* in the manor of Coggeshall with a ditch and hedge of pales, and with gates and locks, and of making therein a park, and to fell therein whatever they will, and of carrying away green and dry wood wherever they will, and of having in the same manner their dogs and the dogs of their men unbound. Wherefore we will and strictly command that the aforesaid monks of Coggeshall may have the liberties aforesaid, in perpetual alms, and in peace freely and quietly, wholly and honorably in all places and things as aforesaid.

"Witnesses:—Geoffrey, son of Peter, Earl of Essex. W. Marshall, Earl of Pembroke. W. Earl of Arundel. Wm. de Breos. Rob., son of Roger. Alberic de Vere. Hugh de Neville. Wm. Brywerre. Given by the hand of Simon, Provost of Beverley and Archdeacon of Wells—at Brehull, 1st Jan., 5th of our reign."

---

* Madox Hist. of Excheq.

HENRY III. granted, among others, the four following charters:—

"*Henry*, &c. Know ye that we have granted, and by this our charter confirmed, to our well beloved in Christ, the Abbot and Convent of Coggeshall, That they and their successors for ever may have *free warren* in all their demesne lands of Coggeshall; so that no one may enter their lands to hunt in them, or to take any thing which to free warren doth belong without the license and will of the said Abbot and Convent or their successors, upon their forfeiture of £10.

"Witnesses:—Ralph, son of Nicholas. Bertram de Crioll. Peter de Geneve. John de Lexinter. Robert de Mucegros. Peter Branche. Bartholomew Peche. Ralph de Wauncery. Rob. le Norreys and others. Given by our hand at Westminster, 26th May, 31st of our reign."

"*Henry*, &c. That they may have *one fair* for their manor of Coggeshall every year, to continue for 8 days, that is to say, on the eve and on the day of St. Peter ad Vincula, [Aug. 1] and for 6 days following, unless that fair may be to the damage of neighbouring fairs. Wit.:—The Rev. Fathers Wm. of Norwich and Rob. of Chichester, Bishops. Wm. de Valence, our brother. John Mansell, provost of Beverley. Rob. Passelewe. Arthur Lewen. Master Wm. de Kylkenny—Archdeacon of Coventry. Ralph, son of Nicholas. Rob. Waler and Anktillus Malore. Jno. de Geres and others. Given by our hand at West., 10th of Oct., 34th of our reign."

"*Henry*, &c. That they and their successors may have *one market* at Coggeshall every week, on Saturday, with all liberties and free customs to such market belonging, unless that market may be to the damage of neighbouring markets. Wit.:—Guy de Lezuignan, our brother. Master Simon de Wanton. W. de Grey. M. John Maunsell. Arcaldus de Sancto Romano. Walter de Merton. Wm. de St. Ermine. Peter Everard. Barthew Le

Bigot. William Gernon and others. Given by our hand at Baduwe. 6th April, 40th of our reign."

"*Henry*, &c. Whereas we understand by an inquisition which we have caused to be made by our well beloved and faithful Rd. de Monfichet, keeper of our forest of Essex, and Simon Passelewe, that it is not to our damage, nor to the detriment or hurt of the said forest, to grant to our well beloved in Christ, the Abbot and Monks of Coggeshall of the Cistercian order, that they may enclose *their woods and heaths* in Toleshunt Tregoz, Inneworth, Childtenditch, and Warlegh Setmel, being within the metes of our forest aforesaid. . . . . We, by a fine which the aforesaid Abbot and Monks have made with us, as much as to us belongs, do grant, and by this our charter do confirm to them, that they may enclose the aforesaid woods and heaths with a small ditch and low hedge, according to the rule of the forest, so that the deer with their young may have ingress and egress freely and without hindrance, and that the foresters both horsemen and footmen may have free ingress and egress in the aforesaid woods and heaths, to survey and keep our deer there abiding, and to make their attachments of the green wood, and hunting and other matters which to their office doth belong. . . . . And we will not that any one who has common in the aforesaid woods and heaths may be deprived of that common by reason of our aforesaid grant. Witnesses:—Guido de Lezuignan, and Wm. de Valence, our brothers. Rd. de Clare, Earl of Gloster and Hertford. Peter de Sabaudia. John Maunsell, Treasurer of York. Hen. de Bathon. Philip Lewel. Rob. Waler. Wm. de Grey. Hubert Pugeys. Master John Maunsell. Walter de Merton. Nich. de St. Meur and others. Given by our hand at Westm. 2nd April. 41st of our Reign."

One of the greatest benefactors of this Abbey was RALPH DE COGGESHALL, knight, who in the year 1276 gave 60 acres of arable land. He was the grandson of Sir Thomas de Coggeshall, who lived in the latter part of the reign of King Stephen. His father's name was also Thomas. The family probably derived their name from the place of their residence, which was Little Coggeshall Hall, not far from the site of the Abbey. This manor he held partly of the Abbots of Coggeshall and Westminster, and of Wm. atte Napleton. He purchased also Codham Hall, near Weathersfield, where he died in 1305. HERBERT DE MARKESHALL also had license in 54 Hen. III., to give to this Abbey 60 acres of arable land in his manor of Markeshall, where he died about 1274.

EDWARD I. granted the following license:—

"Edward, &c. Having ratified and accepted the gift, grant, and confirmation, which RALPH, the son of Laurence of Coggeshal made to God, and to the church of St. Mary of Coggeshal, and to the monks there serving God, of all that tenement with the appurtenances, which the same Ralph had in the town of Markeshall, of the gift of Herbert of Markeshall, to hold to the aforesaid monks in free, pure and perpetual alms, do grant and confirm the same for us and our heirs as much as in us is, as the charter of the aforesaid Ralph which the said monks have, and which we have inspected, fully testifies. In witness whereof we have caused these letters to be made patent:—Witness, myself at West. 10th Nov. 7th of our reign."

The same King also, after referring to the charter of Henry II., confirmed it:—

"Witnesses:—The Rev. Fathers, Rob. of Bath and Wells, and John of Ely, Bishops. Wm. de Valence, our Uncle. Gilbert de Clare of Gloster and Hertford. John St. John. Rich. Fitz John. Roger the Stranger, and others. Given by our hand at West. 18th Feb. 18th of our reign."

In 1291 the rents of the Abbey, according to the taxation, amounted to £116. 10s. 11d., of which £67. 11s. 10d. was from Coggeshall; Markishale, £1. 1s. 11d.; Ferringe, £3. 5s. 4d.* In the presentments of Colchester, 10 *Edw.* II., it is stated that the Abbot holds a market on Saturdays at the village of Coggeshall, to the detriment of that at Colchester.

EDWARD II. ratified all the aforesaid charters,†—

"Except the clause contained in the aforesaid Charter of King Rd., that is to say, we do also forbid that they be impleaded, unless before us or our Chief Justice.

"Witnesses:—Thos. earl of Norfolk, the marshall of England, our most dear brother. Hugh le Despenser, lord of Glamorgan. Thos. Bardolph. Rob. de Monte-alto. Thos. le Blount, steward of our household, and others. Given by our hand at St. Edmunds, 26 Dec., 19 year of our reign."

EDWARD III. made the following grant:—

"Edward, &c. Know ye that since our beloved in Christ, the Abbot and Convent of Coggeshall, have promised to find a monk, as Chaplain, to celebrate divine service each day in the church of the aforesaid House, in honor of God and the blessed Virgin Mary, and for our safety and that of Philippa, Queen of England, our dearest consort, and of our children whilst we live, and for our souls when we shall have departed from this life, We, desiring on that account to regard the aforesaid Abbot and Convent with favor, have given and granted for us and our heirs, to the same Abbot and Convent, and their successors, *one pipe of red wine*, to be received each year at London, at Easter, by the hands of Our Gentleman of the Wine-cellar, or of our heirs, for the time being in perpetuity. In testimony whereof we

---

* Quoted in Dugdale's Monasticon.
† Brit. Mus. Addl. MSS. Inspeximus. 15,553 f. 57·

have made these our letters patent. Witness, myself, at Westminster, 11 January, 18th of our reign, but of our French reign, 5th."

The same King also, in the 51st year of his reign, "granted license to WM. DE HUMBERSTANE and others, to give the manor of Tyllingham Hall, with its appurtenances in Childerditch, Dodingherst, and Southwelde, which lately belonged to William Baude, for finding a wax taper every day before the high altar at High Mass in the Church of the aforesaid Abbey." In the same reign there is allusion to "the repairing of the bridge between the markets of Cogeshale and Branketre," at Bradwell, where a small detached portion of land is still deemed part of the parish of Coggeshall.

RICHARD II. gave license in the 16th year of his reign, to ROGER KETTERICH and ADAM COOK, to grant 20s. rent in Springfield. In this place also HUMPHREY DE BOHUN, Earl of Hereford and Essex, had large estates, part of which, viz., Kewton Hall, was given to this Abbey.

HENRY IV. on the 27th January, in the 9th year of his reign, granted license to JOANE DE BOHUN, Countess of Essex and Hereford, MARGARET, wife of HUGH DE BADEW, Kt., Wm. Bourchier, chevalier, Wm. Marney, chev., Nich. Hunt, chev., Rob. Rikedon, chev., Edmund Peverell, Henry Frank, clerk, Geoffery Colvill, and John Norman, chaplain, to found an Obit in the Church of the Abbey of Coggeshall, for one monk to pray daily for the souls of the said Hugh, Margaret, and

THOMAS COGGESHALL; and they endowed it with £10 per annum, issuing out of 2 messuages, a fulling mill, 240 acres of arable, 11 of meadow, 46 of pasture, 2 of wood, in Springfield and Sandon, called Springfield Harneys and Sandford Barnes.

In the 3rd year of this reign, the Abbot is represented as encroaching on the common of Tiptree Heath, which bordered on his lands; where also there was a Priory of Black Canons of St. Augustine, dedicated to the Virgin Mary and St. Nicholas.

The above are some of the principal grants made from time to time to this Abbey, and by means of which it arose to such importance, that some of the greatest men in the kingdom deemed it no dishonor to hold office in connection with it. HENRY BOURCHIER, Earl of Essex, was chief seneschal or steward; and by deed dated 23rd October, 19 Hen. VIII. the Abbot William appointed JOHN DE VERE in his stead, with an annuity of £3. This was the fifteenth Earl of Oxford, who died at Castle Hedingham in 1539, where a splendid tomb was erected to his memory. The same Abbot, in the 22nd Hen. VIII. granted a lease of *Bowser's* or Bourchier's Grange to Richard Peverell, for forty years, at the rent of £7. 6s. 8d., and in this is the following covenant:—

"Also yt ys agreyd that the sayde Convent shall yerly observe and kepe an Obytt or anyversary within the sayde monastery, upon the last day of Feb., with dirige over-nyght and mas of requiem on the next daye; and to pray for the sowlys of Wm. Peverall and Jone hys Wyff, Wm. Rd. Jone, and Anne, and all crysten sowlys, with V. tapers on the herse, and the bells rynging, and for the said Obytt the sayde Rd. to pay Xs."

The following extracts from the Court Rolls of the Manor contain references of some little interest.*

They begin in the reign of Richard II., who came to the throne in 1377. Shortly afterwards occurred the insurrection of the villeins. Hitherto the peasantry had been entirely dependent on the will of the lord for their personal liberty; they could possess no property of their own, and were compelled to unlimited services: but the spread of intelligence, and a rising spirit of independence, now induced them to demand the abolition of serfdom. One of the chief leaders of the Essex men was John Ball, "St. Mary priest of York, and now of Colchester." He was executed at St. Alban's, less however for treason than heresy; for he was a declared disciple of Wycliffe. The insurrection was quelled; but villenage became gradually extinct: bondmen became free-laborers; the tenants became " copyholders," incapable of being dispossessed whilst they rendered fixed payments or services; as in the following extracts:—

"17 Richard II.—William Fuller surrendered into the lord's hands, two parts of a tenement once called *Herings'* tenement,† to the use of Richard Parker, to whom seisin is granted to hold

* From "Abstract taken out of the Court Rolles of the Mannors of Great Coggeshall and Litle Coggeshall, of all such surrenders and deaths of customary tenants, wherein are expressed as well the yearely rent, paiable for their customary lands and tenements, as the fynes, which they respectively paid to the lord for their admittances to the same." 17 Rd. II. to 38 Hen. VIII. and 9 to 14 Eliz.—in possession of Mr. C. Smith.

† In Church Street, belonging to Mr. Appleford.

to him and his heires, at the will of the lord, by the antient suites and customes. And he gave to the lord for a fyne, 20*d*."

" 20 Richd. II.—At this court came Richard Dodding, and did take of the lord one parcel of land in litle Cherchfeild, over against his tenement, and also a footway from his garden to the Lord's pond, called *Cherch pond*, to drawe water there. To holde to him and his heires, paying yearely to the lord VI*d*." Fine, per donation.

" 1 Hen. IV. (1399.)—The lord granted to Walter Hares a peece of land, lying at the short bregge nere the floudgates of Tye mill,* to hold from Michas. last for 100 years, paying to the lord yearly, Rent, 12*d*. Fine, 4*d*."

" 13 Hen. IV.—The lord granted to Robert Cardinall one messuage, with a little croft of land adjoyning, called the *gate house*. To hold from Michas. last, for 8 years, paying yearly to the *Ranger* [Bailiff] of the Home Grange, 8*s*."

" 7 Hen. V. (1420.)—The lord granted to John Brooke and Mary his wife a messuage, to hold from Michas. last for 10 years, paying to the *Priest of the Abbey*, yerely, R. 8*s*. F. 4*d*."

" 4 Hen. VI. (1426.)—The lord granted to John Cressing and Christian his wife, a messuage in Church Street, to hold from Easter next for 12 years, paying to the *Hog-heard* [swineherd, porcarius] of the Abbey, yerely, R. 11*s*. F. 3*d*."

" The lord granted to John Sawbyn a messuage in Church Street, to hold from Midsummer next for 12 years, paying yearly to the *Singer* of the Abbey, R. 7*s*. F. 4*d*."

" The lord granted to John Lawford a decaied cottage, with a pcell of a garden adjoining, in Stonhey Strete, called the *Crouch house*,† to hold from Easter next for 40 years, paying to the lord, yearly, R. 12*d*. F. 4*d*."

---

* Long since demolished, but there is a meadow still called Tye Mill Meadow.

† House of the Cross; or the house before which may have stood the Market cross, formerly very common in England. It is now the site of the Friends' Burial ground.

"The lord granted to Walter Hares a messuage and a peece of meadow, lying next Sir William Coggeshall's meadow, called Polerd's mead, and one shoppe in the market, to hold from Michas. last for 20 years, paying yearely to the lord, R. 29s. F. per donation."

"2 Edwd. IV. (1462.)—Richard Bullocke died, seised in fee of one customary tent called Moises, holden by the rodde at the lord's will; and that Richd. is his sonne and heire and 7 yeares old, who, by *Robert Fabian* and *John Fabian*,* is admitted tenant, and paies to the lord for a fine 20d.; and they pray to occupy the land untill his full age, and for that license they gave to the lord for a fine, 6d."

"10 Edwd. IV.—The lord granted to Thomas Clerke and Christian his wife, 2 tents, lying together over against Cogshall markett, and a cottage within the market-place, called the *Castell of Gynes*,"† and a garden thereto annexed, R. 32s. F. 20d.

"12 Edwd. IV.—The lord granted to Richard Chapman, sen. a messuage and curtilage adjoining, as it is enclosed, called Lavender, lying over against the markett of Cogshall, betweene the lord's tent, called the Cocke, on the east, and the messuage of Wm. Doreward, Esq., west, paying to the lord, yearly rent, 13s. 4d. Fine, 13d."

"21 Edwd. IV.—The lord demised to John Trewe a field, called *Starlings lese*."

"21 Edwd. IV.—John Windlove died, seized in fee of a tenement called Vernolds, *alias* Heywards, in Cogshall magna,

---

* This was probably the father or brother of ROBERT FABYAN, who was alderman and sheriff of London in the time of Henry VII., and defended the city against the Cornish rebels: he wrote the well-known *Chronicles*, and died at Theydon Gernon in 1512. There is an entry in this Abstract of a messuage in West Street, granted to Wm. Fabian, 5 Hen. V. About the same time Stephen Fabyan purchased a water mill, and the manor of Jenkin's, at Stisted. (See Fabyan's Chron. Preface by Sir H. Ellis, 1811.) There is a farm in Coggeshall still called Fabyan's, possessed by Mr. Skingley.

† In 1665 "a cottage called the Castle of Gaines," occupied by John Cooke, in grant from the King, to Edward Phillips and John Seward.

after whose death noe herriott* falls to the lord, because hee had noe living creature; but hee surrendered it to the use of Christian his daughter."

"7 Hen. VII. (1492.)—The lord, upon John Turner's surrender, admitted John Paicock to a garden and pcell of land, pcell of nether Church field, paying yearly, 1 *clove gilly floure*, 2 *capons*."

"13 Hen. VII.—The lord granted to Thomas Cavill one piece of pasture, pcell of a field called *Ingring-downe*, betweene the lord's bankes, called Robin's brooke and Ingring-downe, paying to the lord, yearely, 9s. and VIl. pepper."

"4 Hen. VIII. (1513.)—The lord granted out of his lands one peece of land or garden, called pcell of *Old church*-feild, lying in Church Street, one head abutting upon Over-church-feild lane, and the other upon the garden and messuage of Agnes Clerke, wid., by the antient rent of 6d. F. one capon."

"5 Hen. VIII.†—The lord granted, out of his hands, to John Bland a cottage and customary yard adjoining, once John Sweetings, in *Gallow Strete*."‡

"38 Hen. VIII.—Robert Whepsted surrendered one messuage with a garden, adjoining Cogshall market."

This is the last entry before the dissolution.

---

* In granting lands the lord sometimes required a *base* service, such as some days' work in harvest: sometimes a *military* service, such as to maintain a horse and arms for his use in the wars, which, naturally, on the tenant's death, devolved to the lord. The last tribute gave place to the custom of surrendering the best beast left behind, whatever it might be.

† Shortly before this, it is stated in the Records of Dunmow Priory—"1510,—Thomas le Fuller, of Coggeshall, came to the Priory of Dunmow; and on the 8 Sept., being Sunday, he was, according to the form of the charter, sworn before John Tils, the prior of the house and convent, as also before a multitude of neighbours, and there was delivered unto him, the said Thomas, a gammon of bacon."

‡ East Street. In all probability it was a place of execution at an early period, perhaps in Saxon times.

The Dissolution.

The dissolution of the monasteries was the result of many causes. The time was past in which they were needed as the only "little sacred islets," where the oppressed, the studious, and the peaceful, might find refuge from barbarism and violence. Although they had been the conservators of learning, they were become the abodes of ignorance and superstition, which the intelligence now spread amongst the people, especially by means of the press, condemned. Their accumulated wealth could not command the reverence which piety had formerly received; but became an object of envy and cupidity to hungry courtiers. They were the stronghold of the Pope in his contest with the King. The Reports of the Commissioners showed that they were full of vice; particularly the lesser monasteries and friaries. The system was rotten in England, and so easily fell before political necessity. First, those whose annual revenues did not exceed £200 were suppressed in 1535: then, three years afterwards, the greater monasteries shared the same fate. The chief agent in the matter was Thomas Cromwell, Earl of Essex: he was aided not a little by Sir Richard Rich, who received Leigh's Priory and other valuable spoils for his pains. Most of the Abbots, seeing that resistance was useless, and induced by the offer of pensions and promotions, speedily gave in their surrenders; and before the year 1538 was gone, thirty-seven of these houses in this county were extinct.

The Abbey of Coggeshall was among the larger Houses; but few of the circumstances attending its last days have been recorded. Its condition in relation to religion and morality was probably very much the same as that of others: there was enough in the report of most of them to make the reader "blush and sigh," as Fuller directs; although what a reverend divine told him is not at all likely to be true.* An instance has been already alluded to, in which some old bones found in Westfield were taken to the Abbey, and laid up in his vestiary by the Abbot, as the relics of some saint. They doubtless wrought miracles not a few. It may have been to the dissolution of this Abbey that *Thomas Hawkes* refers in his conversation with *Bishop Bonner*, who said, "'Where can ye have a goodlier remembrance, when ye ride by the way, than to see the cross?' *Hawkes*. 'If the cross were such a profit unto us, why did not Christ's disciples take it up, and set it on a pole, and carry it in procession with Salve festa dies?' *Chedsey*. 'It was taken up.' *Ha*. 'Who took it up? Helene, as ye say: for she sent a piece of it to a place of religion where I was with the visitors when that house was suppressed, and the piece of the holy cross (which the religious had in such estimation, and had robbed many a soul, committing idolatry to it) was called for; and when it was proved, and all come to all, it was but a piece of a lath covered over with copper, double gilded as it had been

* Fuller's Church Hist. B. vi. s. iii. 8.—S. Marshall lived at Finchingfield, and whatever semblance of truth his assertion had, can hardly be referred to this in preference to other Abbeys in Essex.

clean gold!" *Bon.* 'Fie! Fie! I dare say thou slanderest it.' *Ha.* 'I know it to be true, and do not believe the contrary.'"

Not long before, *John Leland*, who had been commisioned to make a search throughout the kingdom for "records and secrets of antiquity," found in the Abbey Library the following manuscripts :—

"The life of David, King of Scotland, by Ailred, Abbot of Rieval, dedicated to Henry II., and beginning—'Religiosus et pius rex David.'

"Stephen Langton, concerning Penitence—under the person of Magdalen, beginning—'Miserator et misericors.'

"John Godard, concerning the threefold method of calculating: dedicated to Ralph, Abbot of Coggeshall, beginning—'Memini me ad suadelas.'

"Odo, on the five books of Moses, beginning—'Operis subditi materia.' This Odo was a very learned theologian."

The Convent library was generally given to him who obtained the house and lands.

The possessions of the Abbey were far greater than the amount of rental might lead us to suppose; for money was then at least seven times the value that it is now. In the *Valor Ecclesiasticus* (temp. Hen. VIII. vol. vi. p. 10) the amount remaining, after certain deductions, is set down at £251. 2s. The gross income according to Speed was £298. 8s. The great extent of the lands possessed will appear in a following page. All were handed over to the King on the 5th of February, 1538, by the following SURRENDER :—

" To all Christian people to whom this present writing shall come, HENRY, Abbot of the Monastery of the blessed Mary, of

Coggeshall, otherwise Coxhall, of the Cistercian order, in the county of Essex, otherwise called Henry, sole Commendator of the Monastery of the blessed Virgin Mary, of Coggeshall, otherwise Coxhall, in the diocese of London and the convent of the same place, perpetual health in the Lord.

"*Know ye*, that we, the aforesaid Abbot and Convent, with our assent and consent, and with consulted minds, for good and reasonable causes, our minds and consciences especially moving us, of our certain knowledge and mere motion, willingly and freely have given, granted and confirmed, and by these presents do give, grant, render, deliver and confirm to our most illustrious and invincible prince and lord, Henry VIII., by the grace of God King of England and France, lord of Ireland, and defender of the Faith, and on earth the supreme head of the English Church, all our lordship, monastery, or abbey of Coxhall, otherwise Coggeshall aforesaid, and all the circuit and precinct of the same our monastery aforesaid, also all and every the manors, lordships and messuages, gardens, curtilages, tofts, lands and tenements, meadows, feedings, pastures, woods, rents, revenues, services, mills, passages, knights' fees, wards, marriages, reliefs, escheats, bondsmen, villains with their followers, commons, liberties, franchises, jurisdictions, profits of courts, hundreds, view of frankpledge, fairs, markets, parks, warrens, pools, waters, fisheries, ways, waste places, advowsons, ...

"And we do, of our certain knowledge, and with free and willing minds, renounce the same by these presents, and grant this renunciation by these writings. And we, the aforesaid Abbot or Commendator and Convent, and our successors, will warrant against all men for ever by these presents to our said lord the King, his heirs and assigns, the aforesaid monastery, and all and every the manors, lordships, messuages, gardens, curtilages, tofts, meadows, feedings, pastures, woods, underwoods, lands, tenements, and all and every other the premises, with all their members and appurtenances.

In witness whereof, we, the aforesaid Abbot of Coggeshall and Convent to this our present deed here jointly put our seal. Given the 5th day of the month of Feb., in the 29th year of the reign of our aforesaid lord the King that now is."*

After this its last impression the silver seal of the Abbey is broken. The Abbot takes his pension and departs. The monks are scattered, unlamented by those who have been taught to despise their 'super-

* There are no signatures. The seal is now broken as in the above representation, copied from the original in the Record Office—23rd July, 1862. The description in Dugdale is as follows:—
"The common seal of the Abbey on white wax pendant to the surrender in the Augmentation Office, is round. The subject of it is the Virgin and child seated under a rich canopy, with a group of females praying on each side of the Virgin. In base is a double shield, one bearing the arms of France and England quarterly, the other the arms of the Abbey, three cocks. Legend—SIGILLUM......COMMUNE......ECCLE......MONASTERII......DE......COGGESHALE." (See p. 4 ante.) Among the Cotton. MSS. Tib. E. ix. is one consisting of a number of leaves much burnt and mutilated, containing among other things, " Excerpta ex registris chartarum monasterii de Coggeshal."

stition,' or even by those whom their alms have taught to eat the bread of idleness; not without their own regret at leaving this quiet valley, with its dark stream and grove, its sunny park and meadows, and gardens of 'clove gillyflowers,' and fishponds in Pond Wick, its surrounding granges, and the fair prospect of Sunnedon Church, and Monkdown on the right, and the slopes of Ingrydown on the left, the distant fringe of Monkwood, and the little Town, 'with its rows of timber gables and louvres peeping over the fruit trees of the gardens, and the bell turrets of its three chapels and its Guild-hall spiring up here and there:' above all, the old Church of St. Mary, the cloisters and chapter-house, now, alas! given over to the spoilers, and devoted to mean uses.

Just 400 years previously the Convent first assembled on this spot; and here its life of joy and grief, of prayer and labor, had been perpetually renewed. "Here was the earthly arena where painful living men worked out their life-wrestle, looked at by earth, by heaven and hell. Bells tolled to prayers; and men, of many humours, various thoughts, chanted vespers, matins; and round the little islet of their life rolled for ever (as round ours still rolls, though we are blind and deaf,) the illimitable ocean, tinting all things with its eternal hues and reflexes, making strange prophetic music! How silent now: all departed: clean gone. The World-Dramaturgist has written—EXEUNT."

V.

ABBEY LANDS, &c.

Grant to Sir Thomas Seymour.

THE Abbot received £40 from King Henry VIII. on "acknowledging the aforesaid manors to be the right of the same lord and King." The following lands, &c. are enumerated:—

"The Manors of Coggeshall, Tutwike, Bonsers otherwise Bouseys, Holfield Grange, and Busshy Gatehouse, 2000 messuages, 500 tofts, 2000 gardens, 4 dovehouses, 10 water-mills, 4 wind-mills, 10,000 a. of land, 2000 a. of meadow, 10,000 a. of pasture, 4000 a. of wood, 5000 a. of marsh, 4000 a. of furze and heath, 2000 a. of alders, 2000 a. of fishery, 3000 a. of land covered with water, and 200£ of rent, and of the rent of 30 qu. of wheat, 60 qu. of barley, 6 lb. of pepper, 8 lb. of cummin; with the appurtenances in Coggeshall, Childerdich, Tyllingham, Thordon, Warley, Brendwoode, Springfield, Chelmesford, Borham, Tolshunt Tregoz, Tolshunt Major, Inworth, Messinge, Wakeringe, Fulneys, Feringe, Keldon, Bredwell,[*]

---

[*] Among the Benefactors of the Abbey was Sir John Hende of Bradwell juxta Coggeshall.—"17 Rich. II., Bradwell Hall was possessed by SIR JOHN HENDE or Hinde, a very rich man, Alderman of London, Sheriff in 1381, and Lord Mayor 1391 and 1404. He was a great

Patteswicke, Stisted, Revenhall, Colne Count, Halsted Magna, Tey Magna, Braxted, Canewdon, Burnham, Aldern and Fulness; also all the rectories of Childerdich and Coggeshall with the appurts.; also all the advowsons of the Churches of Childerdich and Coggshall, and of the perpetual chauntry founded in the parish Church of Coggeshall in the county of Essex; and of the Manor of Honyby Grange, otherwise Wynston Grange, with the appurts., and of 20 messuages, 10 tofts, 30 gardens, 500 a. of land, 150 a. meadow, 600 a. pasture, 40 a. wood, 200 a. furze and heath, £10 of rent with the appurts. in Wynston, in the county of Suffolk, and of 26 messuages and 26 gardens with the appurts. in the parish of All Saints at Fenn, in the ward of Dowgate and parish of St. Botolph without Aldgate, London, in the city of London."

On the 23rd March, 1538, these lands were granted to Sir Thomas Seymour, brother of the Queen who had just died.

"The King to all, &c. Whereas a certain fine was levied before Justices of the Common Bench at West. in 8 days of St. Hil., in the 29th year of our reign, between us Demandants and Henry, late Abbot of the Monastery of the blessed Virgin Mary, of Coggeshall, by the name of Henry Moore, Abbot and perpetual Commendator, &c.

"Know ye, that we, in consideration of the good, true and faithful service, which our well beloved servant, Thomas Seymour, Knight, hath done to us, of our especial grace certain knowledge

---

benefactor of Coggeshall Abbey; in gratitude for which they engaged to celebrate his obit with the solemnity of a founder. He left 100 marks for repairing the road between Coggeshall and Colchester." Morant.

and mere motion, have given and granted, and by these presents do give and grant to the same Sir Thomas Seymour all the said monastery or abbey of Coggeshall, and all the principal or chief site of the said late monastery of Coggeshall, and all the soil, circuit and precinct of the same, and also all the church, belfry and churchyard of the same late monastery, and all our messuages, &c., of the same, also the rectories, advowsons, and rights of patronage of the aforesaid churches, vicarages and rectories of Childerditch and Coggeshall, and the advowson of the said perpetual chantry founded in the said parish church of Coggeshall."

Sir Thomas Seymour did not possess these lands long, but exchanged them with the King, 12th May, 1541. On the death of Henry he became one of the Privy Council of government during the minority of Edward VI., and afterwards Lord Admiral. He married Catherine, the Queen Dowager; but his ambition and avarice led him to the scaffold, 20th March, 1549. "He was," said Latimer, in a sermon before the young King a few days after, "a man farthest from the fear of God, that ever I knew or heard of in England."

The following were the lands and possessions thus exchanged, according to the Survey returned into the "Court of Augmentations."

	£	s.	d.
Farm of Bowser's in Coggeshall. Rd. Peverell, Farmer of the King his lord, for farm, with the celebration of the anniversary on the last day of Feb. for the souls of all Christians	7	16	8
Farm of Holfield Grange. . Jno. Moygne Gen., Farmer	9	13	4
Farm of Busshegate House. . Jno. Har, Farmer	8	0	0

68 ABBEY LANDS, ETC.

	£	s.	d.
Tolleshunt Major, Manor. . Jno. King, Farmer	34	13	4
Water-mill of Coggeshall. Rd. Clarke, Miller of the King	5	0	0
Rents of Assize [Quit Rents] there, with rents of Tenants, called The Convent rents, with farm of diverse lands, parcel of the lord's lands, &c. .	85	2	2¼
Farm of Home Grange in Coggeshall. . Thos. Choping and Jno. Carnell, Farmers, there . .	48	10	0
Farm of 2 Granges, called Cuddingsell and Tuttewiche [Inworth]. Jno. Paschall, farmer of the king	13	6	8
Farm of Grange, called Kewton Hall, in Springfield	15	0	0
Farm of land and marsh, called Coggeshall Hey.	3	13	4
Rectory of Great and Little Coggeshall. Leonard Smith, Farmer there, of all those rectorial-dues, with the vicarage of Little Coggeshall			
Rectory of High Easter. . William Sorrell, Farmer there	37	0	0
Manor of Chingford Earls, in Chingford, in the County of Essex, in the hand of the King, per exchange with Thomas, Earl of Rutland. Composition of Edward Brooke, Farmer there. . .	24	0	0

These lands were not again granted altogether to one person, but divided into different portions, and so let out or bestowed from time to time.

Site of the Monastery and Abbey Farm.

It was the usual method, on the dissolution of a Monastery, to strip and sometimes utterly demolish the Church and other buildings, except the Abbot's house and offices, which were often allowed to remain for the use of the grantee or purchaser. The Abbey

Church of Coggeshall appears to have stood in the park, and very close to the present mansion or farm house, on the north side; but there now remains no trace of it, except in the unevenness of the ground.* Out of its ruins the mansion was erected; and other buildings on the opposite side were devoted to household or farm purposes. This house was probably built by Leonard Smith, who had a lease of the King for 80 years. The porch was built afterwards, and had this inscription inlaid in freestone:—

R B A
1581

On the 9th December, 40 Eliz. (1598) a lease was granted by the Queen to Matthew Bacon, of "all that mansion-house which Sir John Sharpe, knt. late held, lying within the Monastery of Great Coggeshall, near the Firmary of the Monks, with divers other lands, to hold for 21 years, at the rent of £2. 2s. 2d."

In the Ministers' Accounts of 4 Jas. I. relating to the Rectory of Coggeshall, Richard Benion being then farmer, is the following entry:—

"And he renders an account of £10 for Farm of all those rectories of Great and Little Coggeshall, &c. And also the farm of a house and barn, one called the little barn, the other called ———, situate near the King's high road leading from Great Coggeshall to Kelvedon; together with all Dovecotes, situate

---

* It was planned in the usual form of a cross. "In the summer of 1851, a long-continued drought parched the grass over some of the foundations, which were very near the surface of the soil, and left a plan of these foundations so clearly defined on the field, that it was easy to draw a measured plan of them on paper."—*Rev E. L. Cutts*, Arch. Acc. of the Remains of Coggeshall Abbey.

near the site of the Holm Grange. And also all the Brewhouses, called the Malting houses, as they are now situated between the Bake house and Brewhouse of the said monastery, towards the north & east and the stone wall towards the garden of the convent on the south side, together with the Cistern hall and Kiln house, near the Brewhouses. And also one small curtilage, as is included with the said Brewhouses lying near to them, demised to one Leonard Smith by indenture, dated 28 March, in the year of Henry VIII., for the term of 80 years."

In an inquisition of what was paid for Abbey lands at Coggeshall, 13th Sept. 16 Charles II. (1665), is the following entry in *Ralph Wooley and Thomas Dodd's grant**:—

"Thos. Bromfield, Esq., owner.—The Dairy House at the Holme Grange, together with the Sheepen House, nigh the Gate house on the north side of the King's highway. Rent, £24. 6s. 8d."

"Water mill, with chambers to the same, and the garden called Love's garden, and the other garden called Sandford's garden, in the wast ground in the monastery, £5."

"The Mansion house within the monastery, £2. 2s. 2d."

"John Wildbore, Carpenter.—The house called the Brewhouse with the pasturage of 2 cows in the old park. Rent, 8."

The site of the monastery, together with the whole Abbey Farm, was afterwards in the possession of Sir Mark Guyon, whose daughter was married to Mr. Bullock; and its present owner is the Rev. Walter Trevelyan Bullock, of Faulkbourne Hall.

In the existing remains of the Abbey there is comparatively little to interest the general reader. Within

---

* Other grants were to Geoffrey Morley, Edward Newport and John Crumpton, Lord Zouch and Edward Fulnetby, and Edward Phillipps and John Seward.

the farm-house, which was built out of the ruins of the church and chapter-house, there is a remarkable pointed arch, of plain unmoulded brick, springing on one side from a respond, and supported on the other by a circular brick pillar with a stone capital; built toward the close of the 12th century: there are also portions of two thick walls, which doubtless formed part of the Abbey. Several transition-Norman capitals lie scattered about the premises. The building nearest the farm-house is a covered *ambulatory*, with groined roof, formed of flint rubble with brick dressings, together with stone and Purbeck marble. Adjoining this at right angles is another building of two stories, the upper one of which is reached by means of a wooden stair. There are also indications that the open space between the latter and the little garden opposite was a large room of one story, with a row of stone pillars and arches down the centre. This last may have been the *Abbot's hall*; in such case, the lower story of the building on the south side may have been his kitchen and offices, and the upper story his *great chamber*. It has been conjectured that the room over the ambulatory was the *dormitory*, where the monks slept on rows of pallets down each side, in their full day costume. The detached building on the south is now known as the *monk-house*. It is a lofty room, with open timber roof, and lighted by four lancets on each side; and was probably the *infirmary*.

A flour mill doubtless existed on the site of the present Abbey Mill; and a little south of this are traces of three stews, on a piece of ground called Pond Wick. The course of the river, as already observed, had been altered at a very early period, for the accommodation of the Abbey, which could not have been placed lower, on account of the frequent floods. Although no other traces remain of the church, chapter-house, and other principal buildings, there is sufficient to show with what exquisite taste the Abbey was originally constructed. The wisdom of the monks in selecting its site will be also very evident to any one who walks into the meadow where the old Church once stood, or lingers beside the stream that still continues to flow along its appointed course.

St. Nicholas' Chapel, and the Parish of Little Coggeshall.

At a little distance from the site of the Abbey stands a building which was a Church or Chapel previously to the Dissolution, and has since been used as a barn or hay-house. It is built of flint rubble and bricks, and has a thatched roof. It presents in appearance a pleasant picture to the artist; and the materials of which it is constructed exhibit one of the earliest instances of mediæval brick-making in this country. In form it is a simple parallelogram, having a triplet of lancets under a containing arch at each end, four lancet windows on the north side, and on the south two similar ones, and the remaining jamb of a third, which together with the ancient doorway, were broken

1290.

Coggeshall Abbey, Essex.

away to make the entrance to the barn. On the south wall within, toward the east end, are three *sedilia*,* under brick arches, supported on detached shafts of Purbeck marble; and on the back of the central one the remains of a cruciform *nimbus*, of a chocolate color, which had been painted on the plaster. Probably a figure of the Saviour ornamented each of the three. Near this was a double *piscina*. East of this, again, is a small round-trefoil arched niche of stone, probably used as a *credence;* and on the north wall opposite, another niche, which formed an *ambry* or locker, in which the vessels, &c., used during mass were deposited.

There is no record of the precise period when this building was erected, but its style indicates that it was during the first half of the 13th century.†

Holman quotes the following statement from the *Villare Essexiæ*:—

"Little Coggeshal, which anciently was a parish; and the church was built by the Abbot for himself and monks, who likewise erected *another Chápel* there for their *Villeins* and *Rustics* only, and after the suppression of the house the church was pulled down,

---

* Stone seats under canopies near the altar, where the officiating clergy sat during the intervals of the service: there were most commonly three, for the priest, deacon, and sub-deacon, at high mass.

† "English Architecture:—1. Saxon, to 1066.—2. Norman, 1066 to 1145, use of circular arch in every part.—3. Transitional, 1145-1190, circular and pointed.—4. Lancet, 1190-1245:—5. Geometrical, 1245 to 1315, simple curves, mostly circles.—6. Curvilinear, 1315-1360, tracery of a flowing character, in which the sinuous curve or contra-flexure usually predominates.—7. Rectilinear, 1360-1500, remarkable for the introduction of straight lines."—*Arch. Jour.*

and the bells, as it is said, were carried to Keldon. The chapel was turned into a barn. That village was united to Great Coggeshal and made parcel of it, whence the inhabitants repair to the church of Great Coggeshal."

It has been further stated that it was dedicated to ST. NICHOLAS, and was the parish church of Little Coggeshall.* There are, however, many difficulties, both with reference to this, and to the distinction of the two parishes of Great and Little Coggeshall, which have not yet been satisfactorily cleared up.

The mention of only one name in the oldest documents would lead us to suppose that the parishes were originally one. In consequence of the gift of Godwin to Canterbury in 1046 it became a *peculiar;* for it was a custom to regard the parish in which the Archbishop possessed a manor as exempt from the jurisdiction of the Bishop of the Diocese. But this exemption does not seem to have been extended to the part now called Great Coggeshall: possibly in consequence of the division by means of the river. When the Abbey was settled here its possessions included the greater part of the surrounding land, and about a century afterwards we read of the church of Sunnedon, the vicarage of which was endowed in 1223, and the advowson left with the Bishop of London. Shortly afterwards this chapel appears to have been built by the Abbot and Convent, for the convenience of their

* Morant—without giving any authority. *Mr. Cutts* mentions a tradition that the parish church of Little Coggeshall was further west, on the other side of the lane.

laborers, and retained under their own control. Soon after this, also, the name of *Little* Coggeshall appears for the first time. In the Fines of 46 Henry III. (1262) is found the entry, "That Henry de Bretton held of Guy de Rochford, a free tenement, in Coggeshall *parva*, which Boniface, Archbishop of Canterbury, claimed a relief from, and summoned the said Henry to appear at his court in Bocking" The spiritual jurisdiction of this parish for probate of wills, &c., continued with the Dean of Bocking, at whose court a sidesman was chosen every year, and paid 6*s.* 8*d.* as an acknowledgment, until 1846, when an act of parliament passed, abolishing *peculiars*. Vicarial tithes are paid to the vicar of Great Coggeshall, according to the Commutation, to the amount of £28, part of which, however, is a *Modus*. The parish has not been accustomed to choose churchwardens, but only overseers. In the poor law division both parishes are placed in the Witham Union.

The Chapel seems to have been included at first, with the grant of the Rectory of Great and Little Coggeshall and the Vicarage of Little Coggeshall; but afterwards formed part of the Abbey Farm, and the late Mr. Bullock granted it, together with an acre of land adjoining, to the vicar of Great Coggeshall, for the time being, in perpetuity. It has this year (1862) been cleared of the rubbish within and around it, and several valuable specimens of its architecture brought to light. In an excavation just before the site of the altar, some human bones, together with part of a stone coffin, have been found,* and opposite the door the foundation of a font, built of brick; proving that baptisms and burials were at one period solemnized here.

Rectory of Great and Little Coggeshall and Vicarage of Little Coggeshall.

Soon after the exchange of the possessions of the Abbey by Sir Thos. Seymour, the King appears to have demised the Rectory and part of the Monastery to LEONARD SMITH for 80 years at £10 per annum. Afterwards Queen Elizabeth (4th Dec., 33rd of her reign) granted "The *Rectory* of Great and Little Coggeshall and the Vicarage of Little Coggeshall with all tenths and appurtenances, and a messuage called *le Kils, le Cisterne, le Maulting houses*, and two granaries called the tithe barns" to John Wells of London, scrivener, and Hercules Witham of London, gent. In the following year they sold the Rectories of Great and Little Coggeshall and Vicarage of Little Coggeshall to Richard Benyan, who afterwards granted the same to Richard Bettonson, of Coxall, gent. They were afterwards possessed by Richard Benyan, (Nov. 20, 2 Jas. I.) whose son Richard gave by will, 13th May, 1659, to his eldest son, Henry Benyan, "all the tythes of lands in the Hamlet of Little Coggeshall, great and

* There was also found in another part of the floor the skeleton of an ox. Why it was buried here is unknown. Some coins relating to the Abbey were found near the barn some years ago, and it was not an uncommon thing for 'knowing' people to dig in secret in hopes of finding treasure.

small, and the tythes of those grounds belonging to the Abbey lying in Great Coggeshall, and the Barn and ground in the Abbey lane." Henry (of Markeshall) by will, 18th September, 1673, gave to his brother Charles, in lieu of a legacy left him by his father, his tithes in Little Coggeshall, except a field called *Horse pasture* (or Pope's Leas); and by another deed of the same date he gave "all tythes and other his real estate in Great and Little Coggeshall and elsewhere, to Thomas Stafford, gent., and his heirs, to be sold for payment of his debts, the overplus to the said Thomas Stafford with the chancel of Great Coggeshall, to maintain the same." A law-suit arose about this gift to Stafford, occasioned by the sisters of Henry Benyan. One moiety was purchased by Thomas Cudmore, grandson of Benyan, and another moiety by Henry Abbot. Oliver Johnson of Earl's Colne, as the executor of Joseph Abbot of Copford, (son of Henry Abbot just named,) granted to Samuel Carter, 18th January, 1739, "one half moiety of tithes, glebe lands, of the Rectories of Great Coggeshall and the Vicarage of Little Coggeshall, and advowson of the same vicarage and one half of the chancel of the parish church." It was afterwards possessed by Ezekiel Wood and William Potter, then by Thomas Andrew, afterwards by Mr. Skingley, in whose family it still continues. The former moiety was possessed by Mr. Caswell and Mr. Thoyts, of whom Mr. Charles Newman leased it, and the present proprietor is Thomas Burch Western, Esq., M.P., of Felix Hall.

Neither rectorial nor vicarial tithes are paid by several estates when in the hands of the owner, in consequence of their having belonged to the privileged order of the Cistercians; in some cases the rectorial tithes have been purchased of the lay proprietors.

Manors of Great and Little Coggeshall.

These are separate manors, although they have always been in the possession of the same person. They formerly belonged to the Abbey, and were (12th May, 33 Hen. VIII.) granted by the King to Sir Henry Bromley, Randolph Wolley, and Thomas Dodd. In the first year of the reign of Queen Mary, she granted the manors of Great and Little Coggeshall, Home Grange, West Mill, with the Fishery of the river, to Dorothy, wife of Thomas Leventhorpe, for life, if it should please Her Majesty she should enjoy it so long. In 4 & 5 Philip and Mary, 5th April, the manor of Coggeshall was with divers other lordships in Essex united to the Duchy of Lancaster, and the manor of Little Coggeshall is set down in Witham Hundred; that of Great Coggeshall cum membris in Lexden.

On Sept. 2nd, 1604, James I. granted part of the dismembered manors of Coggeshall to Henry Bromley in fee farm. In a list of the Knights' fees holden of the Duchy is the following entry:—" Manerium de Coggeshall per nomina, &c. concessum Henrico Bromley, Militi A: 2 Jacobi tenendum de Manerio de Enefeild per Fidelitatem." In 12th James I., 10th July, they were granted to Sir James Fullerton and James

Maxwell, Esq., and their rent was £42. 2s. 6d. On the 20th of November, 22 James I., they were conveyed to William Smith and Henry Smith, Esqrs.; 7th February, 3 Charles I. to Thomas Aylett, Esq., of Hovels; 10th April, 1658, to Robert Lovitt and Penelope his wife; afterwards to Augustin Mayhew, Esq., of whom they were purchased in 1693 by Nehemiah Lyde, Esq., of Hackney. He died in 1737, leaving his estates to Richard Du Cane, Esq., who had married Anne his only daughter. Peter Du Cane, Esq., his son, was High Sheriff in 1745, and shortly afterwards purchased Braxted Lodge, where the present lord of the manor, Charles Du Cane, Esq., M.P., now resides.

These manors have usually held separate courts. That of Great Coggeshall was formerly called at the "Shambles," over against the alehouse called the Cocke.* It is only a court *baron*, or lord's court for granting land and maintaining his rights. The court of Little Coggeshall was formerly held between the bridges, in the parish of Little Coggeshall, and is both a court baron and a court *leet*, that is, a court which probably succeeded the *folc-mote* or assembly of the people for redressing injuries to one another, *e. g.* by punishing the drunkard in the stocks and the scold in a ducking-stool.† One of the most respectable men

* Near the *Gravel*. This Inn was granted to Henry Edes by James I., 1614, and in 1616 to Peregrine Gastrell and Ralph Lounds.

† There was formerly a stocks on the Grange Hill. "1682, July 6,—There was a Ducking Stole set up in the church pond." "1680, April 28,—A new pillory set up in Coxall." Old MSS. There was sometimes an inscription, such as—

"HE THAT HIS GOD DOTH FEARE,
"WILL NOT COME HERE."

was chosen constable, headborough, or magistrate.

These courts have a fine certain, viz., two years lord's quit rent for freehold, called a *relief*, and two years lord's rent for copyhold. They are both held on Whit-Monday.

Home Grange, Curdhall and Capons.

Home Grange is situated near the site of the Abbey, and formed one of its granges. It was granted along with the manors to Dorothy Leventhorp. It was afterwards, together with *Great Monkwood* and *Little Monkwood*, in the possession of Sir Henry Bromley, who joined with Randolph Wolley and Thomas Dodd in conveying it to Cyprian Warner and others. In March 25, 1606, it was granted to Edward Newport. An Inquisition of 1665 states the grant to have been to Edward Newport and John Crumpton, and its possessors to be Matthew and Isaac Ellistone.* It was afterwards possessed by Augustine Mayhew, and sold to Mr. Nehemiah Lyde, who also purchased *Curdhall* and *Capons*, and the advowson of the church of Great Coggeshall: all which he left to his son-in-law Richard Du Cane, Esq. Thomas Nicholas was occupier of the grange in 1686, and a manuscript of that date

* 1668.—Henry Benyan granted tithe of Great and Little Sherley [Burnt House?] to Priscilla Ellistone, widow, of Little Coggeshall. Witnesses:—Matt. Ellistone. Isaac Ellistone. A Deed, 1677, mentions John Cox, of Great Coggeshall, Clothier,—Matthew Ellistone, of Little Coggeshall, Clerk,—Isaac Ellistone, of Little Coggeshall, Gent.—and John Cox, son of the first mentioned, (of Mount House), who married Margaret, daughter of Anthony Walker, D.D., of Fyfield.—*Addl. Char. Brit. Mus.*

notes, "1686, July 19,—Thomas Nicholas at the grange began wheat harvest, and most of the wheat hereabouts was had in before Lammas." (Aug. 1.) At the same time William Raven rented Curdhall and Capons. In 1733 the grange was leased to Thomas Unwin, and has been occupied by this family until the present time.

Manor of Little Coggeshall Hall.

This hall stands near the river, on the left-hand side of the road from Coggeshall to Kelvedon. The site of the present house was the residence of a family of knights, who possessed lands in almost every part of the county. Sir Ralph de Coggeshall has been already mentioned as a benefactor of Coggeshall Abbey. He died 33 Edward I., leaving John his son and heir, who held at the time of his decease (13 Edward II.) a capital messuage, water mill, 8 acres and a-half of wood, 203 a. arable, 6 a. meadow, 3 a. pasture, 6*s.* 8*d.* rent, of John Filloll, by the service of half a knight's fee, and the yearly service of 64*s.* 4*d.*,—also 33 a. arable, 1 meadow, 4 pasture, 1 mill, 1 wheel, with a pool and 2*s.* 7*d.* rent of the Abbot of Westminster, by the service of 16*s.* per annum,—and of the Abbot of Coggeshall by knight's service, 44 a. arable, with 3*s.* rent, in socage, 2 granges, 2 chambers, a garden and 5 a. arable, by the service of 17*s.* 2*d.* a year. Sir John de Coggeshall, his son, held the same manor. He was twice sheriff of Essex and Herefordshire, and died 35 Edward III., leaving a son, Sir

Henry, who held this manor of the Abbot of Coggeshall by one knight's fee, and was buried at Coggeshall, 49 Edward III. This is probably the knight to whom there is reference made by *Weever*, who gives from a monumental brass in the parish church,—

......𝕮𝖔𝖌𝖌𝖊𝖘𝖍𝖆𝖑𝖊......𝖒𝖎𝖑   𝕸 𝕮 𝕮 𝕮........

"For which of the name this broken inscription should be engraven I cannot learne; but I find that these Coggeshals, in foregoing ages, were Gentlemen of exemplarie regard, and knightly degree, whose ancient habitation was in this Towne; one of which familie was knighted by King Edward the third, the same day that he created Edward, his eldest sonne, Earle of Chester, and Duke of Cornwall, Anno 1336."

His son, Sir William, Sheriff of Essex, 1391, and of Herefordshire, 1411, died at Codham Hall, in the beginning of the reign of Henry VI. He was the last of the name. The arms of the Coggeshall family were Argent, a cross between 4 scallops, sable.

Sir William de Coggeshall left four daughters, viz., Blanch, who married John Doreward, of Bocking, speaker of the House of Commons; Alice, who married Sir John Tyrrell,* of Herons; Margaret, who married William Bateman; and Maude, who first married Robert Dacres, then John St. George. John Doreward died 16 Edward IV., seized of this manor, "held of

---

* "This town of Coggeshall was the habitation of antient Knights, thence surnamed De Coggeshall, from whose heir general married into the old family of *Tirell*, there branched out a fair proportion of Tirells in this shire and elsewhere."—*Holland's Trans. of Camden.* See also *Harl.* 1137 f. 21 b 1432. f. 14. 1398. f. 6 b. 1541, f. 15. Arms. 1432, f. 5. 1541 f. 1. 1137 f. 18.

the Abbot of the monastery of St. Mary of Coggeshall, by fealty, suit and rent of 20s. by the year." It afterwards came to Sir Robert Southwell, of Filiol's Hall, and on his death fell to the crown. It was granted (20th April, 30 Henry VIII.) to Richard Long, Esq., one of the gentlemen of the Bedchamber, who died 29th September, 1 Edward VI. It afterwards came to his daughter, wife of Sir William Russel, who conveyed it to the use of Sir Thomas Cecil, the youngest son of Lord Burleigh.

His daughter Dorothy brought this estate, by marriage, to Thomas Cudmore, Esq., son of John Cudmore, of Kelvedon, Barrister-at-law, who married the daughter of Mr. Benyan, of Coggeshall. It was afterwards possessed by Mr. Latham, Mr. Blackmore, and Hugh Raymond, Esq., director of the South Sea Company. It was then purchased by A. Abdy, Esq., and D. Matthews, Esq.

The MANOR now belongs to Rev. Walter Trevelyan Bullock. It has a court baron, fine at the will of the lord, and receives customary rents from a large number of premises in Great and Little Coggeshall. The old pound, at Pound Farm, near the King's highway, has been recently destroyed. The HALL and FARM belong to Thomas Burch Western, Esq.

Bourchier's Grange.

This was another grange belonging to the Abbey. It lies in Great Coggeshall, on the way from the town to Markshall and Halstead. It probably derived its name from the noble family of Bourchier, whose chief seat was at Stanstead Hall in Halstead, and who had many halls in the county called after their own name. John de Bourchier had this estate from John de Bucks, in 1326.

"Fines 19 Ed. II. In the octaves of St. John the Baptist. Between John de Bousser, Quer., and John de Bucks, Defor., of one messuage, 85 a. of arable land, 1 a. of meadow, 6 a. of wood, 3 a. of alders, 12s. rent: and rent of 2 cocks, 4 hens, and 2 pulletts: with appurtenances in Great Coggeshall, the right of John de Bousser. The same John de Bousser gave to the aforesaid John de Bucks 40 marks of silver."

In 1321, John de Bousser or Bourchier was made one of the Justices of the King's Bench, and died leaving a son Robert his heir. The latter obtained, 4 Ed. III., charter of *free warren* for his lands in the parish of Coggeshall and elsewhere. He died of the plague in 1349, and was buried in Halstead church, where his father had been interred before him. His son married the daughter of Sir John de Coggeshall. Henry Bourchier was created Earl of Essex in 1461, and his grandson was chief seneschal of Coggeshall Abbey, as already mentioned. The last named was killed by a fall from his horse in 1540.

At what time this estate was given to the Abbey is uncertain. It was leased to Richard Peverell by the Abbot in 1530, and surrendered to the King with the rest of the posessions of the Abbey. Henry VIII., in the 36th year of his reign, granted "the Grange of Bowser's *alias* Bouchier's in Coggeshall, a messuage there, called Helford Grange, Holfield Grange, a grange called Busshegate house with appurtenances, wood and lands, called Buskett Grove, Goldington's Garden and Thornstand Grove," to Clement Smith of Little Baddow. He was the son of Thomas Smith of Rivenhall, and the family derived itself from Sir Michael Carrington, standard bearer of Richard I., in his expedition to the Holy Land; the name having been changed during exile, in the time of the civil wars. He married Dorothy, sister of Sir Thomas Seymour, and died 26th August, 1552, leaving a son, Sir John Smith, heir to his estates. Sir John was a staunch Catholic, and at a time of disaffection in the reign of Queen Elizabeth, attempted along with Thomas Seymour, second son of the Earl of Hertford, to raise an insurrection at Colchester, (12th June, 1596,) but met with a miserable failure and narrowly escaped death. He wrote from his prison entreating forgiveness, and was condemned to remain at his house at Baddow, or within one mile thereof, during the rest of his life.* But long before this, viz., on 9th Septtember, 3 Eliz., he sold his possessions in Coggeshall to Robert Gurdon, of Suffolk, who died 1578. He held "the farm or grange called Bowser's *alias* Bourchier's in Coxsall, £7. 6s. Holford Grange *alias* Holvile Grange, in Coxsall, of £9. 13s. 4d. Bushegate House £10. 6s. 8d., of the Queen in capite, by the 50th part of a knight's fee." It is now the possession of the Hony-

* Hepworth Dixon's Personal History of Lord Bacon, p. 76. Strype Ann. IV. p. 418.

wood family, of the adjoining manor and parish of Markshall.

Holfield Grange.

This was another of the Abbey granges, and is situated north of the road leading from Coggeshall to Braintree. Its name is variously spelt—*Holfield, Holville, Oldfield*. It is now a good mansion, surrounded by a park, adorned by a number of fine elms. A place on the sunny side of the hill, south of this mansion, is still known by the name of the Vineyard, and doubtless produced the wine which supplied the table of the monks. The last vines were rooted up about fifty years ago. On the dissolution of the Abbey it came into the possession of Clement Smith, and then of Robert Gurdon, Esq., as already mentioned, of whom this estate, together with that of Bush-gate-house, was purchased by Henry Osgood, Esq. He converted the house into a good country seat, and made a park around it, and left it to his daughter, who was married to Mr. John Hanbury, a rich Virginian merchant, who cased it with brick, and made other improvements. The present owner is Osgood Hanbury, Esq. It is a reputed manor, and has a pound for waifs and strays.

Hovels.

Adjoining Holfield Grange there is a farm called Hovels. The name was probably derived from Henry

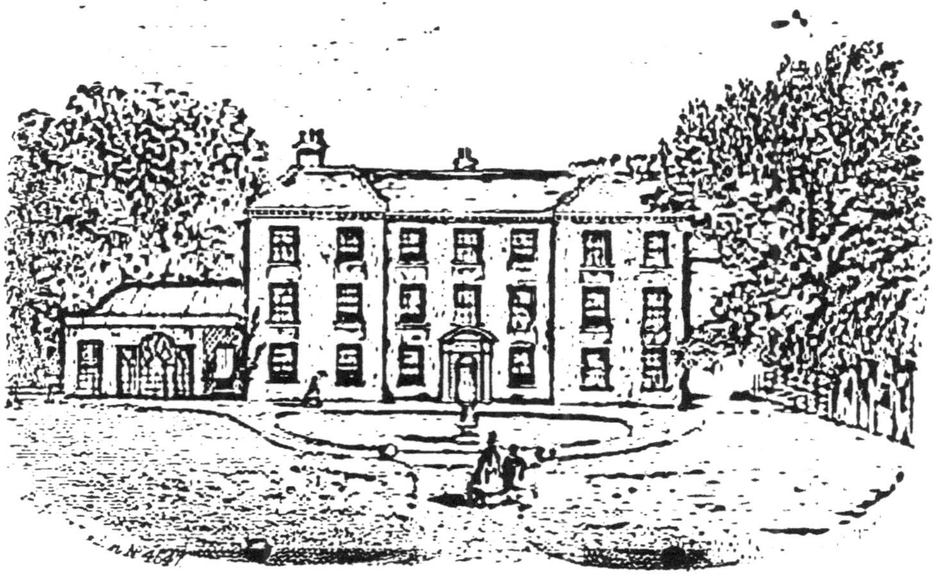

Holfield Grange seat of [illegible]

Hovel, a benefactor of the Abbey. The house is modern, but seems to have been the manor-house of Great Coggeshall. The site of it was purchased of Charles I. by Thomas Aylett, but the royalty was retained in the King's hands. The Aylett family sprang from Boydin Aylett, who had £4 worth of land in Bradwell, in the time of Henry II. Some of them lived at Rivenhall, then at Hovels, whence came the Ayletts of Braintree, Stisted and Braxted. William Aylett (1583) had, among other other estates, "Hoofeilds, Mayesbroome and Mead in Coggeshall." Thomas was buried in the Aylett vault, in the north aisle of the parish church, in 1650, where his son had been previously interred.* It was afterwards, with the land and marsh called Coggeshall Hey, purchased by Thomas Lovett, Esq., who sold it to Thomas Guyon, clothier, whose grandson George afterwards possessed it: then Anne, daughter of the latter and wife of Thomas Forster, Esq.: afterwards Mrs. Elizabeth Lamplow. The present owner is Osgood Hanbury, Esq.

Monk Downs.

This estate stands on the highest part of the parish, east of the town. Great Monk Downs, together with

---

* ROBERT AYLETT, LL.D., born 1583, was one of this family. He was made Master of the Faculties, and afterwards Master in Chancery. He assisted *Laud* in his endeavours against the Puritan clergy in this county, published several poetical works, and was buried in Great Braxted church. Robert Aylett, son of Thomas Aylett, of Hovels, Gent., was buried in Braintree church in 1657. The daughter of John Daniell, of Messing, was married to George Aylett, of Coggeshall, Gent. John Aylett, of Feering, sold some lands [Abbot's Hall, Winstree,] to Sir Mark Guyon.—*Harl.* 1542 *f.* 203 *b.* arms 887 *f.* 17 *b.* 1137 *f.* 19 *b.* 1432 *f.* 4*b.*

Little Monk Downs and Rain Crofts, was part of the Duchy of Lancaster, and granted by James I. (25th March, 1608) to Sir Edward Phillips and John Seward, gent., reserving a fee-farm rent. It was subsequently possessed by Mr. Thomas Bridge, and was sold by Mr. William Sandford to Mr. Skingley, 1783, in whose family it still continues. *Fabyan's, Mount House,* and other premises, belong to the same family.

Other Lands and Tenements.

In addition to those enumerated, there are many other lands and tenements which belonged to the Abbey, either in part or in whole, the history of which is not without interest: nor would it be difficult to trace the story of nearly every one for several centuries by the aid of the Manor Rolls, or the Rentals, or of the Grants of fee-farm rents. The latter arise from such lands of the Abbey as are not contained in the *Manor*, and are specially granted by letters patent to different persons. The amount payable from them at the present time is about £100, which is granted to the support of Sir John Mordon's College at Blackheath.*

Ancient names cling to places with wonderful tenacity, and, along with other traces which still remain, afford a glimpse into their former condition, and the

* "By the will of the donor the persons admitted must be decayed merchants, single men, 50 years of age or upwards, members of the Church of England. There are provided for them each a sitting room, sleeping room and cellar, £6 per month, 28 sacks of coals and 3 dozen candles per annum, servants and medical attendance."

state of the people who once occupied them. One of the oldest houses in the town is at **Market End**,* called in old documents *Maveson's*, and appears to have been a hall of one story, with a bell in the roof. Adjoining it, was formerly the *Crown* Inn. The date of 1565 appears on one house in Church Street, and 1585 on another in East Street : inscriptions of Scripture texts, which was formerly a not uncommon decoration, may be observed in others. The names of some are of uncertain origin and meaning : such as *Earl's Well*, in West Street; *Moses, Bullpits*, in Church Street; the *Butts* field,† *Jackletts Hawkes* and *Jaggards*, in Church Lane; *Ingar Wad* in East Street; *Busket* lands, in Tilkey ; *Wisdom's, Bentfields*, &c. In other cases the names are retained, as in *Canner's Hall* and *Copt Hall*, in Little Coggeshall; but not a trace remains of the buildings to which these names were given.

Bridges.

Besides the bridges which have been already named there is a small one called *Hare's Bridge*, probably from the name of some man who lived there. It crosses the brook which flows from Markshall into the Blackwater. The bridge at Bradwell has been already mentioned at page 53. The following are references to it :—

"Pat. 15 Ed. III., p. 2, m. 5 vel 6. That the Abbot is not

---

* Occupied by Mr. W. Mount.

† Adjoining the churchyard westward, and formerly a public parish playground.

held to repair the bridge between Branktree and Coggeshal. Ibid m. 38 vel 39."

"51 Ed. III; vide Calend. Inq. p. Mort. D'nus Rex. Stratford pons inter mercat' de Cogeshale et Branketre reparand."

The *Blackwater bridge* has been this year entirely rebuilt, by Mr. Gardner, of Coggeshall, under the superintendence of the county surveyor.

The "Short Bridge," between Great and Little Coggeshall crossed the ancient course of the river; but on this being diverted, soon after the building of the Abbey, the "Long Bridge" was built. It has been questioned whether it was quite so early as the time of Stephen: and the bricks now observed in its construction are probably not earlier than the 13th century. It devolved upon the lord of the manor to keep it in repair. After the dissolution of the Abbey, it was repaired by Queen Elizabeth, as lady of the manor and Abbey. In the Bridge Books it is recorded:—

"1618.—Long Bridge in Little Coggeshall, presented to be in decay, and to be made by the owners of the Grange and the Abbey."

"1646, Michas. session.—Presented to be in decay, and to be repaired by Mr. Thomas Osseby, in respect of his manor of Little Coggeshall."

"1649, Epiph. sess.—Pres. to be in decay, and to be repaired by Mr. Thomas Aylett."

"1653, Easter sess.—John Elliston, &c., complaining that £8. 6s. issues, escheated against the parish of Little Coggeshall, for not repairing Long Bridge there, is levied upon them, Ordered that the inhabitants of that parish do make a rate and reimburse them." [Order Book.]

Coggeshall Bridge, Essex.

There was formerly an inscription on freestone inlaid in the upper part of the bridge, on the west side:—

"This Bridge was repaired in the year 1705, at the cost and charge of NEHEMIAH LYDE, Esq., lord of the manors of Great and Little Coggeshall, and of the several fee farmers and proprietors of the lands and tenements, late parcell of Coggeshall Abbey."

The bridge is now kept in repair by the county. The present iron railing has taken the place of the old brick wall on the upper part of the bridge. On the left side of the bridge, in the accompanying sketch, there is a house which is called in old deeds the Rood House. In the little space before it there probably once stood a rood or crucifix, such as was often placed at the entrance of the Abbey demesnes; before which in days long since many a gallant knight and thrifty clothier crossed themselves, in passing over the old bridge, and many a monk and pilgrim knelt and prayed. It was broken down by ruthless hands 330 years ago.

VI.

THE PARISH CHURCH.

Endowment of the Vicarage.

There was a priest in Coggeshall at the time of the Great Survey, as already mentioned; and in the recent restoration of the Church there were found a few fragments of capitals and columns of the Transition-Norman period, which may possibly have formed part of an older Church than the present. This is all that is now known of the earliest ecclesiastical history of this parish. When the manor was given to the Abbot and Convent, whatever tithes had been previously paid were appropriated to themselves; but their vicar or substitute was appointed for the Church and parish of Sunnedon. About a century afterwards, a dispute arose between Eustace de Falconberg, bishop of the diocese, and Benedict the Abbot, which was submitted to the Bishop of Ely, who determined that thenceforth the monks should possess all the tithes of corn (predial or great tithes), and the vicar a mansion, glebe, and all other tithes (small or vicarial), and that the collation of the latter should belong to the Bishop of London.

The following is the "Regulation or Agreement

between the Vicar of Sunnedon alias Coggeshall and the Abbot and Convent there concerning the vicarage portion and other things."*

"To all the faithful of Christ to whom the present writing shall come, EUSTACHIUS, by Divine mercy humble minister of the church of London, eternal health in the Lord.

"Be it known to you universally that when there had arisen a dispute between us and our chapter on the one part, and Benedict, Abbot of the convent of Coggeshall on the other part, concerning the church of Sunnedon, then after many altercations we submitted ourselves, and the settlement concerning the same church, with unanimous consent and free will, to JOHN, by the permission of the Lord, BISHOP OF ELY, promising firmly and in good faith that, ceasing every objection and appeal, we would observe what the same bishop should ordain on this matter— when resignation was made into our hands by the aforesaid Abbot and monks of Coggeshall, of the whole of the right in the said church which they claimed for themselves, having taken counsel of men prudent and skilled in the law, he thus thought fit to ordain, viz., That the monks shall possess for the support of the poor and strangers, in perpetual right, all the tithes of Corn† [garbarum] of the whole parish of the said church, with all the land pertaining to the same church, EXCEPT the capital mansion; and 19 acres in Northfield, near the same mansion; and one acre in the field called Westfield, on the east side, as far as the meadow; and the whole meadow beyond the water course on the north side: and except the tenements which are held of the same Church, by Walter de Rustylford, John Gallicus, William de Fonte, William Bore, John Delbroche, Editha a widow, with their farmers; all which, with all the tithes, profits,

---

* Extracted from the Registry of the Consistory Court of London.

† This has been held to include likewise *hay*, and not a few disputes arose some years ago between the vicar and the lay impropriators as to his right in the tithes of hay.

and all other things pertaining to the said Church, the vicar, who for the time being shall minister in the same Church, shall possess under the name of the vicarage; and shall sustain all burdens, debts and customs: the appointment and collation to which vicarage shall belong to us and our successors in perpetuity.

"But if it shall happen that any messuage or land of the same parish shall be converted into the possession of the said monks, by the act of any one, to the detriment of the said vicarage, the same monks shall be bound by the arbitration of good men, between the vicar for the time being and the monks—Provided that the pension of Rumalicus shall be first fully and truly discharged out of the aforesaid portion—That the said monks shall often attend the celebration of the synods or chapters, unless by reason of any offence committed in the diocese of London, they shall not be deemed worthy to attend.

"And that the aforesaid settlement may be permanently established, we by pontifical authority, and with the consent of our chapter, in confirmation of the same, have thought fit to set our seal to the present writing, under our hand, and the seal of our chapter, together with the seals of the aforesaid Bishop of Ely and the said Abbot and monks, these being witnesses:—Philip de Falconbrydge. Mark Geoffry de Lucy. Reginald de Radenor and others. Done at Raynes,* VI. id. Jan. [8th January], in the second year of our pontificate."

The date of this document is 1223 or 1224. From this time the Bishops of London continued the patrons of the vicarage, until Bishop Ridley by a Quadripartite Indenture, dated the 12th of April, 4th Edward VI., (nine days after he had taken his oath for a bishopric) granted to the King all the manors of Branktry and

---

* Near Braintree, which was originally included under this name. The Bishop of London had a manor and palace there.

Southminster in Essex, Stepney in Middlesex, and the advowson and patronage of the vicarage of Coggeshall in Essex, in exchange for certain other lands of a like value. On the 16th of April, the King, "of his special grace, and in consideration of service, granted to Lord Rich the manor of Branktree, and the advowson of the vicarage and parochial Church of Coggeshall, parcel of the late possessions of the Bishop of London: yearly value, £39. 13s. 4d."* This was the Sir Richard Rich already mentioned as taking part in the dissolution of the monasteries and sharing in their spoils. Among other possessions, he had Tyllingham Hall, near Brentwood, which formerly belonged to Coggeshall Abbey, and had been granted by Henry VIII. to Cardinal Wolsey, for the building and endowment of his colleges, afterwards to Sir Thomas Seymour, who alienated it to Sir Richard Rich. He at first studied law in the Middle Temple, and was at length made Chancellor of the Court of Augmentations. He was created by Edward VI. Baron Rich of *Leighs*, and held *Rochford* and other lands. He took a prominent part in the execution of several of the Essex martyrs under Queen Mary, and continued a papist till his death, which happened 12th June, 1566. The patronage of this living was possessed by his son Robert, Lord Rich, who died 27th February,

* Pat. 4., Ed. VI., p. 1. m. 17. Cole, vol. 41., p. 485. Strype. E. M. II., i. 389. 514. *Newcourt* says (from Grimes' Collections) that Henry VIII., in 38th of his reign, granted the manor and rectory of Coggeshall to Sir R. Rich, to be held in capite by knight's-service, as he did also the Tenth going out of the late Monastery here.

1580-1; and then by his grandson Robert, first earl of Warwick, and his descendants. It was purchased by Mr. Lyde, and thus came into the Du Cane family. The arms of one of this family were formerly on a hatchment in the Church.

Newcourt mentions a Terrier in 1610, in which the vicarage is thus described:—"A vicarage-house, a barn, an orchard, and a garden, and about 19 acres and half and 3 roods of glebe land." The vicarial tithes did not amount to £100 per annum, until about fifty years ago, when by the effort of a new vicar they were greatly increased. By the Award of the Commissioners for Commuting the Tithes, dated the 28th of February, 1851, the amount of small tithes fixed for Great Coggeshall is £350. This is subject to some reservations on account of those Abbey lands which are held in the hands of the owner: such lands as could not at the time of the commutation be proved to have belonged to the Abbey were made permanently liable to great and small tithes, under all circumstances.

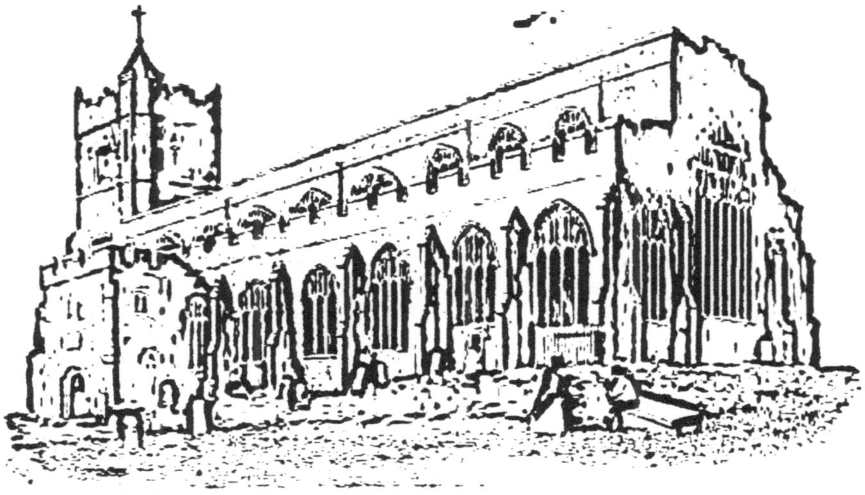

Coggeshall Ch.

General Description of the Church.

The Church consists of a nave and chancel, with two continuous aisles, a south porch, and a square tower at the west end. The walls of the chancel are built of dressed stone; the rest of rubble mingled with bricks. The length of the Church is 119 feet: its breadth 63 feet. It is in the perpendicular style; and was built between the reigns of Edward IV. and Henry VII. inclusive, probably at various intervals.*

The TOWER is the oldest part of the building. It has a west door, and opposite to this a fine arch open to the nave; and is ascended at the south-eastern corner by a staircase turret, the upper part of which having fallen in, was built of brick until the recent restoration. In comparison with the Church it is disproportionately low. A faint line on the tower within the Church, indicates the slope of a former roof; the lead flashing having been cut off close to the wall. Two of the buttresses also stand within the Church. From these facts it has been concluded that the tower was built to a smaller edifice than the present, and that soon after its completion the building of a new and larger Church was commenced.

There are SIX BELLS in the tower, bearing the dates, 1681, 1692, 1733, 1733, 1757, 1806. An old manuscript† notes:—

* *Hatfield*, in his *Architecture of the Essex Churches*, says it was built between 1404 and 1426. He has a fine view of the interior (frontispiece), and some plans, sections of mouldings, &c.
† J. Bufton's Diary, of which a further account and numerous extracts will be given.

"1681, Nov. 18.—Three Bells were run in Mr. Ennew's barn. Dec. 23.—In the night 3 others were run.

"1682, Sept.—The 6th bell and 3rd bell were new run at Colchester.

"1683, April.—The 5th bell was carried to Colchester, and there was made thereof a little bell less than the least before.

"1692, May.—The great bell was carried to London to be new shot, and was brought home again in July.

"1693.—The 4th bell was carried to Sudbury to be new shot, and the rest were chipt to make them tuneable.

"169¾.—The 4th bell was split and carried to Sudbury to be new shot, and brought home about May 7th, 1694. Then it was made too little and was carried to Sudbury to be new shot and made bigger. And was brought home about June 18, 1694; and were first rung after that, June 22, 1694."

The churchwardens' accounts of a more recent date mention:—

"1807, Sept. 10.—To Briant for recasting bell £17. 10s.

"1808, April 17.—To Thomas Hughes' bill for bells, £15. 17s. 1¼d.

"1813, July 14.—Paid the ringers for Lord Wellington, £1. July 22.—Ditto Anniversary. Aug. 3.—Battle of Vittoria. Aug. 12.—Prince Regent's birthday. Sept. 22.—King's Coronation. Nov. 4.—Battle of Leipsic.

"1814, April 7.—Allies entering Paris. April 9.—Buonaparte dethroned."

The PORCH has a fine groined ceiling with boss in the centre, originally a virgin and child, but now cut into a figure of the pelican.* A stair case at the north-west corner leads to the *parvise* (or chamber above) and continues to the leads.

* 1680, Ap. 15.—Thomas Howell, sexton was buried in the church porch.

The NAVE comprises probably the whole extent of the former Church, with its depressed roof. On each side of the present *clerestory* are five windows of three lights; and five arches on each side divide it from the aisles. A gallery was built in 1790 at its west end, and occupied by the school children, but has now disappeared. An organ, erected in 1819, was also placed there. The organ now in the chancel, was given by the direction of Mr. Henry Skingley, in 1839. There is a north door towards the western end; and immediately over it were placed the royal arms of William and Mary.*

The FONT was brought from Pattiswick† and replaces the one which stood here formerly.

The CHANCEL is separated from its aisles by two arches on each side, and deep perpyn walls, one of which has on the north the mark of an arched recess, the other three *sedilia*, opposite the communion table.‡

* "1692-3.—The new King's arms and the Ten Commandments were set up in the Church." Tradition says that the eagle which supports the desk in St. Paul's Cathedral was given in exchange for the former, which were taken down at the commencement of the present restoration and now lie at the White Hart Inn.

† It was there used as a horse-trough, and afterwards stood with flowers planted therein in the garden of Mr. W. Mayhew, M.P., who gave it to the Church; it was repaired, and the former one broken in pieces.

‡ In June, 1550, the Bishop of London held his primary visitation, and directed that the Romish altars should be taken down, and tables substituted in their stead. These tables were placed in the centre of the Church, but afterwards removed to the original position. In the Parish Minute Book is this entry: "1848.—Jan. 9.—A very high wind (the east window being still unglazed) blew down the woodwork in the chancel put up to protect the reredos, breaking the lectern to pieces, and utterly destroying the old communion table, (which was certainly quite unworthy of its purpose, and made of common deal,) the fragments of which were very reverently burnt in the churchyard next day, by the curates, with the churchwardens' sanction."

The clerestory has on each side three windows of three lights. There are in the wall of the north or *St. Catherine's aisle* two windows of three lights, and one of four lights of a different character and later date: the three windows in the wall of the south aisle are like the latter; so is the east window of that aisle. The east window in the north aisle contains paintings of the apostles, and was given by the Rev. C. G. Gretton Townsend. There remain fragments of the *parclose* or screen dividing the chancel from its aisles and chantry chapels; and also the marks of the *rood loft*, on the chancel arch, where the rood or figure of the crucifixion stood. On the north side there is a turret containing a stair, which continues to the leads. The *piscina* on the south wall and the *stoup* or holy-water basin, on the east side of the priest's door, without, have been mutilated: so have the shields with the cross-keys of St. Peter in stone at the foot of the chancel. Underneath the great east window outside is a shallow niche, with under-cusped cinquefoil arch, containing the remains of a rood carved in relief, with St. Mary and St. John, and a pomegranate in each spandril of the arch.

The destruction of these is often attributed to the soldiers of Oliver Cromwell; but it took place for the most part long before, and was done during the Reformation, as an expression of opposition to Popery, of which they were regarded as the symbols. An Act of Parliament of 4 Edwd. VI. enacted that all images in Churches should be defaced. This also applies to funeral monuments, on which were commonly the images of saints, and a direction to pray for the souls of the departed.

Holman (c. 1730) says, " The inside has nothing of that beauty and ornament which its outside promises to the transient observer, but is ill kept and runs to decay:" a state of things which has now been altered. There has been no church-rate since 1835. The chancel was repaired by the lay impropriators in 1847, and during the last ten years the whole Church has been restored, at a cost of about £3,000, the pewing only remaining to be done.*

Funeral Monuments.

" In the floor of this Church and chancel have been several fair grave stones with pourtraitures and inscriptions in Brass, which are torne off by sacrilegious hands, or worn out by frequent calcation, so that the

---

* "In 1678, between Michaelmas and Christmas, 2 new pews were set up in our Church, one for Counsellor Cox, ye other for Mr. Thomas Stafford.

" In July, 1679, there was a new pew, very fine and large, set up in our Church by John Thorne and Thomas Abbot, and was pulled down again in Aprill, 1680.

" In November, 1684, a new pew was set up in the chancel, near the door, by Samuel Sparhawke and Samuel Smith.

"1684, July 16.—Here was a visitation held by the Archdeacon in Coxall Church. Coxall Church was whited and painted."

remembrance of the persons interred had utterly perished, if it had not been for some remains preserved by Mr. Weever and Mr. Symonds* in their collections." *(Holman.)* The matrices of nearly twenty brasses remain, together with some fragments of the brasses. Monuments *against the wall* were not common until after the Reformation.

The Chancel.

A slab on the south side had the figures of a man and two females. The latter only have been preserved: date about 1480. Another has the figures of a man and one of his wives: the original design being two, with two groups of children below and a saint above; scrolls proceeding from the mouths of the females, and a horizontal scroll over the head of the man, and this inscription at their feet:—

Orate pro anima **Gulielmi Goldwyre,**†
et **Isabelle** *et* **Christiane** *uxorum, qui quidem Gulielmus obiit* 27*th Feb.* 1514.

Mary Moder mayden clere
Prey for me *William Goldwye,*

---

* Richard Symonds, born at Black Notley, 12th June, 1617, joined the royal standard, and was at the fight of Naseby, (where his cousin on the opposite side fell,) and afterwards went to Paris and Rome. From early life he was devoted to topographical pursuits. Three vols. of his Collections are now in the Library of the College of Arms: with these I have compared Holman's copy. See *Diary of the Marches of the Royal Army,* (Camden Society.)

† "8 Hen. VII.—The lord granted to William Goldwer one tenement and garden in Church-street, called Cachpoles, to hold by the rodde, at the lord's will, aying to the lord yearly 12*s.* rent: Fyne, 2 capons." Another entry to William Goldwire 28 Hen. VIII.—*Manor Rolls.*

And for me *Isabel* his wyf.
Lady for thy Ioyes syf.
Hav mercy on *Christian* his second wyf,
Swete Iesu for thy wowndys syf.†

There are other slabs, without any fragments of the brasses left, the indents of which show that they were of an earlier date than the above.

On the floor was the following:—

Orate p aia Rici Farrington,
Quondam vicarii istius ecclie qui obyt 8 *die Octob.* 1479.‡

A gravestone of grey marble, with four brass effigies and plate still preserved, with this inscription:—

FOR THE MEMORYE OF JOHN OLDAM OF EAST TILBVRYE GENT WHO DYED THE 24 DAY OF AVGVST, IN THE YEARE OF OVR LORD 1599, & OF HIS AGE THE XXXTH FRAVNCES Y DAVGHTER OF RICHARD BREWNINGE OF WIMERINGE IN THE COVNTY OF SOUTHAMPTON ESQVIRE & HIS LATE WIFE MOTHER TO ONE ONELY DAVGHTER BY HIM NAMED MARYE, HATH SET THIS TO REMAYNE.

Also the following inscriptions on the floor:—

Here lyeth the body of Mr. AMBROSE SUTTON, who departed this life the 15 day of May, A. D. 1688.

........Body of JAMES MULLINGS, who dyed the 7th of Jan. 1726. Aged 40 years.

. the body of MR. JOHN CHIGNELL, who departed this life the 10th day of October, 1720, in the 32ND year of his age.

† Weever. ‡ Symonds.

Here lieth the body of MATTHEW GUYON,
Gent., who died the 3rd day of March, 1678, and in the
46th year of his age.

Here lyeth SR MARK GUYON, Knight,
Anno Domini, 1690.*

North Aisle of Chancel.

In this aisle are several slabs of a family of the name of *Paycocke*.

"Hic jacet Thomas Paycocke, quondam Carnifex† de Coggeshal, qui obiit 21 May, 1461, et Christiana uxor ejus quorum animabus. . . . ."

"**Prey for the sowl of Robert Paycock**, *of Coggeshall, cloth maker, for* **Elizabeth** *and* **Joan** *his wyfs, who died* 21 October, 1520, *on whos soul* . . . ."

"*Here lyeth* **Thomas Paycock**, *cloth-worker*, **Margaret** *and* **Ann** *his wyfs, which Tho. died the 4 of September*, 1518."

"*Orate pro anima* **Johannis Paycock** *et* **Johanne** *uxoris ejus qui quidem* **Johannes** *obiit 2 Aprilis*, 1533. The Creede in Latine is all curiously inlaid with brasse, round about the Tombestone: *Credo in Deum patrem, &c.*" (Weever.)

The last three were brothers. On a large Sussex slab, from which a square brass has been removed, is

---

* See p. 108. There is a small mural tablet in south chancel aisle to Mr. Mark Guyon, late of White Colne, died May 31, 1839, aged 47. Also, in church-yard, several gravestones to persons of the same name John Guyon died Aug. 15, 1781, aged 72. Margaret died Oct. 18, 1778, aged 41.

† '*Butcher.*' Weever adds at the close of the inscriptions, probably with reference to the occupation of several of these persons, " I have not seene such rich monuments for so meane persons."

THE PARISH CHURCH. 105

this merchant's mark of Thomas Paycock, cut upon the stone,—

There is also a similar mark of Robert Paycock. Another slab, probably that of John, has two figures, male and female, with two groups of children beneath, scrolls proceeding from their mouths; above, the virgin and child; underneath, the inscription.

On another slab remains the brass figure of a man in long civil gown, his hands folded in the posture of devotion, and a scroll from his mouth—"**Only Fayth justifyeth**"—and round the ledge a fillet of brass, with the following inscription:—

Here *lyeth buried Thomas Peaycocke, the sonne of Robert Peaycocke, who departed this life the* xxvi^{th} *day of December, 1580, and left behinde him two Daughters, Johan, and Anne, w*^{ch} *Thomas Peaycocke Dydd gyve cc pounds to buy land for the continuall relief of the poore of Coxall for ever.*

   Thou mortall man yt wouldest attayne
    The happie hauen of heavenly rest,
   Prepare thyself of graces all;
    Fayth and repentance are the best.*

---

* Par. Reg. 1584-5, Feb. 14.—Buried John Peaycocke, the last of this name in Coggeshall. The *Manor Rolls* contain numerous references

At the upper end of the same aisle there is a slab with this inscription at its base, on brass plate:—

HERE LYETH BVRYED THE BODY OF GEORGE LAVRENCE, THE SON OF JOHN LAVRENCE, SOME TIME CLOTHIER OF THIS TOWN, WHICH GEORGE DYED THE XIII DAYE OF NOVEMBER. IN THE YEARE OF OVR LORDE GOD, 1594.

Symonds says, " In the vestry belonging to this isle are divers grave stones: but the inscriptions gone. The clerk had it by relation that they did belong to the *Colemans*, that were clothiers. In the window, Arms A. a Rower proper."

On a grave stone of blue marble is this inscription:—

HERE LYETH BURIED THE BODY OF THOMAS AYLETT, GENT., LORD OF THE MANNOR OF COGGESHALL, WHO DEPARTED THIS LIFE THE 19th DAY OF OCTOBER, 1650, IN THE 81st YEAR OF HIS AGE.

Under the north window there was also (in Holman's time) affixed to the wall a plate of brass, which is still preserved in the Church, thus:—

PRIMOGENITO· SVO.
PR CHARISEIMO·
THOMA· AYLET·
HOSPITI
LINCOLIS. ARMIGERO
POSVIT THOMA PATER
SVPERETES.

AB. HAC.

MIGRAVIT LVCI

CLARIO THE 4 AGVST.

ANNO DOMI. 1638.

---

to this family. "3 Hen. VIII.—The lord granted to John Paicock, jun., and his heires, 2 crofts of land lying together at Monkedown gate, called Shepcote crofts. 28 Hen. VIII.—*Emma Buxton*, daughter of Robert

WITH YNCH OF TIME HE TOO YE BEST IMPOVS
OF GREATER HOPES, FREE LOVING AND BELOVID:
HIS LOSE SO SOON VS LEAVES ALL FVL OF SOROW,
HE SETS TO NIGHT, WE FOLLOW HIM TO MOROO.
WHO THVS HIS COVRSE DOTH FINISH IN HIS PRIME,
RVNS THROVGH MVCH BISNIS IN LITEL TIME.*

ANNO - DOMI 1688.

South Aisle of Chancel.

There now remains in this aisle a slab, which had formerly this inscription:—

"*Orate pro animabus Johannis Kebul et Isabelle et Johanne ux. ejus Quorum, &c.* About the verge of the stone in brasse a *Pater noster* inlaid. Upon the middest of the marble this Ave Maria. *Ave Maria, gratia plena; Dominus tecum; Benedicta tu in mulieribus; et benedictus sit fructus ventris tui. Jesus. Amen.*"—(Weever.)

On flat stones these inscriptions:—

"Orate p aiabj **Petri Morseter** de Coggeshall, Mercer, obyt 8 Sept., 1471." (Symonds.)

"Here lyeth the body of **Thomas Cockerell,** Yeoman, who died 20 Sept., 1564." (Symonds.)

Paicock, is admitted to a peece of land or pasture with a way thereto, and to a peece of land with house and a garden, with water pitt thereto adjoining, called Walter Hares, by the surrender of Robert Paicock her father."

* 1650, June 11.—Mr. Nicholas Aylett, gentleman, of London. Reg. of Bur.

Here under lieth the Body of THOMAS SANDFORD,*
late of this parish, Gent., whoe departed
this life y^e eight daye of May, Anno Domini, 1636.

Crest, a boar's head coupe. Nostrils pierced with a boar's bolt.

In memory of THOMAS SMITH, Seedsman, who died August 2nd, 17(8?)1, aged 85 years. And of REBECCA, his wife; who died April 10th, 1775, aged 92 years. Also of REBECCA CL........, daughter of the above, who died July (7th,) aged ( ) years.

Mr. FRANCIS JENISON, died 7th of August, 1840, aged 82 years.

In the same aisle there is an ALTAR TOMB, consisting chiefly of black marble.

Hic jacet corpus THOMÆ GUYON, Gener. qui obiit 24º Novembris Aº. Dom. 1664. Ætatis suæ 72. He bequeathed two hundred pounds to be laid out in land, for a weekely allowance of bread to the poore for ever.

---

* There is in the Church-yard an obelisk over others of this family. They seem to have been "mighty hunters." One of them is said to have requested that Tally Ho! should be called around his grave. See Harl. 1541 f. 216 b. 1542 f. 69, 141. Arms 887 f. 16 b. f. 196, 20, 1432 f. 7 b.

Here lieth the body of THOMAS GUYON, Eldest son of George Guyon, Gent., son of Thomas Guyon, Gent., he was borne the 15th of June, 1652, and departed this life the 13th of June, 1673.

In the south aisle of the nave:—

Here lieth the body of WILLIAM CARTER, Gent.,
who died 12th Nov. 178(5?), aged 72 years.
Also the body of MARY his wife, who died 8th July, 1795,
aged 80 years.

Mural Tablets.

There are numerous mural tablets. On south side of chancel arch, facing the east:—

Memoriæ Sacrum GULIELMI FULLER, Hujus parochiæ
Generosi, Cujus animi probitas Morumq: Integritas
In Deum Pietas Erga Socios Æquitas Omnibus qui Illum
reapse norint Clarissime Effulserunt Has virtutes fervidas
(quod ipse maluisset) Non flammam sed lucem
Eficientes nos visuros Credite posteri
Morti cessit die May 15th Anno { Domini 1748. / Ætatis 68.
Hoc Marmor nitidum Tam charo capiti Grates persolvens
dignas HENRICUS FULLER, Filius ejus superstes
Humillime Dat. Dicat. Dedicat.

One on north side of chancel arch to HENRY SKINGLEY, died August 3, 1793, aged 53, and MARY his wife, died November 13, 1815, aged 75; and the following on south wall of chancel:—

Sacred
To the memory of
HENRY SKINGLEY, ESQR.,
who died July 5th, 1837,
Aged 68 Years.

One on the north wall to ROBERT TOWNSEND, Esq., "an officer in the seven ever memorable campaigns under the late glorious Duke of Marlborough," died November 26, 1728, aged 46. Also the following on south wall:—

Sacred
to the memory of
WILLIAM TOWNSEND, ESQ: ATTORNEY,
who died March 8th, 1789,
in the 65th year of his age.
Also his Brother
CHARLES TOWNSEND, GENT.,
who died May 5th, 1777,
in the 52nd year of his age.

Also WILLIAM TOWNSEND, Esq:
Son of Charles Townsend,
who died March 2nd, 1806,
in the 48th year of his age.
By whose desire this monument is erected.

Sacred
to the memory of
RICHARD WHITE TOWNSEND,
who died July 7th, 1823,
Aged 32 Years.
also of
HELEN EMM TOWNSEND,
who died Sep$^{br.}$ 30th, 1818,
Aged 8 Months.

This Tablet is placed as a small tribute
of respect esteem and regard to the memory
of MARY ANN, the beloved and affectionate
wife af the REV$^{D.}$ N. R. DENNIS, M.A.,
Chaplain to His Majesty's Forces,
and eldest Daughter
of Mr. Townsend, of Ferriers,
She died near Villa de Conde, in Portugal,
on the 8th of March, 1827,
Aged 38 Years.

On north wall—to RICHARD MEREDITH WHITE, died January 3, 1796, aged 58. On south side of chancel arch—to RICHARD WHITE, died March 22, 1806, aged 44. On north wall—to THOMAS ANDREW, Esq., solicitor, died 27th June, 1826, aged 53. Also:—

In Memory of
The Hon*ble* Lieutenant Colonel JOHN GRIME, ESQR.
(late of this Town)
who served in several Campaigns in Flanders,
and the Spanish Netherlands, with
His Grace the late Duke of Ormond,
He was a brave and experienced Soldier,
And King William the III., of Glorious Memory,
at his return from abroad gave him a Pension
for his Life, for his Bravery and courage,
which he enjoyed till his Death,
which happened the 2D day of November, 1714,
in the 74TH year of his age.

Also in Memory of
SAMUEL CARTER, HIS GRANDSON, ESQ.,
(late of this Town,)
who died the 24TH day of Octr, 1773,
Aged 73 Years.

THE PARISH CHURCH.

Church-Yard.

Most of the tomb-stones in the church-yard are of comparatively recent date. At the entrance of the priest's door part of an inscription remains:—

* * * * * *

December ye 20, 1762,
Aged 28 days,
also
JEREMIAH CRUMPTON,
who departed.... June 18, 1764,
Born Jany 14.

South of the Church, on a white coarse marble:—

Here lyes the Body of SUSANNA ABBOTT,
late Wife of John Abbott of Great Coggeshall,
in ye county of Essex, Gent,
who dyed ye 6 of April, 1709, aged 68 years.

The church-yard was enlarged some years ago, by taking in part of the open green adjoining it, on the south. The west side, adjoining the *Butts* field, was formerly set apart for the use of the Baptists, whose chapel was near. Between this and the tower are tombs of the families of *Sandford, Buxton, Godfrey, Abbot, Cox* and others, too numerous to be given at length. Among them is one as follows:—

Here lyeth the body of Mr. THOMAS COX,*
late Minister of Wytham, who dyed ye XXII of May,
A. D. MDCLXXVI, ætatis LXXII.

---

* He may have been a Presbyterian and Conformist. Thomas Cox was admitted by the Commissioners to Great Waltham, 31st March, 1653, and resigned before Michaelmas 1670. Newcourt mentions, at Witham, *John* (?) Cox, cl., presented 15 Sept., 1670, and his successor Thomas Brett, cl., 2nd June, 1676, on the death of Cox.

On a headstone occurs a rude sculpture of the Church, and a mourner walking between two trees, through the church-yard, to a newly made grave, with this inscription underneath:—

Here lieth the body of
SUSAN STEVENS,
who departed this life
March 10, 1749,
aged 59 years.

Few of the inscriptions are sufficiently curious to be specially noticed:* many have become illegible, and several stones have fallen down and perished through neglect.

There are few tombs on the north side; against which there was a very common prejudice.† A portion of the new cemetery joins it on this side, the church-yard having been ordered to be closed since 1856.

Chantries.

There were two chantries in this Church. One was founded by JOAN DE BOHUN, Countess of Hereford,

---

* The "*Excursions in Essex*" (1818) mention a stone to the memory of Thomas Hance, clothier, 1760, containing this inscription, "Lord, thy grace is free, why not for me?" Dying a bankrupt, one of his creditors who had been ruined by him, wrote underneath, "And the Lord answered and said, Because thy debts a'n't paid."

† It was sometimes called "the wrong side of the Church"—partly, perhaps, because of the belief among many early Christians, that the realm of Satan was "in the sides of the *north*," (Is. xiv. 18); but chiefly because the principal entrances were on the south and west, and the graves situated near them would be seen by the living and remind them to pray for the dead. It was appropriated for the interment of the unbaptized, excommunicate, those who had been executed or had destroyed themselves.

in the beginning of the 15th century, or about the time of the erection of the Church. The chapel in which the priest celebrated mass, appears to have been in the south aisle of the chancel. The vault underneath is said, traditionally, to have belonged to this family: it fell in some years ago, but contained no remains.

The other was founded by THOMAS PAYCOCKE, and was in the north aisle.

"By his will he directs that his body is to be buried in the Church of Coxall, before the *altar of St. Catherine:* and bequeaths 100 marks for carving and gilding of the *Tabernacle of the Trinitie* [a small cabinet for containing the host, &c., richly adorned] at the high altar, and another of *St. Margaret* in St. Katherine's Isle, where *the great Lady* [the Virgin Mary] stands: and to the reparations of the Church and bells, and for his lying in the Church, 100 nobles. He wills to a chantry to pray for him and his wife, his father and mother, Jno. and Emma, and for his father-in-law, Thomas Horold of Clare, and for all his friends' souls he is bound to pray for, 500 marks: for a lamp-burning,* and to maintain the said chantry, and 6 poor men to keep the same mass iii. days in the week, on Monday, Wensday and Friday, to pray for the souls before mentioned, and pay the said poor men 18*d.* every week, and every year 100 of wood a-piece, and the priest to sing in Coxhall Church before the altar of St. Catherine. To the friars of *Clare* for a Trental [a service of 30 masses for the dead] 10*s.* To the grey friars of *Colchester,* for a Trental, 10*s.* To the friars of *Maldon,* for a Trental, 10*s.* To the friars of *Chelmsford* 10*s.* To the friars of *Sudbury,* 10*s.,* and 3*s.* 4*d.* to each of the said houses towards their repair. Also other small bequests to several Churches.

* Mortesising [sic.] A Mortere was a light or taper set up in Churches, to burn over the graves or shrines of the dead.

To Anne his wife, 500 marks: and to the child she goeth with, 500 marks; his house that he dwelleth in, and all houses and lands if a son to him and his heires male; in default, his house and lands to remain to Thomas Paycocke, the son of his brother, Robert Paycocke. Constitutes his brothers, John and Robert Paycocke, executors. Probate, 16 February, 1518." [1519.]

In 1545 the property belonging to chantries was granted to the King; but it was not till the beginning of the reign of Edward VI. that it was actually appropriated to the crown. Commissioners were despatched (24th April, 1548,) into all the counties, to take a survey of all such chantries.

"CERTIFICATE of Chantry Lands, 2 Ed. 6 for Essex.
"*Coggeshall in Lexden Hundred.*
"Lands and tenements there put in feoffment by divers and sundry persons to the maintenance of a priest for ever, the said priest to sing mass in Coggeshall aforesaid, and also to help serve the cure. And one Sir *Thomas Francys*, Clerke, of the age of 56 years, having no other premium, and teacheth a school there, of good usage and conversation, is now Incumbent thereof. And the said Incumbent celebrateth in the said Church of Coggeshall. The yearly value of the same doth amount to the sum of £7. Rent resolute null. Goods and chattels none. It is to be considered that the same towne of Coggeshall is a populous towne, and having in it to the number of 1,000 of howseling people, and have no more but the Vicar and the said Chauntrye Priest to minister there, who is not able to serve the same without help.

"One tenement given by one *Hampser* for one yearly obite [service on the anniversary of death] for ever, in the tenure of Robert Miles, worth by the yere 2*s.* 9*d.* whereof to the poor 8*d.* Remainder clear 12*d.*

"Vere, widow, holdeth 5 crofts of land with one meadow for 2 obites, one of *Peacock* and the other of *Coldwires*, worth by the year 16s. whereof to the poor 4s. Rem. clear 12s.

"7 crofts of land and one meadow for the obite of *Rob. Peacock*, in the tenure of John Hilles, worth by the year 16s. Poor 6s. 8d. Rem. 9s. 4d.

"One garden called Godard's garden, given by one *Nesfield* for one obite for ever, in the tenure of John Gooddaie, 2s. 6d. Poor 11d. Rem. 19d.

"— *Clarke*, Taylor, gave one tenement for one obite for ever in the tenure of John Amys by Indenture, worth by the year 3s. 2d.

"*Thos. Randolph* gave a tenement with certain lands called Roodes land for the obite of the same Thomas, in the tenure of Thomas Clerke, and payeth by the year for the same 11s. 4d. Poor 3s. Rem. 8s.

"One tenement given to the founding of one obite for ever, in the tenure of Wm. Lawrence, worth by the year 3s. Poor 12d. Rem. 2s.

"One tenement given by one *Winborne* for one yearly obite for ever, worth by the year 3s. Poor 12d. Rem. clear 2s.

"One tenement given by one *Granger* for one yearly obite for ever, in the tenure of John Heyward, worth by the year 20d. Poor 8d. Rem. 12d.

"One messuage and a garden given by one *Old True* to the maintenance of the lamp light for ever, in the tenure of Henry Warde, by Indenture for term of 80 years yet to come, worth by the year 3s.

"Given out of a tenement with a cottage and a croft of land, called *Vincents*, in the tenure of John Peacock for one yearly obite for ever, by Indenture for term of 100 years yet to come, by the year 6s.

"Item, *one* old *Chaple* in the street there, with a little garden, which is worth by the year 4s.

"Item, one house, then called the *Yield Hall*, and is worth by the year 5s.

"Item, one tenement, decayed, called the Priest's chamber, with one orchard, worth yerely 5s."

To those who were turned out of their foundations, the commissioners were empowered to allow whatever provision they thought fit.

Willis, in his History of Mitred Abbeys, (vol. ii. p. 78), mentions:—

"Pensions paid ann. 1553 to Incumbents of Chantries:— Coggeshall Chantry—To *Wm. Knightsbridge*, Incumbent, £6.
,, To *Thomas Francis*, £5.
"Ann. 1555, here was £9. 6s. 8d. paid in annuities, but no pensions then remaining in charge."

Although it was at first intended to devote the proceeds of the chantries to the founding of grammar schools, most of the property, like that of the abbeys, fell into private hands.

The Parish Register.

The registers kept in the monasteries shared the fate of the other records. In lieu of these Thomas, Lord Cromwell, September, 1538, directed registers of baptisms, marriages and burials, to be kept in every parish; but few were actually commenced until many years afterwards. All clergymen were required, under a penalty, to enter notes and remembrances in their church-books, and in 1597 the Archbishop of Canterbury issued fresh injunctions, and sent persons round to see that they were carried out; which led to the transcript of earlier registers, found in most parishes. The registers of this parish are kept in an old iron-bound circular-headed wooden chest.* Much of the writing is illegible from the damp: in some periods the record is imperfect.

>VOL. I.—On parchment. Baptisms, Marriages and Deaths. Earliest date, 1558. (1 Eliz.) The first pages are evidently transcribed from some older document, and signed at the foot of each page by the vicar, *Lawrence Newman*, and *Richard Constantyne* and *Nicholas Gray*, churchwardens. Mr. Newman died in 1599, and from that time the page is signed by the churchwardens only, and another handwriting appears.

In 1653 Oliver Cromwell ordered that births (not baptisms) and burials should be registered by lay registrars, and the records kept among the records of the sessions; and that persons might be married before a magistrate, on the presentation of a certificate that their names had been duly published. There are several entries of these in the register, signed by *Dionysius Wakering*, magistrate, and *Richd. Harlackenden*, magistrate, of Colne, and always by *John Brightwen*, registrar.

>VOL. II.—On parchment. Labelled 'Marriages,' but including also Births and Burials. From 1653 till about 1680. Extremely imperfect. Many erasures and several years without any entry at all.

* Now at the vicarage.

VOL. III.—On paper. Births, Marriages and Burials from about 1680 onwards.*

In consequence of the decline of the wool trade, there was an Act passed in the reign of Charles II. requiring that all persons should be *buried in woollen*, under a penalty, and distraint was made upon the goods of the deceased, unless the proper affidavits had been made. It is to this that entries of the following kind refer:—

"1678, Sept. 3.—Whereas Francis Pigot a quaker, was buried in *linen*, I notified the default to Richard Shortland, churchwarden, on the day and year above written. Thomas Jessop, vicar of Coggeshall."

"1705, Oct. 16.—Mr. Gouge. Affidavit brought."—*Reg. of Burials.*

---

* From inside of cover of Book of Register of Marriages:—"May 14, 1680,—Mem. I, James Boys, Vicar of Coxall, did, on the day and year above sayd, tith out 400 of faggots in Monk Wood, in that part that belongs to Hovels, it being sold by Mr. Plum standing. Peter Harvey of Coxall, John Ellis, Richard —— of ——, Henry Boltwood of ——, assuring that Mr. Sedgwick and Mr. Owen had tith there formerly."

VII.
ROMAN CATHOLICS AND THE REFORMATION.

Roman Catholic Vicars.

THE bishops of London became the patrons of this vicarage and church from 1223, but the names of the vicars have not been preserved until upwards of a century afterwards. The following list is given by *Newcourt* from the Bishops' Registers:—

RICHARD DE RUSHENDEN, presented 3 id. June, 1330.

WILLIAM SEWALE,* deacon, 6 id. May, 1333.

GALFRIDUS DICTUS CHAPPELL DE BURY.

STEPHEN BROOKS, id. Oct., 1362, per resignation of Gal.

JOHN DE WEADLINGBURGH, 12 kal. May, 1369, per res. of Brooks.

JOHN BELTESFORD.

RICHARD HYDE, 6 Feb., 1384, per res. of Beltesford.

ROGER PHILPOTT.

* In 1377 John Sewale, esq., of Coggeshall, held at Pattiswick, under the abbot of Westminster, one carucate of land. Sir William Walworth, Lord Mayor, who struck down Wat Tyler, the leader of the insurrection of the villeins, left by his will (1385) £20, to John Sewale, of Coggeshall.— *Excerpta Historica. Bentley. p.* 187.

HENRY BURGERSETH or Burghwash, 22 Sept., 1425, per res. of Philpott, presented by the Archbishop of Canterbury [Henry Chicheley :* the only instance of this kind.]

ROBERT WHITE, 18 Oct., 1426, per resig. of B. [White died rector of Ethelburgh, London.]

NICHOLAS HUBERT, 8 Oct. 1450, per res. of W.

RICHARD SPROTBURGH, pr. Nov., 1456, per death of the last vicar.

JOHN SOUTHYN, 3 July, 1461, per resig. of Spr. [Southyn died rector of Copford, 1497.]

RICHARD FARRINGDON, 26 July, 1475, per res. of S. [See Funeral Monuments.]

JOHN GYFFREY, pr. 14 Oct., 1479, per the death of Farringdon.

JOHN BULGEN, A.M., 27 April, 1510, per the death of G.

STEPHEN MYTTON, L.B., 5 Aug., 1534, per the death of B.

HUGO VAUGHAN, L.B., 20 July, 1545, per the death of M.

He was presented by Bishop Bonner, and resigned in 1558. He continued to hold this living during the semi-catholicism of Henry VIII., the protestantism of Edward VI., and the catholicism of Mary, towards the close of whose reign he resigned. He continued rector of Black Notley from 12th July, 1532, till his

* The successor Arundel. Both of them were great persecutors of the English Lollards. *Chicheley* built the addition to Lambeth palace, still known as the Lollards' Tower, from the small room at the top in which they were confined by iron rings, which yet remain fixed in the walls.

death in the reign of queen Elizabeth (1564.) He is mentioned under the name of Hugo Apdd *alias* Vaughan, as vicar of Great Bardfield in 1533, and of Halstead, pr. 19th July, 1537, res. 1540. Also as rector of Gestingthorpe in 1537.

Ridley (chosen bishop on the deprivation of Bonner, 1550,) had granted away the advowson; but on Vaughan's resignation Bishop *Bonner* (restored, 1553,) collated ROBERT STOCKTON, 6th May, 1558, as patron with full right. From his appointment by Bonner it is probable that he was a Roman Catholic; but he continued vicar till his death in 1575, when the advowson fell into the hands of a lay patron, and a puritan became vicar.

Times of Reformation.

"Many ages elapsed" says Hallam, "during which no remarkable instance occurs of a popular deviation from the prescribed line of belief; and pious Catholics console themselves by reflecting that their forefathers in those times of ignorance slept at least the sleep of orthodoxy, and that their darkness was interrupted by no false lights of human reasoning." But this slumber could not continue for ever: and with the awakening of thought came difference of opinion and the struggle for truth. One of the earliest instances of religious persecution, since the Saxons settled in England, was that of the Refugees at Oxford, noted by Abbot Ralph. When brought to trial these men declared that they were Christians, and that the doctrine of the Apostles was their rule of faith; but not agreeing with all the doctrines of the Catholic Church they were cast out by the bishops and King Henry II., and perished of hunger and cold.* About the middle of the next century Wycliffe began to " declare the evil deeds of the friars," and to teach those principles which he gathered from the study of the Bible as the standard of truth. He died in 1384, but his opinions were widely spread by his disciples, the Lollards. They had already suffered much under Richard II., but it was Henry IV. who (although the son of John of Gaunt, the protector of the 'Evangelic Doctor') enacted, for the sake of conciliating the clergy, the infamous statute of *De Hæretico cumburendo*, by which those who taught without being duly authorised, and refused to abjure their heretical opinions, were directed " to be burned in the sight of all the people, to the intent that this kind of punishment might strike a terror on the minds of others."† Among those who were sufferers in this county for Wycliffism, was John Becket of Pattiswick in 1402.‡ Henry V., 'the Prince of Priests,' followed in the steps of his father: but the Lollards continued to increase. During the wars of

* Collier's Eccl. Hist., ii. 263.

† The commons however disliked his thus upholding the clergy, and in the parliament 11th Henry IV, put up a bill to the king to take the temporal lands out from spiritual men's hands, which amounted they said to twenty-two thousand marks by the year, whereof they affirmed to be in the see of Canterbury, with the abbeys of Christ's-church, of St. Augustine, Shrewsbury, *Coggeshal*, and St. Osiis twenty thousand marks by the year, &c. Foxe's Book of Martyrs. Townsend, vol. iii, p. 318. Ex chron. D. Alban (Walsingham) Fabiano et aliis.

‡ Harpsfield Hist. Wyc. 719.

the Roses, the very storm was their shelter. Fragments of the translation of the Bible by Wycliffe in manuscript were extensively circulated; and shortly after Henry VIII.'s accession to the throne, two men of this neighbourhood, William Sweeting, and James Brewster, carpenter, in the service of the Earl of Oxford, were burnt at one fire, for reading the gospel of St. Matthew and denying the orthodox doctrines. Then came the study of the Greek Testament at Cambridge and Oxford—the revival of preaching—the influence of Luther—but above all the New Testaments which the indefatigable William Tyndale had translated and printed abroad, and now sent over to his native land. These were eagerly received, especially by those who met together in secret to strengthen each others' faith, and had learned to say, "We pray in common, and that constitutes a church;"* and not a few found their way into this town and neighbourhood.

In the year 1532, "the image of the crucifix was cast down and destroyed in the highway by Coxhall." This image was probably that already alluded to as standing near the Abbey-Bridge. It is stated by Foxe, "on the testimony of *Gardner* himself." This was Robert Gardner of Dedham, who had joined three other men in burning the rood at Dovercourt, for which his companions were hung in chains, but he himself escaped by flight.†

* At Bumpstead. D'Aubigné's Ref. in England. Edinburgh p. 384.
† "In the same year of our Lord 1532 there was an idol named the Rood of Dovercourt, whereunto was much and great resort of people: for at that time there was great rumour blown abroad amongst the ignorant

The authority of the Pope was replaced by that of Henry VIII., whom he had previously declared Defender of the Faith. Catholics and Protestants were burnt in the same fire: the former for denying the King to be Supreme Head of the Church; the latter for denying the doctrines he enjoined. Yet Evangelical principles gradually advanced. An edition of the Bible was set up in every Church, chained to the desk, and groups of people gathered around to hear it read; but they might not express any doubt of its agreement with the doctrines of the Church, as then received: the last step taken in this reign in the direction of religious freedom. Whilst multitudes were suffering under the " bloody statute" of the Six Articles, the King died, having first bequeathed £600 a year to the priests, to say daily mass for his soul.¹

About this time several instances of ecclesiastical discipline before the Court of the Archdeacon of Colchester are mentioned.

"At the Court held at Coxall, 1540, the parson of Colne Wake was proceeded against for misusing the churchyard, and

---

sort, that the power of the idol of Dovercourt was so great that no man had power to shut the church door where he stood, and therefore they let the church door, both night and day, continually stand open. . . . .
Wherefore these men (whose consciences were sore burdened to see the honor and power of the almighty living God so to be blasphemed by such an idol) were moved by the Spirit of God to travel out of Dedham, in a wondrous goodly night, both hard frost and fair moonlight. They found the church door open, and took the idol from his shrine, and carried him a quarter of a mile from the place where he stood, without any resistance of the same idol. Whereupon they struck fire with a flint stone and suddenly set him on fire, who burned so brim that he lighted them homeward one good mile out of ten." Collected out of a letter of Gardner.—*Vol. IV. p. 707, ed. Townsend.*

allowing persons to die 'without howsill or shrifte throw his defoute, for he is slake and slowe.'"

"At the Court held at Kelvedon. Coxall—Burerissa Garrarde against Robert Rodyn for defamation. Rodyn had to certify of penance, and to receive greater penance if it were not done."—*f* 10 *b*.

"1541.—In the chapel at Kelvedon. Coxall—Johanna Gore is noted by the wardens of the said Church, that she uttered certain words against the Eucharist, the Catholic faith with reference to the praiseworthy customs of the Church of the Holy Mother, and especially in the following English words, viz.,—'the light that is set afore the sacrament of the auter, and the money that is gathered to maynten it, is but a papist fashion and popery.'"—*f* 53.

"1543, 22nd May. Coggleshall.—Thomas Clarke and Richard Trewe had not maide 11 mo torches, nor yet kepede the drynkinge in the parish of Coxsall, accordyne to the laudable use and custome of the same parish."—*f* 111 *b*.

"1543.—Coggleshall. . . . . We present Thomas Paykoke, y^t he hath broken an old awncient and laudable custome of or Churche, in makynge of torches, that haith bene usid every oute of mynd of man. And that the same Thomas is elected to be one of the torchwardyns, and doth refuse to take upon him the same office, accordynge to the laudable custome of the same parishe."—*f* 28 *b*. [*Hall's Precedents*.]

On the accession of Edward VI. the burning of candles, sprinkling of holy water, and numerous other customs, were discountenanced as superstitious, and the images in the Churches were destroyed. A Book of Common Prayer was compiled from the Old Mass Books and other sources, and a first Act of Uniformity passed. Three years afterwards it was revised, and Articles of Religion drawn up. But this attempt to enforce uniformity was productive of much evil, rousing the opposition of the Catholics on the one hand, and estranging the ultra-Protestants or Gospellers on the other. Congregations of the latter met in divers places, and at Bocking 60 persons were arrested, some of whom were sent to prison. Information was sent to the Council by the Lord Rich of others who came together to hear sermons on other days besides Sundays and holidays, and one such congregation probably existed in this town.

The Martyrs.

The first year of the reign of Queen Mary was spent in putting down insurrection, and in preparing to bring back the country to the Catholic church. Ridley was thrown into prison and Bonner restored to the see of London. Both these men are said to have resided occasionally at Feering Bury, a manor near Coggeshall, which formerly belonged to Westminster Abbey, and had been lately bestowed on the see of London. On 28th February, 1554, the bishop issued a monition to all the clergy of the diocese, charging them to note all their parishioners who should not come to confession, and to the sacrament; that he might proceed against them. In the following January the first court was opened for the trial of offenders. John Rogers, the proto-martyr, Bishop Hooper, of Gloucester, Laurence Saunders, of Coventry, Rowland Taylor, of Hadleigh, and John Bradford, were the first who were condemned; and whilst their sentence was being carried out, six others were awaiting a similar fate in the prison of Bonner, five of whom were Essex men, William Pygot of Braintree, Stephen Knight of Maldon, William Hunter of Brentwood, John Laurence of Colchester and THOMAS HAUKES of Coggeshall.

Thomas Haukes.

"As touching therefore his education and order of life," says Foxe, "first he was of the county of Essex, born of an honest stock, in calling and profession a courtier, brought up daintily from his childhood, and like a gentleman. Besides that, he was of such comeliness and stature, so well endued with excellent qualities, that he might seem on every side a man (as it were) made for the purpose. But his gentle behaviour toward others, and especially his fervent study and singular love unto true religion and godliness, did surmount all the rest. Wherein as God did singularly adorn him, even so he, being such a valiant martyr of God, may seem to nobilitate the whole company of other holy martyrs, and as a bright star to make the church of God and his truth, of themselves bright and clear, more gloriously to shine by his example.

"For if the conquests of martyrs are the triumphs of Christ (as St. Ambrose doth notably and truly write), undoubtedly Christ in few men hath either conquered more notably, or triumphed more gloriously, than in this young man : he stood so wisely in his cause, so godly in his life, and so constantly in his death.

"But to the declaration of the matter : first this Haukes, following the guise of the court, as he grew in years, entered service with the lord of Oxford,* where he remained a good space, being there right well esteemed and loved of all the household, so long as Edward the Sixth lived. But he dying, all things began to go backward, religion to decay, godliness not only to wax cold, but also to be in danger everywhere, and chiefly in the houses of great men. Haukes, misliking the state of things, and especially in such men's houses, rather than he would change the profession of true godliness which he had tasted, thought to change the place ; and so, forsaking the nobleman's house, departed thence to his own home, where more freely he might give himself to God, and use his own conscience."

It is supposed that he lived on Market Hill.† His unconcealed opinions, absence from church and asso-

---

* John de Vere, of Castle Hedingham, Lord High Chamberlain of England, 16th earl, son of John de Vere, chief seneschal of Coggeshall Abbey, and appointed by the abbot to hold this office on the death of his father, before which event the Abbey was dissolved. He was buried at Colne Priory, 1562.

† On the site of the house occupied by Mr. Kettle. There is now in my possession, a piece of carved oak, with the initials T. H., which was over the window of the former house: a similar piece has the date 1585. If not the initials of Haukes, they are probably those of one of his children. The house was afterwards the property of Richard Constantyne (p. 119). A family named Hawkes, of Stortford, one of whom was married to Mr. Jacob Pattisson, is said to have descended from the martyr.

ciation for worship with others of similar views, soon made him a marked man. And when he deferred the baptism of a son, who had been born to him, until the third week, because of his dislike to the Roman Catholic ceremonial, he was arrested; probably at the instance of Hugo Vaughan, the vicar, a man whose conscience easily accommodated itself to all the changes of the times; and sent to the Earl of Oxford at Castle Hedingham. The earl not caring to debate with him, and desirous of ridding himself of an unpleasant business, immediately sent him to Bishop Bonner at his palace at Fulham, and committed him to his discretion. On receiving him, Bonner wrote a letter to him that sent the prisoner, with many great thanks for his diligence in setting forth the queen's proceedings, and began the following interrogatories:—

Bishop Bonner.—" What moves ye, that ye should leave your child unchristened so long ?"

" We be bound," says Haukes, " to do nothing contrary to the word of God."

" Why: Baptism is commanded by the word of God," replied the Bishop.

Haukes. His institution therein I do not deny.

Bishop. What deny ye then ?

H. I deny all things invented by man.

B. What things be there that be devised by man, that ye be so offended withall ?

H. Your oil, cream, salt, spittle, candle and conjuring of water.

B. Will ye deny that which all the whole world and your father hath been contented withall ?

H. What my father and the whole world hath done, I have

nothing to do withall; but *what God hath commanded me to do, to that stand I.**

The Bishop then gathered from Haukes that he was acquainted with Knight, (afterwards martyred) of Maldon, and with one Baghet a preacher. Samuel Baghet, vicar of Fordham, who had recanted, was then led in, and Haukes was exhorted to follow his example: but he replied, "I build not my faith upon this man, neither upon you, but only upon Christ Jesus." Other discussions followed between him and the chaplains: and after even-song, Bonner again sent for him and said:—

B. The sacrament of the *altar* ye seem to be sound in.

H. In the sacrament of the altar? Why, Sir, I do not know it.

B. Well, we will make you to know it, and believe in it too, before we have done with you.

H. No, that shall ye never do.

B. Yes, a faggot will make you do it.

H. No, no, a fig for your faggot. *What God thinketh meet to be done, that shall ye do, and more ye shall not do.*

B. Do ye not believe that there remaineth in the blessed sacrament of the altar, after the words of consecration be spoken, no more bread, but the very body and blood of Christ? (pulling off his cap at that word.)

H. I do believe as Christ hath taught me.

B. Why? Did not Christ say, "Take, eat, this is my body?"

H. Christ said so: but therefore it followeth not that the sacrament of the altar is so as you teach, neither did Christ ever teach it so to be.

This was on Midsummer eve, 1554. He was then

---

* These examinations were printed by the writer at greater length from Foxe, in 1857, in a pamphlet entitled "Manly Principles for Young Men."

given into the custody of the porter, and located at his lodge. On the following day the Bishop went to London, for Fecknam was that day made Dean; and on the following morning (Monday), Haukes was summoned again before him and Archdeacon Harpsfield, (booted to ride to Oxford.) In this conference he plainly declared that the *mass* was profitless, *prayers* for the dead useless, and to call upon any or trust to any, save only to Christ Jesus, blasphemy. The books he possessed (he said) were the New Testament, Solomon's Books and the Psalter, and of others, he desired to read only those of Latimer, Cranmer, Bradford and Ridley. "Sir," says Bonner, "it is time to begin with you. We will rid you away, and then we shall have one heretic the less."

The day after "came thither an old bishop, [John Bird, shortly afterwards, 3rd November, put into a living at Dunmow] who had a pearl in his eye; and he had brought with him to my lord a dish of apples and a bottle of wine. For he had lost his living because he had a wife." He said to Haukes, "Alas young man ! you must be taught by the Church and by your ancients; and do as your forefathers have done before you." And when Bonner, after dinner, left Haukes with him to be converted, the old man composed himself to sleep !

The next day Fecknam, the newly made Dean, came and questioned him on the sacrament, the *real presence* in which Haukes denied: and on the following day, when Dr. Chedsey asked him, "How say ye to the Bishop of Rome?" he replied, in the words of the Litany, "From him and all his detestable enormities, good Lord deliver us;" nor did the sermon of the Doctor in the Bishop's chapel serve the more to convince him. "Ye have been with me a great while," said Bonner, the next morning, "and ye are never the better but worse and worse; and therefore I will delay the time no longer, but send you to Newgate." He was then delivered to Harpsfield, with a warrant to the keeper of the Gatehouse at Westminster.

Here he continued till the 3rd of September, when he was brought to the Bishop's palace of London, and asked if he were the same man he was before. "I am no changeling," he replied. "Ye shall find me no changeling neither," said Bonner, retiring to an inner chamber and leaving him standing amidst a crowd of persons, some of whom began to question him. "Beware!" said the parson of Hornchurch and Romford, "that ye do not decline from the Church: for if you do you will prove yourself a heretic." "Even," said Haukes, "as ye do call us heretics that do incline to Christ's church from your church, so are ye all false prophets that do decline from Christ's church to your own church. And by this shall all men know you to be false prophets, if ye say, 'This saith the Church,' and will not say, 'This saith our Lord.'" The Bishop now returned, bringing in his hand a declaration that the mass was abominable and detestable, &c., which he desired Haukes to sign, and on his refusing exclaimed, "It shall be to thy shame for denying it:"

and as in great anger he thrust him on the breast, said, "I will be even with thee, and with all such proud knaves in Essex." Calling for his horse he then rode in visitation into this county.

Haukes continued in prison through the winter, and on the 8th February was cited to appear in the Bishop's Consistory. Several articles were commenced against him, and on the following day, when exhorted by the bishop to return to the mother church, he replied,—" No, my lord, that will I not; for if I had a hundred bodies, I would suffer them all to be torn in pieces, rather than I will abjure or recant." Whereupon Bonner read the sentence of death, and so was he condemned the same day with the residue of his fellows, which was the 9th February.

Four months longer he lingered in prison, and then he was accompanied into the country by others of his native place who had been condemned to the same fate. By the way he used much exhortation to his friends; and whenever opportunity occured, he would familiarly admonish them. They stopped at an inn at Chelmsford, kept by one Scot.* Hither also arrived Thomas Wats, of Billericay, who had been brought before Lord Rich, for not going to his parish-church, and for holding unauthorised religious meetings, and was now on his way to the stake. They were allowed to converse together, and as they were eating meat they

* George Eagles (martyred at Chelmsford, 1557), "was carried to the new inn, called the sign of the Crown at Chelmsford, by the beastly bailiffs, which (some of them) were they that before did their best to take him. And being in the inn, one Richard Potter the elder, an innholder dwelling at the sign of the Cock in the same town, did much trouble him." F. viii. 395.

prayed together, both before and after meat.* They then bade each other farewell, in the anticipation of soon meeting in Heaven.

"A little before his death, certain there were of his familiar acquaintance and friends, who, frequenting his company more intimately, seemed to be greatly confirmed, both by the example of his constancy, and by his conversation; yet notwithstanding, the same again being feared with the sharpness of the punishment which he was going to, privily desired that in the midst of the flame he would show them some token, if he could, whereby they might be more certain whether the pain of such burning were so great, that a man might not therein keep his mind quiet and patient. Which thing he promised them to do; and it was agreed between them, that if the rage of the pain were tolerable and might be suffered, then he should lift up his hands above his head toward heaven, before he gave up the ghost. Not long after, when the hour was come, he was led away to the place appointed for the slaughter, by the Lord Rich and his assistants, who, being now come to the stake, there mildly and patiently addressed himself to the fire, having a straight chain cast about his middle, with a multitude of people on every side compassing him about. Unto whom, after he had spoken many things, especially unto the Lord Rich, reasoning with him of

* "At the stake, after he kissed it, Wats spake to my Lord Riche these or the like words, 'My lord, Beware! Beware! for you do against your own conscience herein: and without you repent the Lord will revenge it: for you are the cause of this my death.'"

the innocent blood of saints, at length—after his fervent prayers first made and poured out unto God—the fire was set unto him. In the which, when he continued long, and when his speech was taken away by violence of the flame, his skin also drawn together, and his fingers consumed with the fire, so that now all men thought certainly he had been gone, suddenly and contrary to all expectation, this blessed servant of God, being mindful of his promise before made, reached up his hands burning on a light fire, which was marvellous to behold, over his head to the living God, and with great rejoicing, as it seemed, *struck or clapped them three times together*. At the sight whereof there followed such applause and outcry of the people, and especially of them which understood the matter, that the like hath not commonly been heard, and you would have thought heaven and earth to have come together. And so the blessed martyr of Christ, straightway sinking down into the fire, gave up his spirit, June the 10th, 1555.*"

* *Foxe.*—Tradition says that it took place in Vicarage Field, West-street. The old wood-cut given in the earlier editions, if possessing little artistic merit, is yet full of spirit and meaning. On the left is the burly form of Lord Rich, mounted on a fiery steed, which is starting back from the gleam of the fire, and looking on with unmoved countenance, surrounded by his men at arms; and near him the priest at whose instance Haukes was arrested. On the opposite side the people are mingled with the soldiers. A poor woman, probably his wife, has a piteous look. An old man, perhaps his father, pleads for his son: another, shrewd and selfish, holds up temptingly a piece of gold between his fingers. In the background is a Church with a row of trees. The flames are bursting out between the faggots, which are piled up in great abundance, and shooting up around the martyr, who stands in the centre of all, fastened to the stake with a chain about his waist, raising his hands aloft, and striking them in triumph. There is also a wood-cut of the 22 prisoners who were led up from Colchester to London.

Three of his letters have been preserved; one to the *congregation*, another to his *wife*, and a third to Mr. *Clement Throgmorton*, who had promised to bring up his eldest son. " I have left for the child," he writes, " certain books which shall be delivered unto you, wherein his salvation lieth, if he learn and practise the same."

Thomas Osmond, William Bamford alias Butler, Nicholas Chamberlain and others.

Six other persons of Coggeshall accompanied Haukes into the county.* They had been apprehended about two months before, and sent up to Bonner by the earl of Oxford and Sir Philip Paris, with the following letter :—

" After our hearty commendations unto your good lordship, this shall be to advertise the same, that the constables of Coggeshall, within your diocese, have brought before us this day 6 persons, dwelling in the town of Coggeshall aforesaid, whose names here-

---

* *Fuller*, (Worthies) in mentioning as a proverb, or rather abusive epithet, an expression, " Jeering Coxhall," adds, " How much truth herein I am as unable to tell as loth to believe; sure I am that no town in England of its bigness afforded more martyrs in the reign of Queen Mary, who did not *jeer* or jest with the fire, but seriously suffered themselves to be sacrificed for the testimony of a good conscience. If since then they have acquired a jeering quality it is time to leave it off, seeing it is better to stand in pain till our legs be weary than sit with ease in the chair of the scorners."

after do follow, viz., Nicholas Chamberlain, weaver; John Wallet, fuller; Thomas Brodehill, weaver; Richard Web, weaver, William Bamford *alias* Butler, weaver; and Thomas Osborne, fuller; for that they, at the feast of Easter now last, have not obeyed to the order of the holy Catholic church in receiving of the sacraments; but obstinately refusing the same, besides the holding of divers other opinions, contrary to the faith of the said church. Wherefore we have thought it good to send the same persons unto your good lordship, further to be ordered as in such case shall appertain. Thus we commit your good lordship to the keeping of almighty God. From Hedingham the first of May, Anno 1555.

"Your lordship's assuredly,
"OXFORD.
"PHILIP PARIS."

In this letter there is no mention of THOMAS OSMOND, who is enumerated as one of the six meeting at Chelmsford; and there is nothing said by Foxe concerning JOHN WALLET here named. The above prisoners were examined on the 17th, and Thomas Osmond, William Bamford and Nicholas Chamberlain made answer to the articles objected against them; and on the following afternoon were condemned and delivered to the sheriffs, "in whose custody they remained until they were delivered to the sheriff of Essex, [William Harris, Esq.] and by him were executed: Chamberlain at Colchester the 14th of June: Thomas Osmond at Manningtree the 15th of June: and William Bamford *alias* Butler at Harwich* the

* "And because this borough had showed itself so early and ready for the Queen, before the coronation even; thus when she was at Framlingham Castle she and her council, out of a more than ordinary care and love for them, sent frequently Dr. Weston, Mr. Alablaster and several other

same 15th day in the month of June." Their execution in different places was for the purpose of checking heresy in those spots where it was supposed to be rife. Thomas Osborne, Thomas Brodehill and Richard Web accompanied them into Essex, but it was to make their public recantation and do penance in the parish church.

William Flower.

Shortly before this, viz., on the 24th April, William Flower *alias* Branch, who had kept a school at Coggeshall, was put to death at Westminster. He was born at Snailwell in the county of Cambridge, and placed in early life in the Abbey of Ely, where he was one of the regular priests until 21 years of age. He afterwards left and became a secular priest, and married Alice Pulton at Tewkesbury, and obtained a livelihood in several places by teaching children. After residing sometime at Coggeshall he hired a house at Lambeth beside London, and practised as an itinerant physician. Crossing the water from his house on Easter day, he came into the church of St. Margaret at Westminster, where he found the priest celebrating mass. In his excitement and zeal he drew out his hanger or wood-knife and wounded him, so that his blood mingled with the consecrated hosts in the chalice, which he at the time held in his hand. Flower was imprisoned in the

---

ministers with arguments and persuasions to them; and that no means may be neglected that might seem but to tend to their conviction and reformation, there was one William Bamford *alias* Butcher [Butler] sent hither to be burnt, and they with the expense of 5*s*. 6*d*. for wood obliged to see him executed, June 15, 1555."—*History of Harwich; by Samuel Dale*, 1730, p. 53.

Gate-house and loaded with irons. He afterwards confessed "that the same his act was evil and naught. Howbeit, as for the matter and cause wherefore he struck the said priest, (which was for ministering of the sacrament of the altar), he did not nor doth mislike himself at all therein." Refusing to recant, he was condemned, and executed in St. Margaret's churchyard. His right hand was first cut off, and "thus fire was set unto him, who, burning therein, cried with a loud voice, 'O the Son of God, have mercy upon me! O the Son of God, receive my soul!' three times; and so his speech being taken from him he spake no more, lifting up, notwithstanding, his stump with his other arm as long as he could."

A great number of Essex men had now suffered. Before the year was gone, Latimer and Ridley were martyred, and Cranmer in the beginning of the following year. "Briars and thorns," it was said, "are only to be burnt." The disappointed and fanatical Queen issued fresh proclamations.

Fourteen men and eight women of this neighbourhood were apprehended and delivered by the lord of Oxford, Richard Weston and others, to the Bishop's Commissary, 29th August, 1556. Among them were CHRISTIAN PEPPER, widow, and CICELY WARREN, spinster, of Coggeshall. They were all driven up from Colchester "like a flock of Christian lambs to London." In passing through Cheapside, the sympathy of the people was so much excited that they came to the Bishop's house at Fulham with about a thousand persons. Bonner sent for direction to Cardinal Pole, who fearing a popular outbreak, stayed his hand. An easy form of submission, not requiring them to violate their conscience, was framed and signed, among the rest, by "Christian Pepper.—Cysly Warren;" but some of the number were afterwards arrested a second time.

Mrs. Honywood.

There were many who deeply sympathised with the martyrs, and visited and comforted them in prison, but did not share their fate. One of the most notable of these was Mistress Mary Honywood, the second daughter of Robert Attwater or Waters, of Royton, near Lenham in Kent. She was born in 1527, and at 16 years of age was married to Robert Honywood of Charing, in the same county. When Bradford was in prison she sent to him, and there are extant three letters which he wrote to his "dear sister in the Lord," and one to her sister Joyce, the wife of Humphrey Hales of Canterbury.* She was present at the burning of Bradford in Smithfield, and so great was the crowd that she had her shoes trodden off her feet, and was obliged to go barefoot to St. Martin's before she could procure a new pair for money.

* Foxe gives the first two: "To Mistress M. H. a godly gentlewoman, comforting her in common heaviness and godly sorrow, which the feeling and sense of sin worketh in God's children." "Another letter, full of godly comfort, to the same person." Myles Coverdale gives the other two: "To my good sister M. H.," and "To Mrs. J. H. (Joyce Hales)." He calls her "Joyce, my good Joyce."—*Letters of the Martyrs*, p. 426 and 822, (ed. 1564.)

Her husband died in 1576, and in 1605 her son Robert purchased Markshall, where she resided during the latter part of her life. On one side of the mantel-piece are the letters R H. O., and on the other, 1609, indicating the date when this part of the building was finished. Thomas Fuller (in his Worthies) tells the following story:—

"Being much afflicted in mind, many ministers repaired to her, and amongst the rest Reverend Mr. John Fox, than whom no more happy an instrument to set the joynts of a broken spirit. All his counsels proved ineffectual, insomuch that in the agony of her soul, having a Venice-glass in her hand, she brake forth into this expression: I am as surely damned as this glasse is broken, which she immediately threw with violence to the ground. Here happened a wonder, the glasse rebounded again, (as some have reported and more have believed), but continued a great time after (short is long to people in pain) in her former disconsolate condition without any amendment. Until at last God, the great clock-keeper of Time, who findeth out the fittest minutes for his own mercies, suddenly shot comfort like lightning into her soul; which once entered, ever remained therein, (God doth no palliate cures, what he heals it holds), so that she led the remainder of her life in spiritual gladnesse. This she herself told to the Reverend father, Thomas Morton, Bishop of Duresme, from whose mouth I have received this relation."

She died at Markshall, but was buried beside her husband at Lenham. In the chancel of Markshall Church there is a marble statue of a woman kneeling, with an open book before her, and this inscription:—

"Mary Waters, daughter and co-heire of Robert Waters, of Lenham, in Kent, Esq., wife of Robert Honywood, of Charange, in Kent, Esq., her onely husband, had at her decease lawfully descended from her 367 children, 16 of her owne body, 114 grandchildren, 228 in the third generation, and 9 in the fowerth. She led a most pious life, and in a Christian manner died here at Markshall in the 93 yeare of her age, and the 44 of her widowhood, the 16 of May, 1620.*

> In memoriam charissimæ ac prentissimæ matris
> suæ officii et amoris ergo sacrum hoc posuit
> illius primogenitus Robertus Honywood, armiger."

Robert her son died in 1627. A manuscript written by him states,—

"My father maried my mother in Febr., 1543, as by her owne speeche affirminge that she was maried at Shroftyde, and the lycence for marriadge is so dated, and that also apeareth true by the indentures of marriadge y^t passed betweene my father and grandfather Waters. My mother also saieth y^t I was borne at Royton uppon M's [Michaelmas] eve's eve was twelve moneth follewinge, wch was ye 27 of September, 1545. And so am I at M's eve's eve, 1612, of the age of 67 yeares." "My mother departed this life at my house in Markeshall, uppon Tewesday, ye 16 day of May, 1620, in ye 93 year of her age, and according to her desyer was buryed in Lenham church, in ye county of Kent, uppon Saturday then followinge."

"Thomas Honiwood was born ther [Bechworth Castell in Surrey] also, uppon Sonday ye xv. of January, 1587 [-7], about 4 in ye morning, and was baptized in ye chappell ther: Sir Tho. Browne myne uncle, Richard Browne of Crandley and his wife wear witnesses." [Nicholls' Topographer. Honywood evidences. vol. i. and ii.]

* Her grandson, Dr. Michael Honywood, used to relate that he was present at a dinner given by her to a family party of 200 of her descendants. There is at Markshall an original portrait of her in the habit of her widowhood, with a book in her hand. On her hat is inscribed— "Ætatis suæ 70," and on the opposite side—"ANO· DNI· 1597." The fragments of the Venetian glass, broken some years ago, are still preserved there.

Marks Hall & Church. Pl. 1.

Early Puritanism, &c.

ACTS of supremacy and uniformity were passed on the accession of Elizabeth: the one declaring the Queen to be head of the Church; and the other enjoining the use of the Book of Common Prayer, as revised and made less ultra-protestant, and forbidding any to absent themselves, under severest penalties, from the place where it was used. In a Convocation of the clergy, held in 1562, the 42 Articles were reduced to 39, and it was decided by a majority of one vote, that the vestments which by the most advanced reformers were regarded as intimately associated with Roman Catholic doctrines, and other ceremonies—such as the use of godfathers and godmothers, the sign of the cross in baptism, kneeling at the sacrament, bowing at the name of Jesus, &c.—should be continued. Then first arose the name of Puritan, which was applied to those who desired a purer form of worship and discipline in the church; and soon a fierce conflict commenced, first on the *vestments*, then on church *government*, and finally on *doctrine*. The Puritans were greatly harassed by Archbishop Parker, but favored by his successor Grindal, who, for encouraging preaching, fell under the royal displeasure * They were again harassed by Whitgift, who issued orders that none should be permitted to preach, unless they subscribed the three articles concerning the Queen's supremacy, the Book of Common Prayer, and the Articles. *Aylmer*, Bishop of London, then (1584) visited every parish of the diocese, with the view of enforcing these orders; and thirty-eight ministers in this county were silenced or suspended.

Among these was LAURENCE NEWMAN, M.A., vicar of Coggeshall. He had been presented to this vicarage 10th February, 1575, by Robert, Lord Rich, son of Lord Rich already mentioned. He refused to subscribe the three articles, and was suspended for half a year.† He died in 1599.

WILLIAM DYKE, a name still better known, was also suspended here at the same time. He was educated at Cambridge, and was preacher at Coggeshall at the time of Aylmer's visitation, and, refusing to subscribe the articles, was suspended along with Mr. Newman. How long he had been here previously is unknown.

---

* Queen Elizabeth is said to have stayed during one of her itineraries at Feering Bury, where there is a pane of glass marked with her initials. I find, however, nothing but a tradition to this effect. The account given of her journey is:—

"1579. Sept. 1.—At Colchester, and there 2 days.

„   „   8.—To Layer Marney, Mrs. Tuke's, and there 2 days."

She probably took Feering Bury in her way.

† Register in Dr. Williams's Library.

"1585, June 20.—Buried Rebecca, daughter of Laurence Newman.
1593.————————Anne————————————————
1599, Mar. 18 ————Mr. Lawrence Newman, vicar of Coggeshall."—*Par. Reg.*

He was at length obliged to leave the county, and then settled at St. Alban's, where his ministry was very useful. "He united with his brethren to promote a more pure reformation of the church, and with this object in view, assembled with them in their private associations. But in this, as in his former situation, the watchful eye of Aylmer was upon him, and he was involved in fresh troubles. Because he continued a deacon, and did not enter into priest's orders, which the bishop supposed he accounted popish; and because he refused to wear the surplice, and troubled his auditory, as his grace signified, with notions which thwarted the established religion, he was again suspended, and at last deprived in the year 1589. The distressed parishioners being concerned for the loss of their minister, petitioned the Lord Treasurer Burleigh, who had been Mr. Dyke's great friend, to intercede with the Bishop in their behalf. But all that the Treasurer could do proved ineffectual. He died about the year 1614."* He was the father of Daniel Dyke, B.D., who died 1620, and of Jeremiah Dyke,† of Epping, both of whom were eminent preachers.

Others of this neighbourhood likewise suffered from the same cause. *Cornwell*, minister of Mark's Tey,

---

* Brook's Lives of the Puritans. Where, however, Daniel is put for William Dyke. Neal i. 284.

† "1584, Oct. 13.—*Hieremy*, son of Wm. Dike, preacher of Coggeshall."—*Par. Register of Baptisms.* He became minister at Epping, and after the decease of his brother, Daniel Dyke, published the treatise written by the latter "On the Deceitfulness of the Heart." He had also a son born at Epping, 1617, named after his uncle, who became chaplain to Oliver Cromwell—one of the Tryers—was ejected from Great Hadham in Hertfordshire—then co-pastor with William Kiffin—and died in 1688.

was suspended for not subscribing, and not wearing the surplice. He was openly reviled by the bishop at Witham, who called him a wretch and a dog, and committed him to his pursuivant. "You shall be *white* with me," said he, "or I will be *black* with you."

On the first attempts of Aylmer, an appeal was made to the Privy Council for protection:—

"We are in great heaviness, and some of us already put to silence, and the rest living in fear, not that we have been or can be, (as we hope) charged with false doctrine or slanderous life; but for that we refuse to subscribe that there is nothing contained in the Book of Common Prayer, and of ordaining Bishops, priests and deacons, contrary to the word of God. . . . . The Apostle teacheth that he which doth doubt is condemned if he eat. Then if a man be condemned for doing a sinful action, because he is in doubt whether it be lawful, and yet doth it, how much more should we incur the displeasure of the Lord, and procure his wrath unto our destruction, if we should subscribe, *being certainly persuaded that there are some things in these books contrary to the word of God.*

"WILLIAM DIKE.
"LAURENCE NEWMAN."
(and 25 other names.)

The Privy Council remonstrated with Whitgift and Aylmer; but it was to no purpose.

The Puritans on the other hand, being refused freedom in ceremonials, advanced to other and higher ground, and many openly declared against the government of the church by Episcopacy, and advocated a *Presbyterian* rule.

Whilst some sought reformation in the church, others advanced still further, and *separated* themselves from it, in order to form distinct communities under pastors chosen by themselves, and independent of external control. This was only a revival in other circumstances of what had long before often taken place.

Shortly after Lord Robert Rich* presented this living to Laurence Newman, his brother (Richard Rich) was committed to prison for having in his possession certain books unfavorable to the existing hierarchy, and for being a great favorer of one Dyke, who in his sermon inveighed against 'statute-protestants, injunction men, and such as love to jump with the law.' Aylmer told the Queen that he had "many great storms with the Lord Rich," who desired him to license Wright to preach in his diocese, which he refused to do. This was Robert Wright, chaplain of the younger Lord Rich of Rochford, and who at his request, gathered in his lordship's hall a congregation, one of the members of which was the mother of Sir Francis Bacon. He was here associated with Greenwood, who afterwards suffered martyrdom. Aylmer succeeded at length in arresting both Lord Rich and his chaplain, and cast them into prison. Thus it had come about that both the son and grandson of the

---

* Son of Sir Richard Rich and father of Robert, Earl of Warwick, who died 1618. Robert, second Earl, was Admiral of the Parliamentary fleet, and a great patron of the Puritans. He was long remembered as "the good Earl of Warwick." He died 1658. His son Robert, third Earl, died 1659, and his grandson Robert, who married Frances, daughter of Oliver Cromwell, died 1657, at the early age of 28. Charles succeeded his brother Robert, and died in 1673, leaving his estate to Lady Warwick during her life. Some account of Lady Warwick will be found in "Home Life of English Ladies in the Seventeenth Century." Also of Dr. Walker, chaplain at Lees and rector of Fyfield, whose only daughter was married to Counsellor Cox, [p. 80, note.]

persecutor under Queen Mary, were themselves the victims of the intolerance of Queen Elizabeth. In her reign also perished in dungeons many loyal subjects and devout Christians, for refusing to act contrary to their conscience, and acknowledge any other save Jesus Christ as Head of the Church.

James I. declared of the Puritans, that he 'would make them conform, or harry them out of the land.' Again the Book of Common Prayer, a new book of Canons, and the Book of Sports, were imposed upon their consciences; and some 300 ministers were deprived for refusing to conform.

One of those most zealous for *Conformity* was JOHN JEGON, Bishop of Norwich. He was the son of Robert Jegon, of Coggeshall, by Joan, daughter of Mr. White, and born here in 1550; where, after having had his education, or at least some part of it, he was removed to Queen's College, Cambridge, and chosen to a fellowship; soon after which he became tutor, proctor, and vice-president. On 10th August, 1590, he was chosen master of Corpus Christi or Bene't College, and held this office twelve years, during which time it greatly prospered under his management.* He was four times vice-

* " He was a most serious man and grave governor; yet withal of a most facetious disposition; so that it was hard to say whether his counsel was more grateful for the soundness, or his company more acceptable for the pleasantness, thereof. Take one eminent instance of his ingenuity. Whilst master of the College he chanced to punish all the undergraduates for some general offence; and the penalty was put upon their heads in the buttery. And because that he disdained to convert the money to any private use it was expended in new whiting the hall of the College. Whereupon a scholar hung up these verses on the screen:—

'Dr. Jegon, Bene't College Master,
Brake the Scholars' Heads and gave the Walls a plaster.'

chancellor of the University. Being chaplain in ordinary to Queen Elizabeth, he was by her preferred to the Deanery of Norwich, (installed July 22, 1601,) and designed Bishop of Norwich, 18th January, 1602; but the Queen dying shortly afterwards, he was confirmed in the office by James I. The following letter, written to him about this time, reveals the course determined on with reference to the Puritans :—

"Right honourable my very good lord.

"Meeting with so convenient a messenger as this my loving cousin, I could not omit my most bounden duty of writing to your lordship at this present. The occurrences of the time, which perhaps your lordship is not ignorant of, are especially about the matter of religion. On Saturday last, being the ix. of this present, there was a petition delivered to his Majesty, by three or 4 Knights of Northamptonshire, in favour of the ministers which resist subscription, whereat his majesty took such deep impression, as the next day, being Sunday, he sat 8 hours in council with the lords. In this meeting he most bitterly inveighed against the Puritans, saying, 'That the revolt in the Low Countries which hath lasted ever since he was born, and whereof he never expected to see the end, began first by a petition for matters of religion, and so did all the troubles in Scotland—that his mother and he from their cradles had been haunted with a puritan divell which he feared would not leave him to his grave—that he would hazard his crown but he would suppress those malicious spirits.' From the puritans he proceeded to the papists, protesting 'his utter detestation of their super-

---

But the doctor had not the readiness of his parts any whit impaired by his age; for, perusing the paper, extempore he subscribed—

'Knew I but the Wag that writ these verses in a Bravery
I would commend him for his Wit, but whip him for his Knavery.'"

Fuller's Worthies, iii. 26. *Muster's History of C. C. Coll. Camb.,* p. 144.

stitious religion, and that he was so far from favouring it, as if he thought his son and heir after him would give any toleration thereunto he would wish him fairly buried before his eyes.' Besides he charged the lords of the council and the Bishops present, that 'they should take care themselves and give orders to the judges of the land, to the justices and other inferior officers, to see the laws speedily executed with all rigour against both the said extremes.' . . . . . And so with acknowledgement of my ever bounden duty, I rest

Your lordship's ever to be commanded,

London, 14th Feb., 1604.   [The subscription torn.]*

He was not much liked in his diocese, on account of his endeavours after strict uniformity, and his reputed penuriousness. So noted was he for a monied man, that the King sent to borrow a hundred pounds of him by way of loan. When his palace at Ludham was burnt down, he purchased an estate at Aylesham, where he built a house and usually resided. He died there, March 13, 1617, aged 67 years; leaving a widow (Lilia, daughter of the Bishop of London,) who was afterwards married to Sir Charles Cornwallis.†

Dr. THOMAS JEGON, also a native of Coggeshall, succeeded his brother as master of Corpus Christi, and was presented by him to the rectory of Sible Hedingham. He was also Archdeacon of Norwich, and in 1608 Vice-Chancellor of the University of Cambridge.

* Peck's Desiderata Curiosa, vol. i. lib. V. f 44.
† Blomfield's Hist. of Norfolk, vol. iii. p. 463. Some account of the fire is here referred to, together with a ballad made at the bishop's death, beginning—
"Our short lord Bishop of Norfo'k, 'twas he
That caused that great fire at Ludham to be;
He could not abide the poor at his gate,
No, nor yet for to see them early or late."
&c., &c.

He died in 1617 and was buried in the chancel of his rectory at Sible Hedingham, where the stone over him bore this inscription, "*Be at peace among yourselves.*"

On the death of Laurence Newman, THOMAS STOUGHTON was presented to the vicarage of Coggeshall by Lord Robert Rich, 12th December, 1600. He was deprived before April, 1606; for what reason does not appear; unless it was that for which a great many Puritans had suffered just before.* He was succeeded by RALPH CUDWORTH, presented April, 1606, Fellow of Emanuel College, Cambridge, B.D. of Oxford in 1610, and afterwards D.D. He was minister of St. Andrew's, Cambridge, whence he removed to Coggeshall. His wife was Machell, nurse to Prince Henry, whose early death was so much deplored. After a short residence, he removed to Aller in Somersetshire, where Ralph was born in 1617. He died in 1624, leaving a widow, who married Dr. Stoughton, by whom the young philosopher was educated and sent to the University.

JOHN HEYLEY was presented 8th March, 1607, and, on his resignation, succeeded by JOHN DODD,† presented 5th May, 1609, who continued here till his death in 1639.

* *Reg. Bap.* "1618, Mar. 20.—Eliz. daughter of Thomas Stoughton." If this was the same, he seems to have continued to reside in the town. The widow of his successor was married to a Dr. Stoughton. A Dr. John Stoughton also was predecessor of Edmund Calamy at St. Mary's Church, Aldermanbury, and died 1639.

† The better known John Dodd the Puritan died 1645. There was a Robert Dodd, M.A., rector of Inworth, ejected in 1662, and died at Weathersfield, 1695. Nehemiah Dodd signed Essex Watchword as minister of one of the classes.—*Lansdowne* 459.

The Register of Baptisms notes:—

"1615, Aug. 13.—Elizabeth, daughter of Christopher Pennock, a Brownist, excommunicated, contemptuous.

"1615, Nov. 5.—Mary, daughter of Moses Ram, an obstinate Brownist.

"1615, Dec. 24.—Martha, daughter of Daniel Pennock, a Brownist."

These persons appear to have held very much the same opinions as the Gospellers and Separatists, for which Wright and others suffered in the reign of Elizabeth. They were popularly called Brownists, from Robert Browne, a clergyman related to Lord Burleigh, who taught with great force the right of Christians to meet for worship, choose their own pastors, and govern themselves according to the New Testament, without interference on the part of the civil magistrate. He was not the earliest,[*] but was one of the least faithful of the advocates of the views generally held by those on whom his name was fastened. Such views were held by those who crossed over, in the Mayflower, to New England, in 1620.

When Archbishop *Laud* endeavoured in the reign of Charles I. to enforce his semi-catholic ceremonies, and sought with great zeal to put down the Puritan Lecturers, multitudes followed in the wake of the Pilgrim Fathers. Thomas Hooker, of Chelmsford, took with him a little colony of Essex men. About the same time also went, among others, Thomas Shepheard,

---

[*] There was a regularly formed Congregational Church in London previous to 1571.—*Congregational Martyrs by Dr. Waddington*, p. 11.

of Earl's Colne,* and Nathaniel Rogers, (son of John Rogers of Dedham, and son-in-law of Mr. Crane of Coggeshall,) "one of the greatest men," says Mather, "that ever set foot on the American shore." Every attempt to subdue Puritanism failed; and after eleven years of misgovernment, puritan and patriot became one in resistance to oppression both in Church and State.

Presbyterians and Independents.

On 6th July, 1639, the Earl of Warwick presented 'that noted Presbyterian,' OBADIAH SEDGWICK, B.D., to the vicarage of Coggeshall. He was born at Marlborough in Wiltshire, in 1600, and educated first at Queen's College, Oxford, and was then tutor in Magdalen Hall, where Sir Matthew Hale was under his tuition; which accounts in some measure for the leaning to Puritanism which that judge evinced throughout his life.† On leaving the University, he became chaplain to Sir Horace Vere, Baron of Tilbury, whom he accompanied to the Low Countries; and

---

* About the time of his leaving Emanuel College, Cambridge, he undertook, at the request of Dr. Wilson, a lectureship in Essex. It was originally intended to set it up at Coggeshall; but at the desire of the people of Earl's Colne, it was established amongst them for three years, at the end of which time Laud compelled him to retire.

† "He was placed under the tuition of Obadiah Sedgwick, who though a noted Puritan, was deeply imbued with classical learning."—*Campbell's Lives of the Chief Justices,* i. 518. When it is further stated that "in the next generation the Puritans in general undervalued human learning," it should in justice be added, so far as there is any truth in this, that both Universities, together with everything that could foster the taste for learning, were closed against them.

returning to Oxford, he was admitted in 1629 to the reading of sentences. After this he became preacher at St. Mildred's, Bread Street, London; but becoming obnoxious on account of his Puritanism, he was obliged to retire. At his institution to the vicarage of Coggeshall, July 15, 1639, the following witnesses are mentioned in the Parish Register:—Neh. Dodd, Tho. Aylet, Rob. Crane, William Gladwine, Tho. Coxe, William Tanner, Richard Shortland, John Alliston, John Sparhawke, Benj. Hawes, Jacob Aylet, Samuel Crane, Thomas Guyon, Richard Shepheard, Joseph Scott, John Pirkeld.

On the breaking out of the civil wars, he again preached at St. Mildred's.*

In 1642 he became chaplain to Hollis's regiment, and in the following year one of the licencers of the press. He was one of the most constant attendants at the Assembly of Divines. On 6th October, 1643, he delivered a speech at the Guildhall " on the occasion of desiring the assistance of our brethren of Scotland in this warre." In 1646 he was preacher at St. Paul's, Covent Garden, and afterwards one of Cromwell's Tryers. He often preached before parliament, and at length, through failing health, retired to his native place, where he died January, 1658, aged 57, and was buried in the chancel of Ogborn St. Andrew, near

---

* "1641, Oct. 19.—Robert, son of Obadiah and Priscilla Sedgwick."—*Reg. Bapt.* He published among other works:—

Military Discipline for a Christian Soldier. London. Oct., 1639.
Christ's Counsel to His Languishing Church at Sardis. London. Oct., 1640.
Thanksgiving Sermon before the House of Commons. London. 1642.
Haman's Vanity. London. 1643.
Speeches at the Guildhall, 6th Oct., 1643. London. 1646.

Marlborough. It is probable that he was also assisted at Coggeshall by his brother, John Sedgwick.

As soon as the King issued his proclamation declaring the Earl of Essex and his army rebels, disturbances broke out at Colchester, and the captains of the trainbands collected aid from Halstead, Coggeshall, Braintree and other places. One of the Parliamentary Committee for the maintenance of peace, and one of the most zealous supporters of the Parliament, was SIR THOMAS HONYWOOD of Markshall. He was the grandson of Mrs. Mary Honywood, and, having been trained up at her feet, it is not surprising that he abhorred intolerance and oppression of every kind. He had come to reside at Markshall in 1627, and was knighted in 1632. Sir Harry Vane was his brother-in-law. At the time of the breaking out of the civil wars he was above fifty years of age; but he threw himself into the Parliamentary cause with all the ardour of youth. He was a principal member of the Essex Committee, and raised a regiment of horse and foot, which was of great service in putting down endeavours made in this county by a party of Royalists. He was at the siege of Colchester, and was colonel of a regiment of Essex men at the battle of Worcester (1651). The same year he was made Doctor of the Civil Law at Oxford. He was member for the county in Oliver's parliaments in 1654 and 1656, and one of his lords of the other house. He died 26th May, 1666, at the house of his son-in-law, Sir John Cotton (grandson of Sir Robert Cotton, founder of the Cottonian Library,) at Westminster, aged 80, and was buried in Markshall Church. In the classification in 1646, he is named along with John Smith as an elder. His wife, who was remarkable for her piety and charity, died in 1681, and was buried by his side. Her funeral sermon was preached by Mr. Livermore, rector of Markshall, Oct. 26:—

"Text—Job xxi. 26. The occasion of this present assembly is plaine before you, being to performe the last piece of service that we can doe to ye body of ye pious and renowned Lady Honeywood. . . . . . I know now you expect I should say something of ye pious lady here deceased. Her light was too great to be put under a bushell. Her works are such as now praise her in the gates. I shall say no more than what may be truly said; and to which you will say Amen. I shall begin with her birth and descent. She came of pious and religious parents, such as were tryed and growne up under persecution. She was the daughter and coheire of John Lamotte, Esq., merchant in London, whose parents came from Flanders, thence driven by persecution. She was piously educated and so she continued all her days, making good that saying, Traine up a child, &c. She was twice married: her last husband was Sir Thomas Honeywood: by whom she had 7 children, of which but two[*] survive her. She stood in severall relations. As a wife she was one of the best of wives, so kind and loving in all respects. I have often heard her say, 'I love a Honeywood,' which she made good by

[*] Elizabeth, wife of Sir John Cotton, and John Lamotte Honywood, (who succeeded his elder brother Thomas, d. 1672) member for the county and sheriff: died 1698, leaving no family: his widow was married to Sir Isaac Rebow of Colchester. Markshall then came to Robert Honywood, Esq., of Charing, and to his three sons successively, Richard, John, and Philip, lieutenant-general of horse (1758), who built the present church. He was the last of the Markshall branch of this family, and devised the estate to his remote collateral relation Filmer Honywood, M.P., on whose death (1809) it came to William Honywood, M.P., (younger brother of Sir John Honywood, Bart.,) who died 1818.

making much of her husband's friends. Take her as a mother and a grandmother. She was a loving, carefull and indulgent one. As to her servants: she was one of the best of ladyes, more like a mother than a mistresse. She was a lady of admirable parts, quickness of understanding, &c. . . . . This noble and never-to-be-forgotten lady is gone from us never to come againe. Let us live so that we may meet her in heaven and live with her in everlasting happiness."—*(Bufton's MS. notes.)*

The county of Essex was almost wholly on the Parliament side; and this town was amongst the foremost in showing its attachment. It was a time of great excitement, and once or twice the place was in imminent danger.

"1642, Friday, 2nd Sept.—This day intelligence from Coggeshall, 7 miles from Colchester in Essex, that train bands had searched the house of Mr. William Sames, of Rivenhall, and there found ammunition for 60 men, and 6 horses, and in plate and money, £800. Ordered that the same be brought to London.*

"26th Oct., 1642.—*Order of the Committee of the Lords and Commons, for the safety of the Kingdom :—*

"Whereas the Lords and Commons in Parliament have chosen the Earl of Warwicke, Generall of the Forces now to be raised. . . . . It is therefore ordered that the Mayor and Aldermen of Colchester, the Bailiffs and Townesmen of Chelmsford, Braintree, Bocking, Coxall and Dunmow, in the county of Essex, &c., shall forthwith procure and raise in their said several towns, and other places adjoining, 2000 horses for Dragooners, or as many as possibly they may, for the service aforesaid, and with all possible speed to send them to London."

Later date:—"Cogshall Mag.—John Pickness houldeth of

* "A Perfect Diurnall of the Passages in Parliament." The oldest newspaper in England, dating from the first year of the Long Parliament.

Mr. Knightly a Papist and Delinquent, p. ann. £12. Cogshall Parva.—Robert Merrills houldeth of the same, p. ann. £12."—[*Registered Lands. Harl.* 5505.]

In the *Committee* for the weekly raising of money for the maintenance of the army, are the names of Jeremy Aylett and ROBERT CRANE.

In 1646 the Parliament ordered a classification of the county, with the names of the ministers and elders. In this there is no minister's name placed opposite Coggeshall; but the elders' names are Robert Crane,* gent., and William Tanner.†

Hitherto Presbyterianism had been the prevailing ecclesiastical government adopted by the Parliament. As the price of the assistance of the Scotch, a modified Covenant against popery and prelacy had been taken. The Book of Common Prayer was set aside; but the Presbyterian system was never thoroughly established in England; and now began to be gradually replaced by *Independency*, which was more advanced in its views of religious freedom, and had several adherents of great energy and influence.

The victories of Cromwell had brought the war to a close. A melancholy episode to which, however, took place in the siege of Colchester in 1648. Endeavours were made by some of the Royalist party in this county in favour of the King's interest: and the Parliamen-

---

* "11 Hen. VIII.—The lord granted ont of his hands to Nicholas Crane, one tenement in Church-street. 14 Eliz.—John Crane surrendered two tenements in Gallows-strete, one head abutting upon the tenement called the Swan."—*Manor Rolls.*

† "May 30, 1678.—William Tanner, clothier, was buried. He lived on his means, and had no children."—*Bufton's Diary.*

tary Committee was seized at Chelmsford. A Royalist army then marched into Essex, and, having pillaged Lees Priory, arrived at Braintree, on Sunday, June 11. To escape a large party of horse and foot, which had been raised by Sir Thomas Honywood at Coggeshall, they left Braintree at nine o'clock in the evening, and, making a detour and travelling through the night, arrived at four o'clock on Monday afternoon within five or six miles of Colchester, into which they were afterwards received. Fairfax speedily followed, and having been joined by Sir Thomas Honywood, laid siege to the town. After eleven weeks of the greatest possible privation and suffering, it was surrendered to the Parliamentary army: the articles of rendition being signed 27th August by Sir Thomas Honywood, as one of the Commissioners.

At this time the vicar of Coggeshall was JOHN OWEN, M.A. He was born in 1616 at Stadham in Oxfordshire, where his father, a strict Puritan, held a small living. At the age of twelve he went to Queen's College, Oxford, where he spent nine years of hard study, and was admitted to holy orders by Bishop Bancroft. He left the University, rather than conform to the ceremonies imposed by Archbishop Laud, and became tutor to the eldest son of Sir Philip Dormer; and then chaplain to Lord Lovelace, whom he left when his lordship threw himself into the Royal cause.

At the same time he was disinherited by his royalist

uncle, to whose estates he had long been designed to succeed. He came to London, and lodged in Charterhouse Yard; but wandered about in uncertainty and mental distress, for he had been sometime awakened to the infinite importance of a personal knowledge of Divine forgiveness and favor; until going into Aldermanbury Church one morning, the minister announced as his text, "Why are ye fearful, O ye of little faith?" which was to him a message from Heaven, and he went forth another man. His first publication (1642) was in opposition to the *Arminian doctrine* which had long prevailed in the Anglican Church, and was the only way to preferment; and was dedicated by him to the Committee for Religion.* " Had a poor Puritan," said he in his preface, " offended against half so many *canons* as they [the Arminian clergy] opposed *articles*, he had forfeited his livelihood, if not endangered his life." Soon afterwards the sequestered living of *Fordham* was conferred upon him, and here he labored as a diligent pastor for three years. He published "The Duties of Pastors and People Distinguished" (1643), and two

---

* Early in the war a committee was formed for the purpose of providing for those ministers of parliamentary sympathies who were driven out of their parishes by the royalist army and fled to London. Ministers of opposite sympathies joined the royal army: many were petitioned against by their parishioners, and proved to be immoral or inefficient, as in several parishes adjoining this: some preached against parliament: and in such cases the committee put other ministers into their places, and allowed the sequestered incumbents one-third of the yearly income. This was done chiefly in 1643 and 1644. None were interfered with for purely religious reasons. In a time of such excitement and violence many doubtless met with hard usage, and some excellent men suffered much. Those who succeeded them were placed there by the government de facto; and with regard to the rights of the patrons and the wish of the people.

short Catechisms (1645). Whilst here, also, he married Miss Rooke.

On March 14, 1645, he was appointed minister of St. Botolph's, Colchester.* On 29th April, 1646, he preached before Parliament at St. Margaret's, Westminster, on the occasion of one of their monthly fasts, for which he received the thanks of the House; and on the publication of his sermon—" A Vision of Unchangable Mercy," &c.—he added " A Country Essay on Church Government."

The report of the death of the sequestered rector of Fordham, when the patron had the right of the presentation of another, led him to accept the invitation of the people of Coggeshall to become their minister; and he was soon afterwards presented to the vicarage by the Earl of Warwick.

" May, 1646.—Whereas the Rectory of the parish of Fordham, by order of this Committee, is sequestered from Mr. Alsopp to the use of Mr. Owen, who, after report that the said Mr. Alsopp was deceased, hath accepted of the presentation of the Church of Coggeshall in the said county, and is minister thereof; and in regard that it is not determined of the said Mr. Alsopp his death, and it is considered that he is yet living, this Committee did, by their order of the 20th May inst., upon the petition of divers of the said parish for the settling of Mr. Richard Pulley in the said Mr. Owen his stead, order the said Mr. Owen to have notice thereof, to the end that the said Committee might

* " Ordered that an ordinance be drawne and executed to the housé, for ye settling of Mr. John Owen, minister of the word, in the Church of St. Botolph's, in Colchester, void by death, in the gift of Sir Henry Audley, Delinquent; and that he shall officiate the said cure in the mean time, and have and enjoy the profits of the said cure."—*Minutes of Committee for Plundered Ministers.* Add. MSS. 15, 670. fo. 77.

be satisfied whether he had left the same; who appearing this day, this Committee has left him to his election, to return to the said chappell of Fordham, or contynue at Coggeshall. It is therefore ordered that the Rectory, and the profits thereof, shall from henceforth stand sequesterd to the use of the said Richard Pulley, who is required to officiate the cure of the said Church as rector, till further order taken in the premises."—*House of Lords and other papers*, 16, 670. 221.

"1646, Aug. 18.—It is this day ordered by the Lords in parliament assembled, that Mr. Dr. Aylett, or his lawful deputy, be hereby authorised and required, upon sight of this order, to give institution and induction to Mr. Owen, clerk, to the vicarage of Coggeshall, county of Essex and diocese of London, void by the resignation of Mr. Obadiah Sedgwick, late vicar there; said Mr. Owen producing the presentation thereunto in the hand and seal of the Right Honourable Robert, Earl of Warwick, and others; and this to be a sufficient authority in that behalf."

About this time he more thoroughly considered and adopted the principles of Independency than he had done before; and he never swerved from them, in honor or dishonor, to the end of his life. On his coming to Coggeshall, he formed a Christian church according to the Congregational order, which continued to assemble in the parish church for nearly twenty years. Never perhaps was this edifice more truly the church of the parish than at this time, when two thousand people constantly assembled in it for worship, and often listened for hours to Owen in the prime of his days.

He was one of the ablest preachers of his time. In profound knowledge of scripture and the human heart he was surpassed by none. Notwithstanding his cumbrous and unadorned style, when excitement animated his calm countenance, and his Welsh fire kindled in his dark eye, he fixed the attention of every hearer, and carried the congregation along with irresistible force. He led their devotions in free prayer with an earnest solemnity, which filled even the most careless with awe. Whilst his dignified bearing, generous nature and gentle manner, won universal respect and love. "He was a man of universal affability," says even Anthony Wood, the enemy of all Puritans, "ready discourse, liberal, graceful and courteous demeanor, that spoke him certainly, whatever else he might be, one that was more the gentleman than most of the clergy. His personage was proper and comely. He had a very graceful behaviour in the pulpit,—a winning, insinuating deportment,— and would, by the persuasion of his oratory, in conjunction with other outward advantages, wind the affections of his auditory as he pleased."

The substance of the Sermons on "Communion," which he afterwards published, was probably preached during his ministry at Coggeshall. In 1647 he published "Eshcol, or Rules for Church Fellowship;" and the year following, "Salus Electorum: a Treatise on Redemption, by John Owen, pastor of the Church of God which is at Coggeshall," dedicated to the Earl of Warwick.

During the siege of Colchester, of which he says he was "an endangered spectator," he became acquainted with Fairfax, who had his head-quarters in Coggeshall;

and preached before the army on the surrender; and again at Romford, September 28, 1648, in memory of the deliverance of the Essex County and Committee. In the first sermon he says, referring to the successes of the Parliament:—

"I hope the poor town wherein I live is more enriched with a store-mercy of a few months than with a full trade of many years. *Note.* No place in the county so threatened: no place in the county so preserved: small undertakings there blessed: great opposition blasted. Non nobis, Domine, non nobis."

On the 31st January following, he preached by command before the Houses of Parliament, on the occasion of the King's execution, "Righteous Zeal: a Sermon, &c." On that tragical event he preserved a deep silence; probably because, though himself convinced of the guilt and utter insincerity of the King, he was yet unable to see the necessity or defend the policy of the deed on which the chiefs of the army had determined. For his sermon he received the thanks of the House, and on its publication appended his essay on *Toleration,* in which he declared it wrong to repress opinion by civil penalties, and laid a foundation on which *Locke,* his pupil at Christ Church, afterwards built. This was at a time when the Independents were in the ascendancy. It remained however for subsequent thought and events to teach even them generally that "The province of the magistrate is this world and man's body; not his conscience or the concerns of eternity," *(Sir H. Vane)* and that "independence and state hire in religion can never consist long or certainly together." *(Milton)*.

He preached before the House of Commons on April 16, 1649, his sermon " On the Shaking and Translating of Heaven and Earth." Cromwell was present and heard him for the first time. On the following day as he waited on Fairfax, Cromwell entered the room, and seeing Owen, came up and touching him on the shoulder said, " Sir, you are the man I must be acquainted with." "That," said Owen, "will be more to my advantage than yours." "That remains to be seen," answered the former, and taking him by the hand led him into the garden. He was going to Ireland, and wished Owen to accompany him to regulate the affairs of Trinity College; and wrote to the church at Coggeshall, urging them to consent to their pastor's absence.

On the 7th of June he again preached before Parliament, ("Human Power Defeated,") when it was referred to the Oxford Committee to prefer him to be head of a college in that University; and the next month he went to Ireland. On his return he preached before Parliament, 28th February, 1650, on the "Steadfastness of Promises;" and soon afterwards joined Cromwell's army at Berwick. He was present at the battle of Dunbar. He frequently preached ("The Branch of the Lord," two sermons,) and held discussions with the Scotch ministers; and then retired to his quiet home. Not long afterwards the following order appeared in the newspapers of the day :

"On 18th March, 1651, the House, taking into consideration the worth and usefulness of John Owen, M.A., of Queen's College, ordered that he should be settled in the Deanery of Christ Church, in Oxford, in the room of Dr. Reynolds."

This terminated his connection with Coggeshall.* Soon afterwards he became Vice-chancellor of the University, and in this office labored with untiring energy. Oxford under his rule became a home of order, learning and piety. His free and generous spirit was proved in his permission of an Episcopalian meeting opposite his own door, and in his defence of Dr. Pococke against the over-zealous interference of the Tryers. He once attended Parliament as member for the University, and in a time of danger raised a troop of 60 horse in defence of the Protector's government. And in addition to frequent preaching he found time to issue several large volumes from the press.

After his displacement from the Vice-chancellorship (1657) he continued Dean of Christ Church till shortly before the Restoration. On attempting after that to preach to a small congregation in his native village, he was prohibited and silenced by the Act of Uniformity in 1662. Whenever he had opportunity he still preached, and afterwards regularly ministered to a congregation in Leadenhall Street. He was a tower of strength to the oppressed Nonconformists; and exerted himself to

---

* "1647, July 25.—Mary, daughter of Mr. John Owen, Vicar."—*Reg. of Bur.*

"1650, Feb. 28.—Mary, daughter of Mr. John Owen."—*Reg. of Bap.*

All his children, eleven in number, died young, except one daughter who was married to a gentleman of Wales, but in consequence of disagreement she returned to her father's house, where she died of consumption.

bring about amongst them a closer union, "which," said he, "I do verily believe will be the *effect*, not the cause of love. There is not a greater vanity in the world, than to drive men into a particular profession, and then suppose that love will certainly ensue." His leisure time was occupied in writing those works which are his most enduring monument. His last work was "On the Glory of Christ." When he was lying on his deathbed at *Ealing*, Mr. Payne, nonconformist minister of Saffron Walden, who had engaged to see it through the press, visited him and told him that the first sheet was printed—to whom he replied, "I am glad to hear it. But oh! Brother Payne, the long-wished-for day is come at last, in which I shall see it in another manner than I have ever done or was capable of doing in this world." He was buried in Bunhill fields, where there was a long inscription closing with these words:—

"In younger age a most comely and majestic form; but in the latter stages of life, depressed by constant infirmities, emaciated with frequent diseases, and above all crushed under the weight of intense and unremitting studies, it became an incommodious mansion for the vigorous exertion of the spirit in the service of its God. He left this world in a day dreadful to the Church by the cruelties of men, but blissful to himself by the plaudits of his God, August 24, 1683, aged 67."

The only word which can now be distinguished, and that with difficulty is—

———Owen———

CONSTANTINE JESSOP appears to have been the immediate successor of Owen at Coggeshall. He was the son of Mr. Thomas Jessop of Pembroke; born in 1602; at 22 years of age student of Jesus' College, Oxford, whence he went to Ireland, and was B.A. of Trinity College, Dublin. He was incorporated at Oxford and M.A. in 1631, and took orders in the following year. "He closed with the Covenanters," says Anthony Wood, "and succeeded Owen in the ministry of that factious town in Essex called Coggeshall. He was sometime priest of St. Nicholas's in Bristol;"* probably previous to his coming into Essex. In the classis of 1646 he is named as minister of Fyfield, where he had been placed in the stead of the sequestered minister in 1643. Here he continued till the close of the year 1647,† when he may have assisted Owen, and continued to minister at Coggeshall after his removal. He died at Wimborne, in Dorsetshire, and was buried in the Church there. Below the Marchioness of Exeter's tomb, a black marble tablet on the wall has this inscription:—

"Here wayteth, in expectation of a glorious resurrection, the body of CONSTANTINE JESSOP, sometime pastor of this place, who, after he had lived 53 years, exchanged this mortal life for an immortal on the 16th day of April, A.D. 1658.
   Constans et fidelis
   Consequitur prœmium.

---

* "So Mr. Thomas Collins told me."—*Wood's M.S. Note.*
† "1648, 8 Nov.—An order for sequestrating the rents and profits of the parsonage of Fyfield, whereof Alexander Read is now parson, to the use and benefit of Constantine Jessop, M.A., a godly and orthodox divine."—*Jour. of Ho. Commons*, iii. 801. "1647, June 4.—Constantine Jessop petitioned to have 2 months to remove, and all the standing crops to be his—petition granted."—*Add. MSS.* 16,671, p. 78. Henry Havers succeeded him in 1648.

The next vicar of Coggeshall was JOHN SAMES. He was probably connected with a family of the same name who held several estates in the neighbourhood, and educated at Cambridge, whence he went in early life to New England. On the breaking out of the civil war he returned, and soon afterwards held the vicarage of Kelvedon.* The exact period of his removal to Coggeshall is uncertain.† On 15th April, 1654, Robert Crane, only surviving trustee of Gooday's charity, appointed John Sames, vicar of Coggeshall, and others, in his stead. On 29th September an ordinance was set forth by the Protector, and confirmed in 1656, appointing commissioners of religion, among whom for this county were Dionysius Wakering, Robert Crane, Sir Thomas Honywood, and Richard Harlakenden,‡ and they had as assistants John Sames of Coggeshall, John Stalham of Terling, Willis of Ingatestone, William Sparrow§ of Halstead, and others.

* "Sept. 9, 1647.—Whereas the vicarage of Kelvedon was sequestered from Peter Dears to Thomas Hempstead, and Thomas Hempstead is deceased, ordered that it be sequestered to the use of John Sames, a godly and orthodox divine."—*Add. MSS.* 16,671, after p. 26.

† There is an entry in the Register:—"1653, Oct.—Collected for Marlborough £17. 1s. 8d." This relates to a great fire which took place in that town. A collection was made in the churches throughout the country, by order of the council for the relief of the distressed. Sames was probably vicar at this time.

‡ John de Vere, 17th earl of Oxford, sold to Roger Harlakenden Colne Priory, where Richard Harlakenden lived. Baxter, in his "World of Spirits," tells the story of a great bell being heard tolling at two o'clock every morning, (as in former times), and how Mr. Thomas Shepheard, who afterwards went to New England, with some other good ministers spent a night in prayer to cast out the devil; and from that time the sound was heard no more.

§ "First awakened by the preaching of Mr. Stephen Marshall. He

In the year 1655 an unusual occurrence happened in the Church. A Public Fast had been appointed to take place on 12th of July, and Willis (Braintree), Sames, Sparrow, Stalham and other ministers were conducting divine service, when a youth of about 18 years of age, named JAMES PARNELL, attended by several children, came into the Church. He was born at Retford in Nottinghamshire, where he worked at his trade. He became the subject of religious impression, and embraced the principles then advocated by George Fox, whom he saw at Carlisle in 1653.

Being a youth of ardent temperament and ready utterance he began to preach. 'Priests,' 'Steeplehouses,' 'Formalists' were unsparingly attacked by this "quaking boy," as he was named from his youth and diminutive appearance. The followers of George Fox were generally of a very different spirit from that of the Friends of the present day. In the delirium of new freedom in religion many ran into unwarrantable excesses; and the excitement of the times stirred within them a spirit of intense antagonism, not always to existing evils, but often in utter disregard of social order and propriety. Parnell had been already imprisoned at Cambridge. On coming into Essex he freely preached from place to place; and in Colchester, Halstead, and elsewhere, entered the Churches, and

---

was early in declaring for the Congregational way, and a great correspondent of Dr. Owen's. As much reputed through the country for a preacher as Mr. Rogers of Dedham had been sometime before." Mr. Stalham wrote, among other works, a piece against the Quakers. The above-named ministers were all ejected by the Act of Uniformity.

declaimed against the ministers and those who were of their views. Coming into the Church at Coggeshall as above mentioned, and hearing some of his opinions reflected upon, he undertook their defence. With reference to what one of the ministers said of those who followed any teaching but of Scripture, that "they were building upon a sandy foundation, and were appropriately named *Shakers*;" he called him a false prophet and a deceiver. Great confusion and disorder arose, and Parnell left the Church; and when a crowd of persons gathered around him without, and some "gave out threatening speeches leading to the breache of the peace," Justice Wakering came and placed his hand on Parnel's shoulder, saying, "I arrest thee in the name of the Lord Protector." He afterwards preached to the people in a Friend's house, and was then committed by Dionysius Wakering, Herbert Pelham, Thomas Cook and Richard Harlackendon to take his trial at the Chelmsford Assizes; when he was fined by Judge Hills £20 for contempt of the Magistracy, and £20 for contempt of the Ministry. In default of payment he was placed in the castle of Colchester, where the gaoler and his wife appear to have dealt hardly with him. Here he was visited by Fox, George Whitehead, Stephen Crisp and others. During his confinement he wrote, among other things, several letters full of bitter invective. Under what he deemed a direction of the Spirit, he declined to receive any food for ten days; and soon afterwards died. Anne Langley and Thomas Shortland, his intimate friends, gave evidence before the Jury at the inquest, "that he was not suffering under any illness, but had voluntarily abstained himself from food, in obedience to a command."* Upon this and other evidence they brought in their verdict:—

"We do find that James Parnell, through his wilful rejecting of his natural food for ten days together, and his wilful exposing of his limbs to the cold, to be the cause of the hastening of his own end, and by no other means that we can learn or know of.

JOHN GAEL, *Coroner.*
JUDE TAYLOR, *Foreman.*
JOSEPH SMITH."†

He was doubtless a youth of intelligence, earnestness and strong will; and his death is to be regretted; but it can be attributed to little other than his own misdirected zeal and strange self-delusion. Order was as much needed to be enforced in public worship then as it is now: and in instances of the like nature, a certain yet it may be a different and milder remedy would at the present time be applied.

Little can be inferred from the above concerning

---

* "We being as careful and inquisitive as we could to find out the truth, we asked her if he were sick, or complained of not being able to take his food. She answered, 'Nay, nay. He was well. He was strong.' We asked her if it were a wilful act of him to reject his food: she answered, 'he denied will, and stood not in his own will.' We, not knowing how to speak in her language, we asked her if it were a free voluntary act. She answered, 'Yea, yea. It was free. It was free. He had freely offered himself up, and that he had done it in obedience unto a command.'" To the same purport was the letter of Thomas Shortland, afterwards written.

† *Fruits of a Fast*, by James Parnell. Oct. 19, 1655. *A true and lamentable Relation of the death of James Parnell, Quaker*, who wilfully starved himself in the prison of Colchester. 1656, May 7. *The Lamb's Defence against Lyes.* 1656, June 5.

piety or liberty under the rule of the Protector. "It is certain," says Bishop Kennet, "that the Protector was for liberty and the utmost latitude to all parties, so far as consisted with the peace and safety of his person and government." He was in advance of most men then living in enlarged views of religious freedom; and a few years longer of his administration would probably have removed many if not all of the evils which still clung to the National Church. But when his strong hand was removed, all was brought into confusion again.

If the treatment of Parnell be regarded as an act of *persecution*, it only adds another to the long train of proofs which history exhibits of the danger of "grafting the sword upon the crook," or entrusting to any man or class of men authority over religious belief.

"If thou doubt me, mark
"The blade: each herb is judged of by its seed."

IX.

CONFORMITY.

On the restoration of Charles II., many ministers who had been sequestered were restored to their livings, and two years afterwards an Act of Uniformity was passed, which came into operation on St. Bartholomew's Day, 24th August, 1662. Very many ministers who had held livings under the Commonwealth and Protectorate, and who were of Puritan sympathies, conformed to the conditions henceforth imposed on those who ministered in the Established Church, rather than relinquish their ministry. Of this class was the first vicar of Coggeshall after the passing of the Act.*

THOMAS JESSOP was formerly minister of Winwick, in Lancashire, and after his ejectment (1660) conformed, and was presented to the vicarage of Cog-

---

* *Newcourt* mentions *Nathaniel Ranew* as presented 1st March, 1660, by the Earl of Warwick. There is here probably some mistake; for he was ejected from Felsted in 1662, where also the Essex Watchword names him minister in 1649. He had been educated at Emanuel College, Cambridge, and was minister at Eastcheap. On his ejection he removed to Billericay, where he had license to hold a meeting in 1672, and died soon afterwards. He was well beloved by the Earl and Countess of Warwick, who allowed him £20 a year during his life. The old Earl Radnor, some time lord lieutenant of Ireland, had great respect for him, and admitted him to his intimate acquaintance. He published in 1670 a little work entitled "Solitude Improved by Divine Meditation."

geshall by the Earl of Warwick, 3rd October, 1662. Most of those who had formed the congregational church, which since Owen's ministry had met in the Parish Church, left it on account of the enforced ritual, along with their pastor John Sames the ejected vicar, and met together elsewhere. Mr. Jessop continued here until his death. Some notes of his sermons have been preserved, and indicate that he was a man of some learning.

"1665, Feb. 16.—Sermon preached by Mr. Constable [of Earl's Colne] at the Buriall of Mary Jessop, daughter of Mr. Jessop."—*Bufton.*

"1670, April 6.—Sermon preached at ye funerall of old Mr. Jessop, by Mr. Tabor [of Kelvedon.] 'We are here come to performe the last office of love for a brother deceased, whom ye lord of life and death hath gathered to the grave in peace. He was one whose goodness shined forth and burned in zeal to God and religion. He much lamented the differences among Christians and the contempt of God's worship; he desired and prayed that they that professed themselves the subjects of the Prince of peace were of more peaceable spirits, and when I had any discourse with him he would exhort us to walk close with God, and keep up our communion with him. But I will return to my text.'"—*Bufton.*

"Mr. Thomas Jessop. Citizen of London."—*Reg. of Bur.*

This was probably the father of the vicar.

"1673, Jan 14.—Mrs. Mary Jessop, wife of Mr. T. Jessop, minister of Coggeshall."—*Reg. of Bur.*

"1673[4], Mar. 10.—Thomas Jessop, minister of Coggeshall and Elizabeth Calandrine of this parish."—*Reg. of Mar. Markshall.*

"1679, Jan. 31.—Mr. Jessop buried without a sermon."*— *Bufton.*

JAMES BOYS, A.M. was presented 16th Feb., 1679, by Daniel Finch, Henry St. John, and Thomas Barrington, (sons-in-law of the Earl of Warwick.) He continued vicar forty-four years. He was a faithful pastor and able preacher. He wrote "A Practical Exposition of the 39 Articles, to which is added a Sermon on I John v. 7.," (London. fol. 1717) and left behind him an infinite number of sermons of his own composition. *(Morant.)* Some account of funeral sermons preached by him will be given on a subsequent page.

"1682, Nov. 26.—Mr. Boys' brother's son of 11 years old died at the vicarage of the small-pox, and was carried to Colchester to be buried."

"1683, Sept. 5.—Mr. Boys was married to a kinswoman of Mr. Thomas Keeble's. Her name was Bennet. Her father was a poulterer in London."

"1685, Nov. 11.—Mr. Boys had a son buried, three days old."

"1685, Nov. 18.—The first wife of Mr. Boys was buried. 6 gentlemen carried up ye pall, with white hoods and night veils, and Mr. Livermore preached at her funeral, and I was gone to London."

"1688, Sep.—Mr. John White was married to Mrs. Ann Boys."

"1692, Apl. 5.—Mr. Boys was married to the Lady Guyon." [Widow of Sir Mark.]—*Bufton.*

He died 10th October, 1725, and was buried under the communion table, where there is this inscription:—

* Calamy says "He died at Coggeshall under some scandals."

Exuvias hic Deposuit
Reverendus Vir
JACOBUS BOYS, A: M:
Hujus Ecclesiæ per XLIV Annos
Vigilantissimus Pastor
Qui per totum Sui Ministerii cursum
Vestigia premens Apostolica,
assiduo conatus est.

MEDEMIAN EN MEDENI DIDONAI OROSKOPEN

INA ME MOMETHE E DIAKONIA.

Nat: VIII^{vo} Martii MDCL.
Ob^{t.} X^{mo} Octobris MDCCXXV.

Adjoining this there is another inscription:—

ANOTHER DORCAS
or the
Remains of DAME DORCAS GUYON,
who departed this life, October ye 2ND,
1714, aged 58 years,
waiting the happy summons of
Tabitha arise.

On her left hand lyeth
DORCAS BOYS, her Daughter, who
Dyed November ye 2ND 1714,
Aged 20 Years.

There is a mural tablet on the north wall of the chancel to the memory of Counsellor Boys, who resided in West Street:—*

"Here lies (near the remains of his ancestors), the Body of MR WILLIAM BOYS, Gent. Eldest Son of the Revd. Mr.

---

* Now the residence of Mr. George Swinborne. Two or three peculiar traditions linger about the memory of Mr. Boys, who was somewhat eccentric.

James Boys, late Vicar of this Parish. He married Hester, the youngest daughter of John Cox, Esq., and Ann his Wife, who was the daughter of Major General Haynes, of Copford Hall, in this county. John Cox, was of Emmanuel College in Cambridge, and of Gray's Inn, London, Barrister at Law, and (late) of Mount Hall, in this parish. A Gentleman justly esteemed and respected as an Eminent and able Councellour, an Honest and Upright Man and a good Christian. HESTER, wife of the said M̤ṛ WILLIAM BOYS, departed this life, May 30TH, 1742, Aged 53 years, and was buried in this Chancel. Where by his own desire his Remains are also Interr'd, after a Long life spent in Piety and good works, his great care and study in particular was to instruct the poor and ignorant in the knowledge of their Christian Duty. Witness the many Good Books he dispersed for that purpose, Witness that charitable Donation to the Parish of Great Bardfield, to perpetuate the same pious design to the end of the world. Thus lived this good Man, and thus he died July 25th, 1768, aged 83 Years.

"Beatus servus ille, quem, quum venerit Dominus ejus invenerit ita facientem.

"The Revd. Mr. John Harrison, Nephew and Executor of the Deceased, to testify his respect to his memory caused this Monument to be erected."

On the death of Mr. Boys, GILBERT BURNET was presented by Richard Du Cane. He had been previously minister at St. James's, Clerkenwell. He died of apoplexy at Coggeshall, 28th January, 1746.

To him succeeded JOSEPH GULLIVER, A.M.* presented June 27, 1746, by Peter Du Cane, (died 1803.) Mr. Gulliver is said to have had so loud a voice that it could be heard at a great distance without the Church.

* I have in my possession a copy of an agreement between Mrs. Anne Gulliver, widow, and Joseph Cox, dated 23rd July, 1783. Josias Gulliver, A.M. was vicar of Messing in 1700.

HENRY DU CANE, son of the patron, was afterwards presented to this living. He resided at the Grange; and is yet remembered as a man of great kindness of disposition. He was not accustomed to preach at Coggeshall, but did duty latterly at Marks Tey; and died at Witham.

At this time the curate was JOHN DUDDELL, who lived at the Vicarage and taught the Hitcham School. After having resided in this town for many years, he became rector of Wormington; but during the later years of his life partial blindness unfitted him for the discharge of his duties; and he returned to Coggeshall, and died at a house in the Hamlet, at an advanced age. He was greatly respected and beloved in the parish; and if not accounted by some so strict a churchman as many, since he was often present at the Independent Chapel, listening to the week-night lecture, and at a private prayer-meeting in the house of a Nonconformist; yet few excelled him as a Christian. On the wall of the south aisle is this inscription:—

Sacred
to the memory of
The REV^D JOHN DUDDELL, Rector of
Wormington, Gloucestershire, and for
Thirty-three years Curate of this Town,
who died January the 8th, 1826,
Aged 82 Years.
And also to
MARGARETT, his WIDOW,
who died the first day of November, 1833,
Aged 85 Years.

By whose daughter Ann, the wife of
HENRY SKINGLEY, ESQ.,
this monument was
erected.

The next curate after Mr. Duddell was JOHN BULL, who, like his predecessor, was remarkable for his piety and charity. On a flat stone east of the Church is an inscription:—

In Memory of SUSANNA, Daughter of
The Rev. JOHN BULL, sometime Curate of this Parish,
and Mary his wife,
Who died 31st March, 1810, aged seven years.

The next vicar was RICHARD MANT, M.A., (afterwards D.D.) who was born on 12th February, 1766, at Southampton, where his father was master of the Grammar School. He was admitted in 1789 to the foundation of Winchester College, afterwards entered Trinity College, Oxford, and then became Fellow of Oriel. In 1804 he became curate at Buriton, and in 1808 removed to Crawley, then to Southampton. One of the pupils whom during the first years of his ministry he received to prepare for college, was Mr. Henry Du Cane; and by his cousin, Peter Du Cane, (died 1823) he was presented to the vicarage of Coggeshall, and was instituted 2nd May, 1810.* Whilst the vicarage house was undergoing repair he resided in the house of Mr. Du Cane, at the Grange. He de-

* "One of his predecessors had been Dr. Owen, and he left behind him at Coggeshall a leaven, the effects of which subsisted above a century. Besides this the family of the lord of the manor, the Du Canes, claimed descent from Oliver Cromwell himself."—*Memoirs of Bp. Mant; by the Ven. W. B. Mant, M.A., Archdeacon of Down*, p. 71.

clined to join with some of his parishioners in the prayer-meetings at which they desired his attendance. One of his first endeavors was to urge in his sermons the necessity of children being brought to be baptized, and shortly after he published *Two Dialogues* on the same subject, which led to a controversy concerning "Regeneration by Baptism," and a pamphlet was published by the Nonconformist minister in opposition to his views.* He exerted himself greatly to promote the education and general welfare of the parish. In 1812 he delivered the *Bampton Lecture* before the University of Oxford, which brought him into public notice. Two of his lectures were reprinted as tracts. In the following year he became chaplain to the Archbishop of Canterbury, Dr. Sutton, and removed to Lambeth, keeping a curate at Coggeshall till his resignation. During his residence at Coggeshall he published three volumes of sermons for parochial and domestic use. In the year of his leaving he also published a sermon preached at Colchester for the benefit of the National Schools. He then commenced editing, in conjuction with the Rev. George D'Oyly, an edition of the Bible, which the Society for the Promotion of Christian Knowledge had determined to publish; and

* In a subsequent publication Dr. Mant says, "I believe it to be the doctrine of the Bible, and I am sure it is the doctrine of the Church of England. This doctrine, however, is virtually at least, if not actually, denied by some ministers of our Church; and it is denied in terms which charge the maintainers of it with blindness and ignorance, with innovating on evangelical truth, with being opposers of the doctrines of the gospel, and patrons of a heathenish superstition. . . . The nonconformist ministers who quitted their stations, assigned this reason in common with others for their nonconformity, that the Church clearly teaches the doctrine of real baptismal regeneration."—*Bampton Lectures*

continued to labor upon it in the *Lollards' Tower.*' In 1815 he was collated to the rectory of St. Botolph, Bishopsgate, by the Bishop of London; and afterwards received from the Archbishop the benefice of East Horsley, in Surrey. In 1820 he was made Bishop of Killaloe and Kilfenora; and was translated to the see of Down and Connor, 22nd March, 1823, where he continued till his death, which took place the 2nd of November, 1848. He was buried in the church of Hillsborough, where his wife had been previously interred. He wrote numerous volumes, chiefly in support of the doctrine and ordinances of the Established Church, for which he had a boundless veneration; but will probably be longest remembered as the author of several excellent hymns, which he bequeathed to the church universal.

EDWARD WILLIAM MATHEW was the next vicar. He removed to Bury St. Edmund's, and subsequently retired to an estate, which had come to him at Pentlow, where he died.

HENRY STEPHENS was curate about this time.

The living was presented in 1834 by Peter Du Cane, M.P. for Stanning, Sussex, to his nephew PERCY SMITH, who in 1835 resigned, and removed to the donative of Pattiswick, of which he is now incumbent.

The next vicar was ARTHUR CAPEL JOB WALLACE, M.A., of C. C. College, Cambridge, eldest son of the Rev. Job Wallace of Braxted. He was previously curate of Hadleigh: resigned this living in 1839, and was presented to that of Monk's Eleigh.

The succeeding vicar was HENRY ELEY, who resigned, and removed to Broomfield near Chelmsford.

The National School was built in 1839, on the site previously occupied by the Work-houses. Towards its erection, &c., the Lords of Her Majesty's Treasury granted £200, (December 24th, 1839), and the Committee of Council on Education £125, (June 16th, 1847).

In 1841, WILLIAM JAMES DAMPIER, M.A., was presented to the vicarage. During the last ten years, the Parish Church has been restored, chiefly through his unceasing efforts. Mr. Dampier has issued several publications, among which are:—

"Faithfulness and its Recompense." A Funeral Sermon. In memory of Ann White, who died 15th Nov. 1846, aged 93. Burns.
"The Sympathy of Christ." Bell and Daldy.
"A Memoir of John Carter." Parker. 1850.

From the last the following account is taken. JOHN CARTER was born at Coggeshall, 31st July, 1815, and, after having been at a dame school, had two years education in the Hitcham charity school. He then worked at the silk weaving. One Saturday night, in the month of May, 1836, he, and some of his companions in mischief, went to the rookery at Holfield Grange, for the purpose of carrying off the young birds. In climbing one of the lofty trees, when about 40 feet from the ground, he missed his hold and fell to the ground upon his back. He was taken up senseless, but not dead... The blow, however, inflicted a serious injury to the spine, so that he was henceforth deprived of all power of feeling and voluntary motion below the neck. The muscular power of the neck itself was retained, and no permanent mischief was sustained by the organs of the head. The fifth, sixth and seventh of the cervical vertebræ were thrust out into an arch, and the seventh dislocated, so that the spinal cord, without being severed, suffered severe compression, such as to deaden completely the nerves of *motion* and *sensation*, yet not such as to injure the nerves connected with the respiratory and digestive systems, by which the functions of life were carried on. In this condition of paralysis he lived 14 years, and his intellectual faculties appeared not the least affected. Whilst lying on his back he read a great many books; and, from a suggestion in one of these, he began to employ himself in drawing and painting, by means of a pencil or brush held between his teeth, and a small light desk, on which his drawing paper was fastened, adjusted on his breast. In this manner he executed several works, in line drawing, which display considerable artistic talent. He could also write well with pen and ink. Specimens both of his drawing and writing are given in the above-mentioned memoir. During his illness he became a sincere Christian, and died in faith, 2nd June, 1850.

Since Mr. Dampier became vicar, the following curates have been successively appointed:—W. Wigson, John Sutton, Frederick A. Iremonger, T. A. Griffinhoofe, Edward L. Cutts, B.A., and J. W. Browne, M.A.

X.
NONCONFORMITY.

Ejected Ministers.

WHENEVER laws were ordained contrary to conscience and the word of God, Nonconformity became a necessity for those who would obey God rather than man. It existed accordingly where the least scope was allowed for freedom of thought; and every attempt to bring the laws of the state into harmony with the individual conscience, and to silence its voice, alike failed.

During the twenty years which preceded 1662 there were placed in the parish churches men, of whom the least that can be said is that they were faithful pastors and able preachers. All of them were ultra-protestant in doctrine; many were in favor of Presbyterianism or a modified Episcopacy; and many were Independents. Charles II. was restored under most solemn engagements "that no man should be molested for his religion;" but as soon as the Restoration was effected all these were put aside. First of all (1660) three hundred ministers were ejected from their livings to make room for the restoration of such as had been sequestered, and without regard to the character or competency of the latter. Then all the objections urged against the re-establishment of unmodified Episcopal authority and the Book of Common Prayer, were overruled, and an Act was passed, which required each minister who had not been ordained by Episcopal hands to be re-ordained, and to declare publicly his unfeigned assent and consent to all and everything contained in the Book of Common Prayer, as now set forth,* &c.; and on neglect or refusal pronouncing him *ipso facto* deprived of all his spiritual promotions. Unable, without disregarding the supreme claims of conscience, to comply with such requirements, above two thousand ministers† ceased to minister in the Established Church, from Bartholomew Day, 24th August, 1662. Another shade was thus added to the previous darkness of this day,‡ by the privation and suffering into which these men were driven. The Conventicle Act was afterwards passed, forbidding more than five persons besides the family to meet for religious worship, under severest penalties.

About this time the *plague* visited this country, and

* The alterations made were of the following nature:—The Book of Bell and the Dragon inserted in the Calendar—the words "rebellion and *schism*" in the Litany—"Priest" and "Deacon" substituted for "Minister"—Absolution ordered to be pronounced by the priest alone—kneeling at the Lord's supper—*Charles* styled "our most religious King." The Nonconformists, many of whom were in favor of a Liturgy, had many objections to the prescribed forms. Among other things they said, "We cannot in faith say that every child that is baptized is regenerated by God's holy spirit." "The words of the burial service cannot in truth be said of persons living and dying in open and notorious sins. These words may harden the wicked and are inconsistent with the largest rational charity."

† William Rastrick, in a MS. Index, (date 1734) in a library at Lynn, gives 2257 names.

‡ The massacre of 10,000 French Protestants in 1572.

carried off great numbers of people in this neighbourhood. It does not appear to have been severe in this town, if it prevailed at all. At Braintree, on the contrary, 600 persons died within a short period; and in the vestry of that parish a memorial on parchment, containing the names of charitable contributors towards the distress, mentions "The Inhabitants of Coggeshall —£35." Several of the ejected ministers ventured into vacated pulpits, to preach to the excited people. The *Five-Mile Act*, however, forbade them to come within five miles of any place where they had previously ministered, or of any borough or corporate town. Great numbers of Nonconformists were fined and imprisoned; but meetings were secretly held. When the Conventicle Act was revived in 1669, enquiries were sent to every parish concerning such meetings; and the returns, partial and imperfect, are preserved at Lambeth.

"Coggeshall. Hard to be suppressed. (Ministers) Mr. Sammes. Mr. Lowry."

The next entry is:—

"Wethersfield. Mr. Cole, now in Chelmsford Goal."

In 1672 Charles II. issued his Declaration of Indulgence, and above 3,000 licences for religious worship were taken out.

"License to John Sammes, to be a congregational teacher in the house of John Croe at Coggeshall.—1st May 1672."

"License to Thomas Lowry, to be a congregational teacher in his house at Coggeshall, in Essex."

"The house of Thomas Lowry in Coggeshall to be a Meeting House."

"The house of Matthew Ellistone at the Grange in Little Coggeshall to Matthew Ellistone.—13th May."

"William Grove, in his house at Coggeshall, licensed to be a congregational teacher.—May, 1672."

"Thomas Millaway, of Coggeshall, Essex, licensed to be a general congregational teacher.—22nd July, 1672."

The Nonconformists in this place were too numerous to meet in one spot. The *Test and Corporation Acts* immediately followed the Indulgence; afterwards came other persecutions. It does not appear, however, that in this town, beyond having their assemblies broken up, the Nonconformists suffered greatly; for the magistrates, and others upon whom the execution of the laws devolved, were themselves of the same mind as the offenders. The attempt of James II. to bring back the country to Roman Catholicism, led to the Glorious Revolution of 1688, and the Act of *Toleration:* but the Act of Uniformity and other laws against Nonconformists were still continued.

JOHN SAMES was one of the ejected ministers, as already stated.* Most of those who formed the congregational *church* of which he was previously pastor left the Parish Church, and met together elsewhere,

---

* *Palmer* says, "After the loss of his living he and some of his people went to Church, but others of them not being satisfied to do so, and the minister at the same time reproaching them in public for not being present in time of divine service, he desisted and set up a separate meeting, and died pastor of a gathered church there. He was a man of good learning and valuable ministerial abilities, but melancholy to an excess."

"1656, July 2.—(Born) Deborah, daughter of John and Anne Sames, vicar.

"1672, Dec. 16.—(Buried) Mr. John Sames."—*Par. Reg.*

"1689, Nov. 29.—I first heard old Mrs. Sames was lately dead."—*Bufton's Diary.*

as circumstances permitted, and were ministered to by Mr. Sames, Mr. Lowry, and others. He died soon after the Indulgence was granted, and his funeral sermon was preached by Mr. Lowry.

"The notes of ye sermon preached at ye funerall of Mr. John Sames, by Mr. Lourey, Dec. 16, 1672.

"Text—Isaiah lvii. 1-2. We have been burying the greatest riches of the town, the jewel of the town; but we do not know whether ever we shall outlive the following storm of judgments, to regain such a pearl again. It is the great sin of a people, that when the righteous are removed by death they think they have done their last duty; but their last duty is to sit down and consider their loss, and what will be the sad consequences of such a dispensation. . . . . We must not be troubled upon the personal account of this man, for he is gone to rest and peace, from all the troubles of this world. Death to him is gain. . . So that we are not to lay to heart his loss, but our own loss. Such as sat under his ministry and were refreshed by his doctrine, should mourn and lay it to heart; and the town should lay it to heart; for he was the salt as it were of the town, and the light of the town. He shined among you in his doctrine and conversation. Some men's death is but a cipher, and a hundred ciphers signify nothing; but the death of some is as a figure, and a figure of 1 and three ciphers stand for a thousand. He was a messenger of a thousand, and ought to be laid to heart more than the death of a hundred or thousand wicked persons. . . . . . Some men are not at all affected with such a dispensation as this. They may persecute the righteous when they are alive; but when they die, they lay them in their graves, and hide them in the dust, and forget them, and their hearts are hardened it may be against their widows or children. A righteous man is excellent; but they are willing to have him buried out of sight. They do not see that a righteous minister in a place is the greatest advantage: nor foresee that such a hedge or fence is taken away that the judgment of God may take hold of them.

"But yet there are gracious souls that do see the feet of the righteous servants of God to be beautiful: they open their hearts and their doors to them: they see God in such messengers, and when they are removed they see that it is an irreparable loss, except God make it up. God will take care of such a poor flock, though they be a flock of slaughter. And though their shepherd is gone, yet God will provide them another. Is there no more in the world? Yes: but you must go to God for one by prayer. Those that are sorrowful to see so many congregations without a soul-saving ministry, the Lord has made a promise to comfort them; as in the third of Zephany, 12-17. . . . . . Now doubtless this friend which we have been burying was a righteous man. I could not only judge him to be righteous, but eminently righteous. He had a rich propriety in God and Christ, and he had a gospel spirit in his prayers and preaching. He was spiritual in his worship and spiritual in his conversation, and he had that wisdom from above that made him pure and peaceable, gentle and easy to be intreated: his wisdom did not carry him forth to strife, envy or contention. Again, he was of a plain spirit; he had a plain honest heart. And verily he was profitable to old, to young, to this company and that company, and he was communicative of any good he had. He did not handle the word of God in craftiness. He was patient: and of a free and public spirit. He was tender-hearted to his people, and to all; and he had a spirit of government in his family, and walked conscientiously. How careful was he! He ordered his family, and therefore was the more fit to order the church.

"Therefore our loss is great, now such a righteous man is taken away. You that are *sinners* have a great loss. He warned you of Hell, and of being drowned in the world. You that were his *church* have a great loss. He carried you in his warm bosom. Christ make it up to you. You *young men* have had a great loss. He was kind to young men, and tender of their souls. The Lord make up our loss. And let us all endeavour to be righteous men and women; and then God will either take us from a day of trouble, or hide us in a day of trouble. And the Lord grant that we may be truly affected and humbled under this dispensation."—*Bufton's MSS.*

THOMAS LOWRY was a Scotchman. He succeeded Mr. Meighen, who was sequestered at Great Braxted, and afterwards went to Harborough in Leicestershire, (inducted Feb. 24, 1649,) and received a moiety of Whitworth rectory to supplement his salary, which was very small. He declined to be lecturer at Maldon, to which he had been appointed June 12, 1649. On his ejection, he came to reside at Coggeshall.* He preached in his own house. An extract has been given from his funeral sermon for Mr. Sames. He preached another at the funeral of Mrs. Brockwell, at the close of which he said:—

"Now this woman whose funeral we solemnize was in my apprehension a pious, prudent, profitable, sober and peaceable woman. If she was not so good, and so pious and prudent as she did show for, you that are without a fault throw the first stone at her. Though her life might be somewhat obscure and reserved, yet I cannot but think 'the root of the matter' was in her. Then whatsoever things are honest, and lovely, and of good report, that were in her, let us do, and the God of peace shall be with us."

His own funeral sermon was preached by Mr. Gouge, April 2, 1681:—

* "1661, May 28.—Obadiah, sonne of Tho. and Bridgett Lowrye, vicarii.
"1662, Sep. 28.—Robert, sonne of Thos. Lowrye, vicarii."—*Reg. Bap.*

"Text—Psalm xci. 16. I have read concerning a king that in the bequeathments of his will he made a deed of gift of all from the heavens to the centre of the earth. Such is the riches of God and the infiniteness of his love, that unto his servants he gives all from the centre of the earth to the centre of the heavens; he gives them what is sufficient upon earth, and what is saving in heaven; he gives them throne blessings and foot-stool blessings; and so you find the largeness of God's heart to his people, both in upper and nether springs, in eternal and temporal distributions of love, an assurance of which we have in these words, ' With long life will I satisfy him, and shew him my salvation.' Observe, First, Life is one of the primest flowers that grows in nature's garden. Secondly, It is God that is the fountain and spring of life. Thirdly, Length of life, and satisfaction with it, is a further blessing which God bestows upon his godly people. . . . . Although the departure of our reverend friend and brother ought to be matter of greater sorrow than I see among you; yet God honoured him with a double crown, a crown of long life on earth, and I question not but with a crown of salvation in heaven.

God did satisfy him with life, by the life of grace and taking him up into his love; and God did afford him a competency of outward things to the last. This is *life*, when a man has his name written among the living in Jerusalem. Let churches be reviled and contemned, yet they are the Jerusalem of God; and to be enrolled a true member in a true church is a glory next to the glory of heaven. Thus our friend in his last sickness, upon some discourse of his hopes, gave that for one ground among many others, 'Lord, I have loved the habitation of thy house and the place where thine honour dwelleth.' This servant of God was one that laboured much among you; but what is there of his labours to be seen? You have had able ministers among you; there has been much seed sown among you; but where is the harvest? If ever you would honour any minister, honour him by receiving his labours into your hearts and lives. God hath 'watered' you with *wine*, yea, with the *blood* of many of his servants; but if this blood be found amongst an unprofitable people, it will be dreadful for you at last.

"Ye that remain, children of the deceased servant of God, remember his counsels and example, and do not wound him now he is dead. Let it not be his reproach afterwards, that any of you should prove a wicked son or an ungodly daughter. . . . So let us live, that God may satisfy us with long life for evermore."—*Bufton's MSS.*

MATTHEW ELLISTONE was probably a native of this town, where the family had long resided. He lived here in 1646, and on the 3rd of September in that year was appointed by an ordinance of the Lords to Stamford Rivers, in the stead of Dr. John Meredith, who had been deprived the 6th of May, 1643. On his ejection, he returned to Coggeshall and lived at the Grange, where he had licence to hold a meeting for worship in 1672. He was a Presbyterian.

"The notes of the sermon which was intended to have been preached by Mr. Elliston, at the Burial of old John Picknet at Kelvedon, Sept. 6, 1675. But he being then hindered, he preached it the Sunday after, being the 12th September, 1675.

"Text—Phil. i. 15. You find the Apostle in a straite at the penning of this text; and I was in a straite; straites of time as to my sermon and meditations: and some of you know I was in a straite when it was intended to be delivered, *by reason of an unkind and unchristian opposition.* That which was then hindered is by relations desired to be the discourse of the day.
—*Bufton's MSS.*

In 1677 *(see p.* 80 *note)* he is mentioned as Matthew Ellistone of Little Coggeshall, clerk, in connection with

Isaac Ellistone of the same place, probably his brother, and lived there until his death.

"The notes of the sermon preached at the funeral of my cousin, Isaac Ellistone's wife, by Mr. Burwell, Nov. 13, 1674."

"The notes, &c. of my cousin, Mr. Isaac Elliston, by Mr. Burwell, April 3, 1678."

"1678, 5th Oct.—My cousin Sam. Sparhawke's wife was buried. She was old Mr. Burwell's daughter, Minister."—[Probably Mr. JEREMY BURWELL, ejected at Hertford.]—*Bufton's MSS.*

"1693, May 3.—Buried Matthew Ellistone."*—*Markshall Reg.*

THOMAS BROWNING was born of pious parents at Coggeshall, about the year 1634, and was sent to Oxford at sixteen years of age. Here he "chose the worst companions and despised the best instructions; and after some years left, and became tutor in Col. Sydenham's family. There was so much religion here that he quickly grew weary of it and left, and chose rather to embrace a vain and uncertain course of life." On attending Westminster Abbey, he was greatly impressed by sermons of Mr. John Rowe, the pastor; and afterwards of Mr. Thomas Weld of New England, and Mr. Pinchback, assistant of Dr. Manton. About this time Mr. Sames met with him in London, and induced his parents, whom he had estranged by his former life, to invite him and his wife to reside with them at Coggeshall. He became a member of the church, and was at length encouraged by Mr. Sames

* A Mr. Thomas Ellistone preached at Maldon and thereabouts until his death.—*Palmer.*

to devote himself to the ministry, and preached his first sermon on Matt. i. 20. in his pulpit in the Parish Church. Going with Mr. Sames to a commencement at Cambridge, they met with Mr. Beverly of Rothwell, who was seeking a minister for an adjoining parish of Desborough; and Mr. Browning, after preaching there, was invited to become pastor in 1657. Here he continued faithfully discharging his duties for five years.* In all his work he followed the advice once given him by Dr. Owen,—" Study things, acceptable words in course will follow."

He was ejected among the two thousand, preaching his farewell sermon on 2 Cor. xiii. 14. The people of Desborough and Rothwell gathered together to form one congregation under his ministry, at Rothwell, where he had licence to preach in 1672, and continued during the rest of his life.

"Some soldiers came one Lord's-day, April, 1682, to break up a meeting, and to take Mr. Browning of Rothwell. The constable advised them to be well-advised in what they did, 'for,' said he, 'when Sir —— was alive, he eagerly prosecuted these meetings, and engaged 8 soldiers of the country troop therein, whereof myself was one. Sir —— himself is dead; 6 of the soldiers are dead; some of them were hanged, and some of them broke their necks; and I myself fell off my horse and broke my collarbone in the act of prosecuting them, and it cost me 30s. to be

* Mr. Beverly says in his Diary—"1658, May 13. Pretty cheerful till Brother Browning's return from Essex, who told me the sad news (among some other more refreshing) that there was some discord in the New England churches: Mr. Stone turned classical. O what a fountain of tears broke my heart forthwith out into, to conceive that Satan should infest those precious churches which the Lord had hitherto so gloriously carried as on eagle's wings."

cured. It hath given me such warnings, that for my part I am resolved I will never intermeddle with them more.' This story he repeated several times that day, which shews how readily conscience, when a little awakened, construes the Divine Providences to be acts of judgment and admonition."*

Mr. Browning was on one occasion arrested and imprisoned in Northampton Gaol; from which place he wrote the following with other letters to his church:

" My dear Brethren and Beloved,

"I salute you in the Lord, and make mention of you to him with joy, counting it my most happy lot, next interest in His love, to have so great a share in yours. . . . . We have peace in the midst of trouble, and quiet in the day of war; because 'this man is our peace even while the Assyrian is in the land.' God has been a little sanctuary to us in our scatterings, and has over-ruled that which was designed for our ruin to our help. O my brethren! methinks I am with you, weeping with you, joying with you, praying with you, and hearing with you. It is *true* fellowship my soul has with you at a distance. I long after you much in the Lord, yet rejoicingly stay his good pleasure. I would not come out a moment before his time. I would not take a step without his direction. I am wonderfully well; better and better. The cup of afflictions for the Gospel is sweeter the deeper: a stronger cordial the nearer the bottom — I mean death itself. O the joy unspeakable the glorious and dying martyrs of Jesus have had! How full freight have been their souls in their passage to their port! I tell you, if you knew what Christ's prisoners, some of them, enjoyed in their gaols, you would not fear their condition, but long for it. And I am persuaded, could their enemies conceive of their comfort, in mere vexation of heart they would stay their persecutions. 'Therefore, my brethren, my joy and crown, stand fast in the

* Conformist's Plea for Nonconformists, Pt. iv. p. 83.

Lord.' Rejoice greatly to run your race: fear not their fear: sit loose from the world: allot yourselves this portion which God has allotted you, through many tribulations to enter into the kingdom of heaven. Come the worst is death, and that is the best of all. . . . My brethren, do not budge. Keep your ground: the scripture is your law: God is your king. Your principles are sober, your practices are peaceable. Your obedience to superiors known in those things wherein your obedience is required. If men have nothing against you but in the matters of your God, rejoice and triumph in all your persecutions. . . . I exhort you all to walk in the faith, fear, love and joy of the Lord. Study your mutual edification. Fear nothing of events till they come: only fear offending God with a neglect of your duty. There is no shadow like the shadow of God's wings; therefore keep close to God. Ps. lvii. 1." "T. B."

Reference to his death is made in the church-book of Rothwell:—" Mr. Thomas Browning, pastor of this church, was gathered to his Father's house in peace, in an awfully persecuting day, May 9, 1685, having served his Lord in this house with much pains and many tears, with much presence and success, about 23 years." He was buried in Rothwell churchyard, and was succeeded by Mr. Richard Davis.*

ROBERT GOUGE became pastor of the church after the death of Mr. Sames. During the interval Mr. Lowry preached, as before observed.

* *Monuments of Mercy*, or some of the distinguished favours of Christ to the Congregational Church at Rowel, as handed down in the ministry of Mr. John Beverley, and Mr. Thomas Browning, remembered. By MATTHEW MAURICE. London, printed for R. Hett, at the Bible and Crown in the Poultry, near Cheapside, 1729.

Palmer says—" His tomb yet remains with a Latin inscription. The late Mr. Moses Gregson, who married a descendant of his, communicated to the Editor some extracts from his Diary, which discover an ardent piety."

Mr. Gouge was born at Chelmsford, and sent by Lord Fitzwalter to Christ's College, Cambridge, where he had for his tutor the celebrated Henry More. On leaving the University he went to Maldon, where he preached and taught a school. From thence he removed to Ipswich, where he is spoken of as pastor of a congregational church, August 17, 1658.* He was silenced in 1662; and came to Coggeshall about the year 1674.

"1675, May 26.—The notes of ye sermon preached at the funerall of old Mr. William Cox by Mr. Gouge.

"Text—Gen. v. 24. . . . I hope our dear friend whom God hath taken away in these respects did walk with God. He was, but is not. God hath taken him. Alas! you lament the death of the man; will you desire to live the life of the man? an humble, mortified, friendly, fruitful life as he did? I see a treasure withdrawn, and the stock is lessened. Did not I see a corner-stone falling out of the building? You children of a good father, take heed how you carry it, take heed of taking your liberty. Methinks there is a gap made now: I pray God, let his spirit fall down and make up the breach; for the family, the town, the church, have a great loss. *I am a stranger among you, and in part a stranger to you.* God hath taken away many candles, many lights from us. I am afraid God is provoked by us. Remember pride does not eat out the heart of religion and the love of your souls to God, and therefore think of it, and the Lord grant we may make a good use of this solemn stroke of God, superadded to the strokes of former days.

"1675, July 17.—Funeral Sermon of Nicholas Merrills,† by Mr. Gouge.

* Letter from Samuel Petts, of Sandcroft, to Slater, at St. Katherine, near Tower Hill. Peck's Desid. cur. ii. 505.

† "1704, Dec. 28.—Died Mrs. Merrills, formerly wife of the worthy Mr. Dodd.—*Bufton.*

"1676, May 16.—Funeral Sermon, John Bowyer's second wife.
" 1678, Oct. 29.————————Old Widow Sach.
"1679, Nov. 12.————————Old Nurse Newton.
"1679, Nov. 6.————————Wife of Thomas Brewster.
"1680, Jan. 27.————————Daughter of Mr. Samuel Richardson, servant of Mrs. Cox."

The old church book contains the following allusion to Mr. Gouge; but it was not written till the year 1775:—

" Mr. Sammes shared the same fate as the 2000. By this very solemn providence the people became scattered as sheep without a shepherd: for many of them could not sit down to his successor as he maintained both another faith and another order. But the Lord, who is the watchful keeper of his people, sent them a gatherer of the dispersed remnant, in the person of the Rev. R. Gouge. As now they were cast out of and become dissenters from the established church, and so could not meet where they formerly did, they hired a barn in East Street, which they converted into a meeting-house."

This house, situated on the north side of the street, now belongs to Mr. F. Hills. It was then the property of ISAAC HUBBARD, who was a deacon of the congregational church.* This good man died in 1687. Mr. Gouge shortly afterwards published a little volume entitled " The Faith of Dying Jacob, or God's Presence

---

* The Manor Rental shows that Mr. Hubbard owned this place. He lived on the site of the Mechanics' Institute, Church Street. An old manuscript, including a statement of Mr. Hubbard's effects, and of the subsequent building of the present Chapel, has—" Gave Mr. Gouge a pair of spectacles with silver bands:" and—" There were some old boards that came from the old meeting-house that were carried to the new meeting-house."

"1681, Oct. 18.—Mr. Isaac Hubbard brought home his third wife.
"1684, Oct. 80.—Old Mrs. Smith, Mr. Hubbard's sister, was buried.
"1687, Dec. 6.—Mr. Isaac Hubbard was buried."—*Bufton.*

with his Church notwithstanding the Death of his Eminent Servants: being several sermons from Gen. xlviii. 21, occasioned by the death of Mr. Isaac Hubbard, with the memorials of his life and death, and advice to his son. London. 1688."

"EPISTLE DEDICATORY to the Church of Christ at Great *Cogshall* in *Essex.*

" You are a people whom the Lord hath honoured with many successive able Pastors, Mr. *Obadiah Sedgwick*, Dr. *Owen*, Mr. *Sams:* All which Lights the Lord hath taken up into his upper Chamber, after their shine upon Earth to shine in Heaven; after their Labours with men, to take their rest in the Bosom of their God and Saviour. You are a people whom the Lord hath preserved marvellously in the stormy, cloudy and dark daies that scattered many others. You have had but a few drops of those tempestuous showers that drowned others. A garden inclosed, a spring shut up, a fountain sealed have you been: Your bow yet abideth in strength, though I am well aware how the Archers of Hell and Earth have shot at you. You have seen the goings of God in your Sanctuary, and every one of you may speak of his glory. The Lord hath much thinned your glory and comfort, by the decease of many Principal Members, though after the fall of the leaf, you have had sweet after-springs and budding stems, that you remain as green Olive-trees in the house of your God: So let his spiritual glory remain fresh upon you. You have continued in a close adherence to the Lord, and his Worship, not mixing with the world, and thereby have lost little: in your keeping the word of his patience, he hath kept you from the hour of temptation that hath tryed the Earth, when greater damage hath attached others in their neutral, treacherous compliances. The Pillar of Cloud and fire, hath given you a safe conduct to this present break-day of the Glory of God, and the Jubile of rest and liberty, universally extended in this Nation from its Bondage, and where is the fury of the Oppressor? The Lord cause this springing glory to shine to a perfect day, and prevent new darkening Clouds. For above the space of fourteen years, the Lord hath placed me, unworthy me, among you: And to the praise of his glorious name, you have seen the workings of his blessed Spirit in your confirmation, and others conversion: In which years, through the various tryals Divine Providence hath exercised me with, and the many personal infirmities that have attended me, you have born up in your Christian ingenuous respects to me, as also in your assistance, according to your abilities, to my civil expences, wherein I have yearly spent the whole revenue of my little Own that I had in this world, which had not been, but for the failure of some other hand, of what was at first proffered at my coming to you; though the disturbing exigences of late times, conduced much to that failure. This indeed in some fits of exigence, hath proved some little uneasie temptation to me, to think of some other supply: Which at present I wave in duty to God, and true love to you. The last blow the Lord gave us, was that deep one, by the decease of our dear and honoured Brother Mr. *Hubbard*, which becomes the occasion of this small book. He was a good Copy, I hope many will write after him, and not let that goodly picture drop out of their hearts or lives: He gave you good conduct in all your affairs, and prospered, for the Lord was with him: 'Twas amongst his very last words, the Lord hath the residue of Spirits, let us pray that that living, flowing, renewing Spirit may flourish among us, with the encrease of Gifts and Grace. By reason of my many occasions, some months are pass'd since this Christian deceased; but I remember *Vespasian's* Motto on his coin, *sat cito si sat bene*. 'Tis soon enough, if well enough. I design not many words to you, 'twill be better, that what concerns the Glory of God and our mutual comfort, be expressed in our continued fellowship.

"So, finally Brethren, Farewell, be perfect, be of good comfort, be of one mind, Live in Peace, and the God of love and peace shall be with you.

"Yours to serve in the Gospel of Christ,
"R. Gouge."

Of Mr. Hubbard he says:—

"He was never so unchristian as to make all anti-christian who differed from him, as if none could get to heaven but went in his congregational path. God's eternal truth was dearer to him than liberty or life. His card, pole-star, canon he walked by, was the word of God. Wheresoever he separated from others it was because they first separated from truth. His conversation was in Heaven. The solitudes and arbours of holy retreated meditations he found to be gates that let in the inward world, Heaven's suburbs and sunlight. At home his conversation was pious and profitable. In the church: he cared for the things thereof with singular prudence and exemplariness, as a sound, able Christian, and almost a Divine. He was eyes to the blind, and feet to the lame. He was charitable and tender-hearted. He was contented, meek and humble. Death met him nigh at home, whose imperious necessity he had prevented by the daily resignation of himself to Heaven's commission. In the last year of his life he was much solacing his soul in the foreviews of future glory, much reading that piece of his ancient reverend Pastor, Dr. Owen, about the *Glory of Christ.* Thus having finished his course upon earth, having oft fetched his God down to him, he was taken up to his God."

Mr. Gouge resided at the upper end of Stoneham Street. He had some relatives here, one of whom was named Samuel Gouge, a lawyer. He had also a son, named Thomas Gouge, who was born at Ipswich in 1662, and became pastor at Amsterdam: on returning to England, was pastor of the Independent Church at

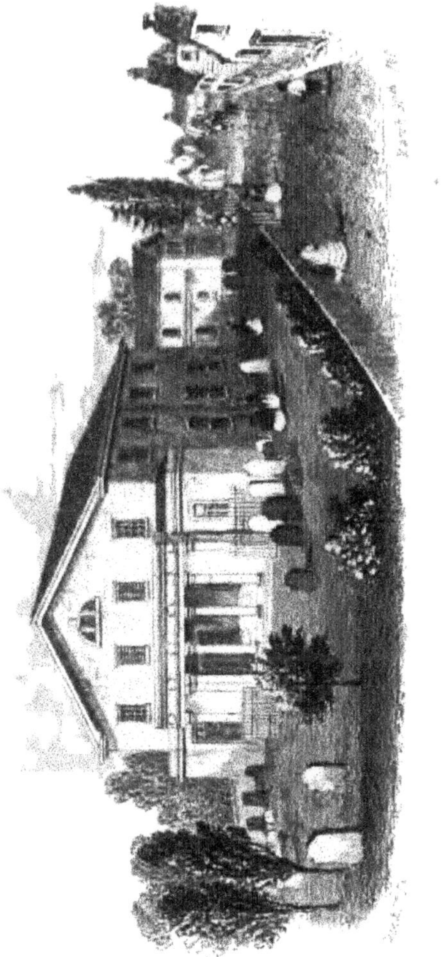

the *Three Cranes*, near Thames Street, and died 8th January, 1700. *Dr. Watts* says that the three greatest preachers in his younger time, were Mr. John Howe, Mr. Stennet, and Mr. Thomas Gouge, whose strength lay in the illustration of scripture; and dedicates one of his Lyric poems to his memory. Mr. Gouge outlived his son, and died in a ripe old age at Coggeshall, where he was buried October 16, 1705.*

Independent Chapel.

About the time of Mr. Gouge's death, EDWARD BENTLEY† was chosen pastor of the church. There was a meeting of congregational ministers at Coggeshall in 1706,‡ either at his ordination, or for conference on denominational matters. The spirit of intolerance toward Nonconformists once more burst out under Queen Anne, and with the cry of "The Church is in danger!" inflicted further but not enduring civil disabilities.

It was now determined to remove from the old meeting-house in East Street, and to build a new one. On 20th of April, 1710, two tenements in Stoneham

---

* "1680, Apl. 27.—Mr. Thomas Gouge was married to a rich gentlewoman of Chelmsford.

"1689, Oct. 31.—Mr. Thomas Gouge brought home his second wife from London.

"1689, May 19.—Mr. Samuel Gouge, a lawyer, was buried."—*Bufton.*

"1693, June 6.—Child of Mr. Thomas Gouge.—*Reg. Bap.*

"1709, May 18.—Mrs. Gouge.—*Reg. Bur.*

† 1703, Nov. 17.—Edward Bentley and Mary Bird, both single persons of Coggeshall.—*Reg. of Mar. Markshall.* 1710, April.—Child of Mr. Bentley.—*Reg. Bur. Coggeshall.*

‡ Diary of Mr. Harrison, Wethersfield.

Street* were purchased for this purpose, of Henry Ennew, by Isaac Buxton, of Great Coggeshall, clothier, Thomas Nicholls, of Little Coggeshall, yeoman, and William Brown, of Little Coggeshall, gentleman. A croft adjoining these tenements was also purchased of Ennew by the above-named, and Edward Bentley, John Barnard, senior, of Great Coggeshall, draper, John Cooper, of Kelvedon, gent., Thomas Porter, senior, of Messing, gent., William Raven, of Little Coggeshall, yeoman, Thomas Porter, junior, of Easthorpe, yeoman, and William Barrick, of Feering, yeoman. The contract for building is still in existence. The chapel was built by Thomas Crosby, of Bocking, and was to be 45ft. long, 36ft. wide; also a vestry 12ft. square, galleries, pulpit of oak, and pews of the same kind as those in Bocking meeting-house, which had been built just before. Amongst the church-papers there is also a list of subscribers' names, in which the largest contributors mentioned are—Nehemiah Lyde, Esq., Richard Du Cane, Esq., Mrs. Grimes, T. and I. Buxton, Thomas Nicholls, Edward Bentley, and others.

On the 9th of March, 1715, the Chapel was put in trust, "to be used and enjoyed as a meeting-place for

---

* Called or known by the name of "Old Ales." Being at the end of Church Lane, it is probable that in the olden time the people resorted hither from afternoon prayers to their sports and pastimes. *Whitsuntide* especially was employed in these *Church-ales.* Both old and young met together, bringing their provisions: there was dancing, shooting at *butts* [probably in Butts field nearer the Church], and a general carousal. Sometimes there were collections made for the poor and other objects. The times had changed and the spot was applied to another use. A chapel registered in the Registry of the Bishop of London, as a meeting-house for religious worship of Protestant Dissenters from the Church of England commonly called Independents, 81st August, 1710.

the worship of Almighty God, by and for the people of that congregation or society for the time being of which the said Edward Bentley is now pastor or minister, or whereof his successor or successors for the time being shall be pastor or pastors, and all such other persons as shall attend the ministry there." The trustees were—Isaac Buxton, Thomas Nicholls, William Brown, Nehemiah Lyde, of Hackney, Esq., Richard Du Cane, of the city of London, Esq., Edward Bentley, clerk, John Taylor the elder, John Barnard, of Messing, gent., Moses Richardson, of Pattiswick, gent., Richard Brewer, of Great Coggeshall, yeoman, William Barrick, of Feering, yeoman, and Jeremiah Raven, of the same place, yeoman.

One of the principal agents in building the Chapel was ISAAC BUXTON, son of Thomas Buxton.*

"Thomas Buxton was a man of great piety and meekness, great tenderness and humanity, a Nonconformist, narrowly escaping imprisonment for his profession—a very industrious and thriving man. He died of a paralytic stroke in his 70th year. Judith Gunton his wife, born in 1661, was a zealous, godly woman, earnest to instil instruction into the minds of her grandchildren, who were cast by providence, through the bad

* The name first occurs at Coggeshall in the time of Henry VIII. (page 106, note). Thomas Buxton was buried there, 26th April, 1592: his son William in December, 1624: and grandson Thomas in 1646. The last named claimed and received from the Herald's College in 1684, the arms borne by the family of the same name settled before 1478, at Tybenham in Norfolk. His son *Thomas* died 1718, aged 70. From the above-named Charles Buxton, the late Sir Thomas Fowell Buxton was descended. Travers Buxton, Esq., of Camberwell, is a descendant of the above-named John Buxton. An interesting letter exists, written by Charles Buxton, to "his loving brother John Buxton, Esq., at Coxall," dated, London, Aug. 19, 1746, containing an account of the execution of the two rebel lords, Kilmarnock and Belmerino.

health and early death of their mother, [Elizabeth, died 1713, aged 40] into her care. Their only child, *Isaac Buxton*, joined to a fine person, a very keen active temper in his business, [a clothier] and was very successful. As he was alive in trade, so he was alive in the cause of religion. Zealous in his Nonconformity, he was the chief manager in and promoter of the building of the meeting-house, now belonging to the protestant dissenters in Coggeshall. He was born in 1672, and died of the palsy in his 60th year. He left 5 sons, *Thomas, Isaac, John, Charles* and *Samuel*, all of them men of sincerity, great honesty and sound sense. They received a good education, and were strict Nonconformists. I knew four of them. Thomas, John and Isaac left trade, the first two were clothiers, the last a draper and grocer, and retired upon their fortunes. Samuel died a young man, and Charles, in the trade of an oil merchant, raised a considerable fortune and retired a few years before his death. All the above are buried in the church-yard at Coggeshall. My mother, Anne Bentley, [2nd wife of Thomas Buxton] who died when I was in my 10th year, was the only daughter of Joseph Bentley of Leicester, mercer, and Anne Tinville his wife, and was niece of the Rev. Edward Bentley, Dissenting minister of Coggeshall."—*Manuscript of Anne*, (died 1798) daughter of Thomas Buxton; wife of Jacob Unwin, brewer, and mother of Thomas Unwin, and of the late Mrs. Buxton, who died at Camberwell at the age of 95. Another daughter of Thomas Buxton was married to William Forbes, Esq., who died at Coggeshall 1818.

A list of Nonconformist churches, &c., in 1716, (written from materials collected by Lord Barrington, of Little Baddow, in connection with some political matters,) mentions the Independent Chapel of Coggeshall as having " 700 hearers, 43 voters for Essex, 19 gentlemen." On 8th February, 1727, the following new trustees were appointed: John Brooks, of Feering, Thomas Buxton, John Buxton, Joseph Thetford, George Abbot, John Savill, of Feering, Edward Sach, of Great Coggeshall, Abraham Cook, Robert Salmon, George Brett, of Little Coggeshall, Thomas Porter, of Inworth, gent., Isaac Buxton, junior, of Great Coggeshall, draper, Edward Brooks, of Feering, and John Willsher, of Mark's Tey. Other documents of the same period, relating to the Chapel, likewise exist.

In 1734, April 23, Mr. Ford of Hedingham preached here a sermon before several ministers. It was published under the title of " National Guilt: a just cause for National Humiliation."

" Mr. Bentley," says an old record, "was a lively, zealous, and useful minister; and was continued for upwards of 30 years, when he also went the way of all living; though with this glorious addition, that *he died in the Lord.* His remains were interred at the foot of the pulpit stairs; and to the honour of his memory it is to be recorded, that he was a builder of the Lord's house in a double way; not only by his preaching, but by his purse, being a generous contributor to rearing the temple in which we now worship." (1775.) An inscription still remains in the aisle of the Chapel:—

> Here lieth the Body of EDWARD BENTLEY,
> Who departed this life June 9, 1740,
> Aged 60 years.
> 2 Tim. iv. 7, 8. " I have fought the good fight,"
> &c.

Before his death he had been joined in the pastorate by JOHN FARMER. He was born at a village near Shrewsbury, where his parents, who were persons of reputation and piety, resided. His grandfather by his mother's side was Hugh Owen, who was silenced by the Act of Uniformity, but afterwards preached in Wales. He received his education from Dr. Charles Owen, at Warrington, one of those early Tutors of the ministry among the Nonconformists who sought to compensate for the lack of the training of the Universities, which had been shut against them. He afterwards pursued his studies under Dr. Doddridge, and was chosen Dec. 30, 1730, assistant to Mr. Rawlin, of Fetter-lane; where he continued till his settlement at Coggeshall, March 28, 1739. Here he remained for about seven years, and then retired to London. Few excelled him in thorough acquaintance with the Greek Testament. He published a volume of sermons which possess considerable merit, and present a remarkable contrast to the doctrinal errors and dead morality of preaching that prevailed to so large an extent before Wesley and Whitfield began their labors, under the shadow of the toleration won by the struggles of the early Nonconformists.

Mr. Farmer was unfitted for extensive usefulness by several eccentricities of temper. During the latter part of his life he was dependent for his subsistence in great measure on the benevolence of his friends, particularly of his younger and more celebrated brother, Hugh Farmer of Walthamstow (born 1714).

who conveyed it to him in such a manner that he never knew whence it came.

After Mr. Farmer left NICHOLAS HUMPHREY became pastor; but he remained only two years, when he removed to Bergholt, near Dedham, at Michaelmas, 1750, and succeeded Rice Williams. There he continued five years, when he was attacked with fever, which terminated in insanity, from which he never recovered. Edward Hickman was invited to become pastor of the church at Coggeshall. A paper signed by about thirty of the congregation, March 25, 1751, "showing our approbation of the church's invitation to you" still exists. But he appears to have declined coming.* "The clouds then hung very heavy, and gloomy were our prospects: two ministers living that had been our pastors, and yet the church destitute. After long waiting, Providence appeared once more to smile, in sending us our present dear and worthy pastor, the Rev. Henry Peyto."

HENRY PEYTO was the grandson of Samuel Peyto or Petto, of Catherine Hall, Cambridge, ejected from Sandcroft in Suffolk, and afterwards pastor of a congregation at Sudbury: an eminent mathematician, and author of several useful works. He first preached at Coggeshall, Nov. 10, 1751, and was ordained in the following year.

Previous to his coming there had been some inattention to the church books, or these books were

* Some disagreement, about this time, led several persons to leave the church: and a minister named Royce, preached to the secessionists until his death, when they returned.

lost. The *Registers* of Baptisms, &c. commencing at this time were conveyed to the Registration Commission, 10th July, 1837, and are preserved at Somerset House.

Stoneham Street. Independent. Founded 1665 [?]

1. Baptisms 1752—1776 (kept by Mr. Peyto.)
2.   ,,   1775—1785 (kept by Mr. Andrews.)
3.   ,,   1786—1821 (kept by Mr. Andrews, Mr. Fielding, and Mr. Wells.)
4. Burials 1802—1818 (kept by the clerks of the Meeting, Nat. Plumpstead and F. Hunwick.)
5. Baptisms and Burials 1821—1837 (by Mr. Wells.)

The following New Trustees were appointed, 16th October, 1755:—

Robert Salmon, sen., Great Coggeshall, clothier; Thomas Unwin, sen., Little Coggeshall, yeoman; William Unwin, sen., Great Coggeshall, clothier; Thomas Unwin, jun.; William Unwin, jun.; William Sandford, draper; Edward Powell, clothier; John Abbot, wool-card maker; Jonathan Peacock, Stisted, yeoman; Edward Sach; Thomas Babbs, jun., wheelwright; William Newton, sen., maltster; Thomas Lay, clothier; Edward Walford, baker; Ephraim Willsher, yeoman; Daniel Halls, salesman; George Day, jun., draper. In 1764, considerable repairs were done to the Meeting-house.

Mr. Peyto continued pastor for about 25 years; and his careful ministry was attended with much success.

"On Thursday, about eleven o'clock a. m., we were deprived of our dear old pastor, the Rev. Henry Peyto. He quietly fell asleep in Jesus, after having gone in and out before us nearly 25 years. At his earnest request our other pastor, Mr. Andrews, preached his funeral sermon the evening after his interment, from the text, *I know in whom I have believed*. Thus we are now without our good old shepherd, whom, as we were exhorted the Sabbath after, we hope to remember, whose faith to follow, considering the end of our conversation."—*Church Book*.

His wife was the niece of John Mason, M.A., of Cheshunt, author of the "Treatise on Self Knowledge," (son of Mr. Mason of Dunmow), and his daughter was married to Peter Good, minister of Epping, an excellent scholar and able preacher: another daughter was married to Mr. Unwin. In the parish church-yard is this inscription :—

"Here lies interred the body of Miss Mary Peyto, daughter of the Rev. Mr. Peyto of this town, who departed this life, Oct. 7, 1772, aged 27 years.

> 'Heaven gives us friends to bless this present scene,
> Resumes them to prepare us for the next.'

Also the body of the Rev. Henry Peyto, who died, Nov. 7, 1776, aged 74 years. Also Love Peyto, his wife, who died, June 4, 1779, aged 64 years. Also of Mrs. Elizabeth Mason, who departed this life, Dec. 23, 1784, aged 81 years. Also of Mr. Stephen Unwin, formerly of this parish, clothier, and late of Black Notley in this county, who was suddenly called from time to eternity, Jan. 20, 1806, aged 63 years."

MORDECAI ANDREWS was ordained Sept. 5, 1775, as co-pastor to Mr. Peyto, and "the venerable pastor, trembling beneath his infirmities, stood forth to testify his full approbation."

He was the son of Mr. Andrews of Spitalfields, and

became member of the Independent church at Stepney. He studied at Mile-end Academy, (removed to *Homerton* about this period,) one of the tutors of which, Dr. John Conder, assisted in the solemnity. Mr. Towle of Aldermanbury, Brewer of Stepney, Davidson of Bocking, Winter, (his assistant,) Bingham of Dedham, Lombard, and twenty other ministers, were present. The names of the deacons were Edward Evans and Haddon Rudkin, who, along with the pastor and other members of the church, had sent a circular inviting the attendance of neighbouring ministers. The number of members was about fifty, forty of whom had been received into the church by Mr. Peyto; at the close of Mr. Andrews' ministry the number in communion was about eighty, only one of whom, William Hume, survives in 1862.

"1776.—Besides two discourses on the Sabbath, on some one day in the week we have a preaching lecture alternately with a historical lecture on the rise and progress of the Gospel in England from the earliest days.

"Every Thursday the children assemble to be catechised.

"The year opened with the usual exercise of the dear little ones, who repeated 300 texts of Scripture which had been preached upon chiefly in our own town during the past year, all Dr. Watts' songs for children, and all Dr. Doddridge's Principles of the Christian religion."

1777, May 13.—The following new trustees of the Chapel were appointed:—

"John Godfrey, surgeon; William Babbs, gent.; Habbakuk Layman; Fisher Unwin, brewer; Jordan Unwin, (of the Grange); Stephen Unwin, clothier; Edward Sach; John

Wright of Feering; Henry Shetelworth, sen.; John Raven Thomas Babbs; Haddon Rudkin; Edward Evans."

"1783.—Three new deacons were chosen, viz., Mr. Thomas Heward, [died Jan. 12, 1815, aged 75, see Tablet at entrance of chapel], Mr. Wright, [died April 28, 1823], and Mr. Raven.

"Mr. Edward Sach left a legacy to the poor."

"WILLIAM KEMP admitted a member of this church," [afterwards went to Homerton College; then co-pastor of Mr. Hobbs of Lion Walk Chapel, Colchester; finally pastor at Terling, where he died 1844.]

"1784, July 11.—THOMAS EISDELL dismissed to become pastor over the congregational church at Abbots' Roothing, according to their united call and desire."

"1794.—ISAAC ANTHONY admitted member," [went to Homerton College; then pastor at Bedford; his son Isaac Anthony was pastor at Hertford; F. E. Anthony, M.A., classical tutor at Western College, Plymouth, and Thomas Anthony, B.A. of Bury St. Edmund's, are his grandsons.]

"1795.—JOSEPH DENNEY admitted member," [went to Homerton College; afterwards pastor at Kingston: died Dec. 3, 1805, aged 28.]—*Church Books.*

Mr. Andrews was one of the first in this neighbourhood to establish SUNDAY SCHOOLS. A meeting was held for the purpose on 24th Nov., 1788, Mr. Du Cane the vicar, Mr. Andrews, Mr. Jacob Pattisson, and Mr. Thomas Unwin being the chief promoters. About 200 children were collected, arranged in companies of 25 each, and taught in different places by teachers, who received one shilling and sixpence a week for their trouble; attendance at Church or Chapel being left to the choice of their parents. Governors were also appointed, who met at an inn once every month to manage the business; Mr. Heward, secretary.

All went on well for some months; there was no dispute about Bibles, Testaments and spelling books; but when it was thought necessary to introduce the Church Catechism, the Independents preferred the Catechism of Dr. Watts; one hundred of each were therefore ordered; but at the end of the year the union was amicably dissolved. The next year a subscription was opened for providing the children with Sunday-clothes of green baize, and white collars. The following year a united anniversary took place, (Sept. 14, 1790.)

"This morning the governors and the children, with their teachers, of the several Sunday schools assembled on Market Hill, and from thence about quarter-past 10 the procession began, preceded by the Rev. Mr. Duddel and the Rev. Mr. Andrews, and 6 governors—then the band of music—the Sunday schools in order two-and-two, with their teachers, attended by the rest of the governors and a vast concourse of people, proceeded to the Church, where an excellent sermon was preached by the Rev. John Hallward, vicar of Assington. The collection amounted to £40. 2s. 0d. The procession returned from Church in the same order, going on until they arrived at Mr. Walford's field in Church lane; tables were spread, booths erected, and a good dinner provided for the children, and the governors waited upon them to cut their victuals and give them their beer. In the evening the principal inhabitants met at the Chapel Inn, supped together, and spent the evening in harmony and love, and parted in friendship and peace."

Still the schools continued separate; and after some years it was thought advisable to appoint one master for charity Day and Sunday Schools; and out of these arose the existing British and Sunday Schools.

Mr. Andrews resigned in 1797, and went to Southampton, where he died September, 1799. He was the father of Dr. Andrews of Camberwell.*

In the vestry there is a mural tablet in memory of Hannah Andrews, (first wife of Mr. Andrews), who died Oct. 22, 1776, in the 22nd year of her age. The tombstones in the burial ground are of a date subsequent to this, and bear the names of Unwin, Pattisson, Denney, Gardner,† Andrew, Johnson, &c.

JEREMIAH FIELDING succeeded him. He was born, 24th December, 1773, at Harshead, a village near Ashton-under-Lyne, and studied at Hoxton Academy. He was ordained pastor at Coggeshall, 12th June, 1798, the following and other ministers being present, Dr. Simpson (Tutor), W. Bentley Crathern of Dedham, Reynolds of Hoxton Square, Hobbs of Colchester, Ray of Sudbury, Stevenson of Castle Hedingham, William Kemp.

"1799, 18 Dec.—Mr. Jacob Pattisson elected Deacon." [died, Nov. 9, 1806, aged 43. His son, F. U. Pattisson, Esq., chosen Deacon in 1842.]

"1801, 3rd July.—JAMES SPURGEON admitted member." [afterwards dismissed to Clare to become pastor of Independent congregation; now of Stambourne: grandfather of the Rev. C. H. Spurgeon.]

"1802, April 26.—Peter Good and Fisher Unwin [died 1821] elected Deacons."

---

* Some account of Dr. Andrews is given in Paxton Hood's " Lights of the Temple."

† M. Gardner died 1817; father of Dr. John Gardner, author of the " Great Physician," " Domestic Medicine," and other works.

"1806, April 4.—Alexander Good admitted member." [1813, Oct. 24, dismissed to church at Bergholt, having accepted pastoral charge.]

"1812, May 3.—William Archer chosen Deacon."

"1815.—William Till and John Raven chosen Deacons."

About this time disagreements arose between Mr. Fielding and some of his congregation, which led to the publication of pamphlets displaying little of the spirit of charity on either side. Some thirty persons left the 'Great Meeting,' and met for worship in a warehouse, fitted up for the purpose, in East Street, and continued to do so until Mr. Fielding left. After leaving Coggeshall he resided eight years at Little Moor in Derbyshire, and died at Partington in Cheshire, May 20, 1840. He was buried in Rusholme Road Cemetery, Manchester. He was a man of considerable learning, and an eloquent preacher: in more genial circumstances, his life would have been much brighter and more extensively useful. He published a work in two volumes, entitled, "Eugenius, or the Infidel reclaimed."

ALGERNON WELLS was born at Peckham, 11th Sep., 1794. When seven years of age he was sent, in accordance with the will of his father, whose death had occurred just before, to a school at Gildersome, near Leeds, kept by John Ellis a member of the Society of Friends. From very early life he was thoughtful and pious. He became a member of the congregational church at Chatham, afterwards assisted Dr. Redford in a school at Uxbridge, and went from thence to

Hoxton Academy. Before he had completed the usual period of study he was sent to preach to the new congregation at Coggeshall; and after preaching for some weeks accepted their invitation to become pastor, February 12, 1818. Some arrangement having been made, in consequence of which Mr. Fielding retired, they returned to the former house of worship: and at the request of the re-united church, Mr. Wells was ordained, April 6, 1819; when there were present Dr. Harris of Hoxton, John Hooper, A.M., J. Blackburn, Alexander of Norwich, Thomas James, Thornton of Billericay, Stephenson of Hedingham, Morell of Baddow, Savill of Colchester, Crathern of Dedham, David Smith of Brentwood, Heward of Clare, [son of the late deacon,] J. Hunwick* of Kelvedon, and others.

The difficulties of his first settlement were soon overcome by the wisdom and love with which he devoted himself to his work; and he continued to labor here, amidst the respect and love of the people, for nearly twenty years. He married Miss Eliza Godfrey, daughter of Mr. Godfrey, surgeon, who survived him some years.

The Chapel was enlarged in 1818, and again in 1834; in the latter case at a cost of about £1000. In 1837 it was registered for the solemnization of marriages. In 1819 Mr. S. Unwin and Matthias Gardner [died 1835, father of Mr. M. Gardner, chosen 1851]

---

* He attributed his conversion to the preaching of Mr. Bull, curate of Coggeshall. After preaching in a room at Kelvedon, (where formerly there had been a lecture by the ministers of Coggeshall and Witham,) a church was formed in 1820, of which he became pastor. He died 24th March, 1841.

were elected deacons : and in 1835, John Clemance*
[died 1836; father of Mr. J. A. Clemance, chosen 1851]
and Stephen Bridge [died 1838]. One hundred and
twelve members joined the church during his ministry.
This however represents very inadequately the success
that attended his labors. Nor was his influence confined to his own congregation and neighbourhood, but
was felt throughout the county. Missionary effort in
Essex was greatly promoted by his zeal and energy.
Few could so effectively address an assembly, when
the subject was one in which he felt an interest; none
could reconcile discordant opinions and feelings more
effectually.

He had the 'charity that never faileth;' and, 'even
weeping,' diffused the same spirit amongst others.
His great worth was best known to his own family
and church, but it was at length well known throughout
the denomination. Having been invited to become
the secretary of the Congregational Union of England
and Wales, and of the Colonial Missionary Society, he
resigned his charge June 3, 1837, and left amidst
general regret. "His name is still among the people
as a household word; and the loving recollection of
him the country round, is a proof at once of his holy
consistency, his sympathetic intercourse, and his successful labors."† While at Coggeshall he published :

"Jesus Christ the Author of His People's Resurrection and
Eternal Life. A Sermon on occasion of the death of Mrs. Lydia

---

* Father of Rev. Clement Clemance, B.A., of Nottingham.
† Life and Immortality, &c. A Funeral Discourse, by the Rev. T.
Binney. London. 1851.

Unwin,* late of the Grange, preached 26th December, 1820." *London.* 1821.

"Allegiance to Christ, Liberty of Conscience—Two Sermons, from Matt. xxiii. 8. and I Kings iv. 25. preached on 24th August, 1828, the Anniversary of the Ejectment of Nonconformists, and the year of the Repeal of the Corporation and Test Acts." *London.* 1828.

"Sermon, on occasion of the death of Mr. Thomas Unwin, jun. and Mr. Isaac Unwin, preached 28th May, 1832." *Braintree and Coggeshall.*

"Sermon, on occasion of the death of Mrs. Mary Godfrey, preached Nov. 24, 1833." *Braintree and Coggeshall.*

"On Animal Instinct: a Lecture, delivered before the Mechanics' Institute, Colchester, Nov. 25, 1833." *Colchester.* 1834.

"Ministerial Devotedness Recommended, Charge delivered at the ordination of the Rev. W. J. Unwin, M.A.,† at Woodbridge. April 21, 1836." *London.*

"When the Congregational Union was first projected he did not feel quite sure that it was allowable or safe. Having early imbibed the spirit of the old Independents—brave and true men, though exaggerating somewhat personal rights and individual liberty—he was a great friend to freedom, civil and religious; very jealous of ecclesiastical usurpation; and hence his fear of the proposed movement. He attended one of the early meetings of the Union, not so much as an objector as a doubter, proposing difficulties and seeking

* Daughter of Mr. Everett of Capel in Suffolk, and wife of Mr. Thomas Unwin. Her daughter, Mrs. Lydia Death, died 18th June, 1831, and in the following year her sons, Thomas the eldest on 19th May, aged 28, and Isaac on the 28rd of the same month, aged 16.

† Previously member of the church at Coggeshall; now Principal of Homerton College.

their solution—the ultimate result of which was that he became its devoted secretary himself! In this office it is hardly possible to award him excessive praise. His wise suggestions, his efficient plans, his judgment in council, his prudence in action, his talent for correspondence, his beautiful addresses—printed or spoken, his bearing and deportment, spirit and tone—everything belonging to him, within him, and about him, marked him out as one whom God had peculiarly qualified for that kind of work which he did so well, and of which therefore he was called upon to do so much."

Being desirous of preaching regularly to the same congregation, he undertook, in addition to his other duties, the pastorate of the church at Upper Clapton, in 1839, where he continued until his death. A new chapel was about to be erected, when he was laid aside from his work. During his illness he dictated a tract on "The House of the Lord rebuilt," and soon afterwards died, 29th December, 1850; and was buried in Abney-park Cemetery.

The words which he uttered to one of his congregation who visited him not long before his decease, form his best memorial:—

"I have finished my tract 'The House of the Lord Rebuilt,' and I am weaving another, and shall hasten to think it out. I am anxious to record the thoughts gathered together while lying here. It will be on the GLORIOUS GOSPEL. And, my dear friend, if it please God, I hope to be able to preach *that* to you as I have never yet done! Not that I reproach myself with having concealed or forgotten it. No; but more than ever I would fain speak of it, as I have thought and felt here. I would make it the first thing, the pre-eminent! All gathered knowledge, all history, all poetry, all pleasant thoughts and happy things—all that I have, and am, and know, and think, shall range round and illustrate, but be subordinate to this—the Glorious Gospel! The more I think of it in my long and quiet pondering, the more precious and needful it becomes to me! Yes; I will have it written, but I long to preach it; and if it please God, I will preach it as I never did yet. That is, dear sir, after all, the one thing—the Glorious Gospel."

JOHN KAY was born at Abingdon, in Berks, June 18, 1813. Being apprenticed in Birmingham, he became hearer of the late J. A. James, and member of his church; and after a short probationary course of instruction, entered Highbury College in 1835. He was ordained pastor at Coggeshall, June 6, 1839, the following and other ministers being present:— Algernon Wells, Dr. Halley, Thomas Craig, John Alexander, Stephen Morell, Robert Burls.

In 1841 new school-rooms were built on ground purchased of John Newton Hunt,* and made over to

* J. N. Hunt was a conveyancer at Coggeshall: he was born in London, 14th May, 1776. "My grandfather was a dissenting minister at Hackney; his grandfather was ejected from Lutton in 1662. My maternal ancestor was a Dr. Harrison, who had the living of Pentlow, and was probably 'among the faithful found' at the time when the Rev. W. Hunt was ejected." He was apprenticed to a grocer at Colchester: afterwards clerk in the Bank of England. He wrote one or two pamphlets at the time of the French Revolution. In 1810 he came to reside on some property belonging to his family in Coggeshall. "In the establishment of a Lancasterian school for the children of the poor, my endeavours were crowned with success: although it would have been more satisfactory if the good vicar, Dr. Mant, would have concurred in forming one school for all the poor in the town, instead of having a rival institution, adapted only for those belonging to the Church of England." He published several

F. U. Pattisson, Esq., Mr. Jacob Unwin, Stephen Unwin, jun., Joseph Denney, Jacob Pattisson, Harold Giles, M. Gardner, J. A. Clemance, H. Moore, Wm. Beard, Thomas Kettle, and John Sach, in trust "for the erection of school-rooms for the education of children, without excluding any on account of any religious distinction of sect or party." At the same time another piece of ground, on which the building as since enlarged stands, was conveyed to other trustees —S. Unwin, F. U. Pattisson, Jacob Unwin, S. Unwin, jun., Joseph Denney.* In aid of the erection £118 was granted by the Committee of Council on Education, 5th Jan., 1842, since which time these schools have been entirely sustained by voluntary contributions; and contain (1862) in Boys' Day School, 80 children; Infant School, 110; Sunday School, 600.

Mr. Kay continued here nearly 16 years. During his ministry one hundred and fifty persons joined the church. He was a man of high Christian principle, a faithful preacher, and kind pastor; in consequence of his retiring habits not widely known, but wherever known greatly beloved. And when the Chief Shepherd called him to his rest, he was borne to the grave

---

small works,—'The Spirit of Christianity' (1810). 'Translations of the Epistles of Paul by Philalethes.' 'Devotional Exercises.' An Edition of Watts' Hymns. Fugitive Pieces. Suggestions on the Law of Real Property, &c. He usually attended the Independent Chapel, but differed from many of the views generally regarded as orthodox.

* On 18th August, 1845, the following new Trustees of the Chapel were appointed:—F. U. Pattisson, T. C. Swinborne, Harold Giles, Wm. Beard, C. Moore, Thomas Kettle, Joseph Denney, Joseph Sach, J. A. Clemance, S. Unwin, jun., Jacob Unwin, Fisher Unwin, George Beard, jun., H. Moore, Alfred Denney, W. L. Oliver, Matthias Gardner.

amidst love, honor, and respect.* In the burial ground, east of the chapel, is this inscription:—

Sacred to the memory of the
Rev. JOHN KAY,
For 15 years pastor of the Independent Church, Coggeshall:
who died Oct. 14, 1854, aged 41 years.

There are mansions exempted from sin and from woe,
But they stand in the regions by mortals untrod;
There are rivers of joy, but they roll not below;
There is rest, but it dwells in the presence of God.

BRYAN DALE, M.A. (of Western College, Plymouth, and the University of London) was ordained 18th October, 1855, when there were present, Samuel Newth, M.A., Thomas Craig, J. Reynolds of Halstead, (deceased), John Carter, W. J. Unwin, M.A., of Homerton, T. B. Sainsbury, B.A., George Wilkinson, J. Hill, M.A., J. Waite, B.A., D. Flower (deceased), Henry Gammidge, C. Riggs, P. H. Davison of Wandsworth, E. H. Jones of Bridgewater, and other ministers.

The Society of Friends.

James Parnell's preaching in 1655 has been mentioned on a preceding page. Five or six years afterwards George Fox was at Coggeshall, "not far from which there was a priest convinced of the truth of the doctrine held forth by him and his friends; and he had a meeting in his house."† By this

---

* Two sermons on occasion of the decease of the Rev. John Kay: by Rev. J. C. Rook of Thaxted, and Rev. William Griffith of Hitchin. Coggeshall, 1854.
† Sewel's Hist. of Friends, i. p. 489.

time many in the town and neighbourhood had adopted the same views. After the Restoration they shared in the sufferings of the other Nonconformists, and were forbidden, not simply to preach in the churches, but also to assemble for worship in private houses. As soon as the Indulgence was issued, they availed themselves of the liberty, and began to build meeting-houses. On 21st April, 1673, premises at Coggeshall were purchased of John Raven and Daniel King of Hedingham, wool-combers, by Nathaniel Sparrow of Stisted, Richard Pemberton, clothier, Robert Adams, William Savill, John Radley, John Clark, Robert Ludgater, Robert Harvey of Great Braxted, and John Garrett: and the present meeting-house was erected.

In 1693, September 25, Joseph Drywood and Thomas Scarlett granted a lease for 480 years to John Drywood, clothier, William Ludgater, grocer, John Jenkins, card-maker, Richard Pemberton, jun., clothier, Isaac Anthony, wool-comber, John Stacey, wool-comber, Robert Ludgate, jun., fellmonger, Wm. London, baker, and William Cook, baker, of "a parcel of land called Ayworth's or Crouch's, abutting on an orchard belonging to a messuage called Sewal's or the Chapel, and upon a pond there situated, for a burying place of the people called Quakers, who shall die in or near Coxall."*

* "In April, 1698, the Quakers made a new burying-place in Crouches.
"1678, Jan. 11.—Thomas Larke, comber and Quaker, was buried.
"1678, Nov. 21.—George Guyon, clothier, took to him for his wife his maid, Martha Bowman.
"1688, Oct. 18.—Geo: Guyon, clothier, Quaker, was buried."—*Bufton.*

In 1786 an additional piece of ground was given by O. Hanbury, Esq., for the same purpose, in accordance with the intention of his late father, Osgood Hanbury, (buried there Jan. 20, 1784, aged 51,) "out of great respect for the people called Quakers." He was interred in this burial-ground Feb. 18, 1852, aged 86. Great numbers of the Friends were buried here formerly: in 1856 it was closed, and another piece of ground purchased near Tilkey.

John Turner, 28th January, 1710, gave three tenements near Short Bridge, in Little Coggeshall, unto Edmund Raven and William Candler, upon trust to distribute the rents among poor friends called Quakers.

The number of the Friends in the town has of late been gradually diminishing. Their decrease generally would be viewed with regret by every friend of freedom, unless he believed that the truth to which they have borne witness, and the good they possessed, had become as truly the possession of others.

The Baptists.

Towards the close of last century the Baptists had a small chapel in Vane Lane, Church Street. Robert French, and afterwards Mr. Hutchinson, preached there to a very few persons. They then removed to a Chapel in West Street. In 1815 William Payne (now deceased) was their minister, and afterwards several others in succession. In 1855 a new Chapel was erected in Church Street; but the old place was still occupied by several persons who remained behind, until it was sold in 1862. Mr. Collis preached for some time both at the old and new Meeting, and the present minister is Mr. Powell.

The Wesleyans.

For many years the Wesleyan Methodists have had a small Chapel in East Street, where worship has been regularly conducted. But this form of Nonconformity has never taken very strong hold of the people of Essex.

Two hundred years have now passed away since the last Act of Uniformity constituted our Established Church what it is; and during this period has so operated as to sever the sympathies of one-half of the country, and produce great social discord in almost every parish. The Nonconformists still allege the same reasons as at first; and, reviewing the course of history and the present condition of religion in England, most of them have come to the conviction that it would be for the promotion of truth, piety and social concord, if the existing relation of Church and State were altogether terminated. "However political considerations and reasons of State may require Uniformity, yet Christian and Divine accounts look chiefly at UNITY."*

* Bacon.

XI.

THE CLOTHING TRADE, &c.

THE wool trade was largely cultivated by the monks. "All the world," it was said, "was clothed from English wool wrought in Flanders." As early as the time of Henry I. certain Flemings, driven out of their own country by an encroachment of the sea, settled in England, and in the following reign the *manufacture* of cloth extended more or less throughout the kingdom, so that dealers in Norwich and other places paid fines to the King, that they might freely buy and sell dyed cloth. Markets and fairs were established for its promotion! In the reign of Edward III. it was still further advanced, partly by the endeavours of his Queen, Philippa of Hainault, who established a manufacturing colony at Norwich in the year 1335, and paid to it several visits. A monastic chronicle says, "Blessed be the memory of King Edward III. and Philippa of Hainault his Queen, who first invented clothes." It is probable that the monks of Coggeshall shared in the benefit of such endeavours of the Queen, for whom they founded a chantry. In the 14th year of the same reign there was granted to the King a subsidy of the ninth of corn, wool and lambs; and in the returns the ancient tax of the church (according to Pope Nicholas' Valor) was stated, together with the true value of the ninth, on the oath of parishioners. In consequence of war and a severe winter, the value was in many cases not so much as in the former instance.*

"Coggeshale. Tax, £20. Valuation of the ninth, £12. 6s. 8d. For the ninth in this Vill. Simon atte Gate, Walter Wydeweson, Thomas Vincent, John atte Stocke and John Ballard, are chargeable with £20, which is the tax. And, moreover, it was found by 12 jurors that the value is not more than £12. 6s. 8d., and so the tax avails not for £7. 13s. 4d., as appears in the present council by the same jurors, on account of the causes in the same.

"Teye ad Ulmos (as far as the Elms).† Without tax. Valuation of the ninth, 66s. For the ninth in this village John Mot, John Permont and John Blakenham, are chargeable with 66s."—*Inquis. Nonarum, p.* 319.

Various laws were passed, both with reference to the exportation of wool and its manufacture at home. Kent was famous for its broad-cloth, Norfolk for its fustians, Suffolk and Essex for bays and serges. In 13th Richard II. an act was passed, setting forth that plain clothes were wrought in divers counties, and tacked and folded together, and did not agree with the part shown, to the great deceit and damage of the merchants, and the slander of the realm; and enacting that no plain cloth so tacked or folded should be set

---

* "Under Edward III. Colchester, which was the centre of a large district, and ranked but nine towns in the kingdom superior to itself, contained only 359 houses, some built of mud, others of timber, and the number of inhabitants was only 3000."—*Eccleston's Eng. Antiq.* p. 199.

† Probably the Elm Farm, now belonging to Travers Buxton, Esq.

to sale, but that it should be *open* so that buyers might see it *as was used in the county of Essex;* and in 8th Edward IV. another act was passed prescribing the length and breadth, and weight of Essex cloth.

The manufacture was early introduced into this town, and added largely to the wealth of the inhabitants: as appears from the monuments of several persons engaged in this trade. In the 1st year of the reign of Queen Elizabeth, (c. 14), there was an act passed for continuing the making of woollen clothes in divers towns in the county of Essex. After reciting 4 and 5 Philip & Mary, by which no cloth should be made to sell but in a market town where it had been made for ten years last past, and allowing certain other places to do so, among which was Goddelmine in Surrey, it goes on:—

"And for as-muche as the Townes or Vyllagies of Bocking, Weste Barfolde, Dedham and Cockshall, in Essex, bee fayre large Townes, and aswell planted for Clothe making as the said Towne of Godlemyne, or better, and fewe Townes in this Realme better planted for that purpose, and have been inhabited of a long time with Clothe makers, wch have made, and daylye doo make, good and trewe Clothe, to the greate Comon Weale of the Countrye there, and nothing prejudiciall to or for the Comon Wealthe of this Realme: Be it therefore ordeyned and enacted by thaucthoritee of this pnte Parliament that y^t shall be lawfull to all and every suche person and persons which nowe do inhabyte or dwell, or hereafter shall dwell, in the sayde Townes or Villages of Bocking, Westbarfolde, Cockshall and Dedham, or in any of them nowe using or exercising, or that hereafter shall use or exercise, the Feate or Misterye of making, weaving or rowing of Clothe or Carseye, by the space of 7 yeres at least, or have been prentyse therto by the sayd space of seaven years, and inheryte and dwell in the sayd Townes, and to use the making, weaving or rowing of Clothe or Carseye, as before this tyme they might have doone yf the sayd acte had never been made; Annything in the sayd acte to the contrary therof made, or any other acte, statute or lawe, heretofore made, or hereafter to bee made, to the contrarye hereof, in annywise notwithestanding." [Also 37 Eliz. c. 23.]

A great impulse was given to this trade when Philip the Second of Spain sent the Duke of Alva to crush the reformed doctrines spread in the Netherlands. "The most independent and spirited, that is the most active and skilful part of the manufacturers, disdaining to submit to a tyranny by which they were oppressed in their most valuable rights, fled from their native country, and finding a refuge in other European nations, carried along with them that knowledge and dexterity in manufactures, and those habits of industry which they possessed in so eminent a degree." (1568.)* Great numbers came into the Eastern counties of England, and settled at Norwich, Colchester, and elsewhere.† Their presence also greatly strengthened the Puritans.

In 1575 there was a petition presented by the inhabitants of Coggeshall, and other poor clothiers, to the council, stating " that now no opposition is made

---

* Prof. Millar—quoted in Bischoff's History of Woolen Manufactures, vol. i. p. 45.
† Several foreign coins and Nuremburgh tradesmen's tokens have been found in Coggeshall, from time to time. Some of these are in the possession of Mr. C. Smith, who has likewise numerous silver coins of the Edwards, Henry VII., Elizabeth, James I. and other Sovereigns, found here.

to Mr. John Hastings' patent for the making of freesadoes after the manner of Harlaem, but that they are most unjustly vexed by him to their utter undoing."

Norden (1594) says—"There are within this shire these especial clothing towns: Colchester, Brayntree, Coggeshall, Bocking, Hawsted, and Dedham. Cogshall is specially famous for the most rare *whites* there made, exceeding any cloth in the land for rare fineness, and therefore called Coggeshall Whites. It is governed by 24 headboroughs, of whom are chosen two constables, for the time being chief governors of the town."

A cause similar to that which brought the manufacturers to this country drove many of their descendants away. Unable to conform to the rigorous injunctions of Archbishop *Laud*, they fled to New England and Holland; and thus the trade of the county was considerably lessened. During the Commonwealth it revived, and in 1653 is said to have arrived at the highest pitch it ever knew. At this time several wealthy clothiers resided at Coggeshall, one of whom, Mr. Thomas Guyon, 'the great clothier,' left at his death above £100,000. From the year 1648 to 1672 '*tradesmen's tokens*' came into use. They were small copper coins issued by tradesmen, and containing their names, and some figure or motto: they served as a kind of advertisement, but being only payable at the shop of the issuer, were very inconvenient, and at length suppressed. The following were issued at Coggeshall:—

THE CLOTHING TRADE.

Obv. THOMAS BECKWITH
Rev. Coggeshall in Essex. } in centre { Tallow-chandlers' arms
His half peny. T. A. B.
[Initials of his own and wife's christian name and surname.]

Obv. SAMUEL COX, of
Rev. Coggeshll. in Essex. } in centre { A hand holding a pen.
T. G.   A farthing.

Obv. THOMAS GVYON. in
Rev. Coggeshall. 1667. } " { A rose.
T. G.   A farthing.

Ob. WILLIAM GVYON 1670
Rev. In Coggeshall in Esex } " { A fleur-de-lys.
His half peny. W. R. G.

Obv. JOHN LARK of
Rev. Coggeshall. 1667. } " { St. George and the dragon.
I. L. M.   A farthing.

Obv. MOSES LOVE. Stay
Rev. Maker. of Cogshall.
[1657.] } " { A shuttle.
M. L.   A farthing.

Obv. ROBERT PVRCAS
Rev. in Coggeshall. } " { The Grocers' arms.
R. A. P.   A farthing.

Obv. BENIAMIN SAMSON.
Rev. in Coggeshall. 1665. } " { Samson.
B. E. S.   A farthing.

The figure of Samson standing with a robe over his shoulder and loins, holding a jaw-bone in one hand: it is a play on the issuer's name, which is frequently met with in these pieces.

Obv. AMBROSE SUTTON.
Rev. in Coggeshall. 1665. } in centre { Crest; on a cushion a greyhound's head, with a coronet on its neck.
A. S. S.   A farthing.

Obv. JOHN DIGBY.
Rev. Cogsall.   Grocer. } " { A fleur-de-lys.
I. D.   A farthing.*

Those who were occupied in the clothing trade forme

* From "Tradesmen's Tokens," &c. by W. Boyne—except the last.

a company or GUILD, (*gildan*=to pay) and paid into a common fund for the benefit of distressed members. The place of their meeting was called a Guildhall. There was an annual procession in honor of Blase, bishop of Sebaste in Cappadocia, the reputed inventor of the art of combing wool, and beheaded in the Diocletian persecution after having had his flesh torn off by instruments resembling those used in this craft. The last procession of this kind in Coggeshall, is said to have taken place about 1770, when a Mrs. Rowe rode in a carriage as "Peace and Plenty."

Certain orders were agreed upon, and confirmed by the Quarter Sessions of the Peace, for the "trade and mystery of the Clothiers, Fullers, Baymakers, and New Drapers in the town of Coggeshall." They were of the following nature: that none should use the trade unless they had been apprenticed seven years—that none should be apprenticed unless one of their parents had 40s. a year freehold—that one journeyman should be kept for every three apprentices, &c. Fines were imposed on those who absented themselves from the guild; and warrants were issued by Justices of the Peace requiring the wardens of the company and the constables of the town to prosecute all intruders into the trade and offenders against such orders. These orders were signed in 1664 by Richard Shortland, Mat. Guyon, Mark Guyon, John Guyon, Wm. Gladwin, Wm. Cox, Jo. Cox, Jo. Gray, Jo. Sampson, sen., Ben. Sampson, Paul Pemberton, Robert Nicholas, Peter Pridmore, R. Neele, T. Purcas, J. Rodly, sen., T.

Keeble, R. Sheppard, W. Clark, S. Harvey, Ambrose Sutton. The wardens for the Fullers in 1659 were N. Gladwin and Wm. Hatton; in 1698 Robert Nicholas and John Andrews; in 1710 John Hatton, jun., and John Phillbricke; and in 1799 William Mayhew* and Mark Cowell. The feoffees for the Fullers in 1659 were John Rodly and William Clark, jun., and the stock—£22. 11s. 6d. In 1799, F. Lay and J. Seex, the last named in the book of orders, divided (Nov. 14, 1800) the remaining stock among about 30 persons.

Special efforts were made from time to time against intruders, and in 1686 a subscription was set on foot, and a new warrant obtained. An address to the fulling trade at Coggeshall says:—

"We do not design to prevent our neighbours' children learning the trade, provided they be bound to it as the law requireth. We desire that we may be more constant in frequenting and upholding the guilds: and then be careful to choose such wardens and feoffees as will stand up for the good of the trade. This is a true account of our minds.

"From such as would our rights invade,
And would intrude into our trade,
And break the laws Queen Betty made,
Libera nos Domine."

"In August, 1688, I wrote the following verses 'Of Blase' in a Book for the Combers:—

---

* His son WILLIAM MAYHEW, wine merchant, purchased an estate belonging to the Gladwin family, called *Wybores* (at one time the *Green Man*), and resided there: now the property of Mr. C. Smith. At the time of the passing of the Reform Bill he became a candidate for the representation of Colchester. Spottiswode his opponent was returned, and voted against the bill; but Mayhew petitioned against his return—succeeded—and took his place just in time to vote in favor of the bill, which was carried by a bare majority.

> ' Judicious auditors with love we greet,
> To *blaze* our patron's memory 'tis meet,' &c.

And after these some verses of my own composing:—

> As in all ages have been some that stood
> Most nobly to promote the public good,
> So in the present age some are inclined
> The good of this our Fulling trade to mind, &c.

"1699, the following verses I made for the Bellman, for the Guilding morn:—

> This day there will a noble feast be made
> For all amongst us of the Fullers' trade,
> This ancient custom they do still uphold,
> Which hath been used from the days of old:
> Their wardens for next year will chosen be
> By voice of those who of the trade are free."—*Bufton.*

The clothing trade in the Eastern counties began to decline about the close of last century, and to go northward, where abundance of water-falls, coal and iron, afforded facilities not to be obtained here. A good trade in 'bays and says,' which were exported to various parts of the world, continued at Coggeshall at the commencement of the present century, but ceased soon afterwards.

XII.

PUBLIC CHARITIES.

In earlier times, when the laborer was entirely dependent on the lord, and could claim as a right food and shelter in sickness and old age, Public Charities were unknown. But when this condition of things was changed, poverty became common. On the dissolution of the monasteries, which had extended their hospitality both to the diligent and the idle, the healthy and the sick, great numbers were cast upon the country desirous of obtaining their living at the expense of others. Most severe measures were adopted to prevent the evils which followed. In the first year of Edward VI. it was enacted "that if any person should bring before two Justices any one who lived idlingly or loiteringly by the space of three days, they should cause him to be marked with a hot iron on the breast with a V [vagabond], and adjudge him a slave for two years."

Various modes were also adopted to mitigate the prevalent distress. Voluntary collections were directed to be made in most parishes, on behalf of the aged and infirm; and fuel sold to the poor at prime cost. An Act of 27 Henry VIII. directed "that every preacher, parson, vicar and curate, in sermons, confessions and making of wills, should exhort the people to be liberal for the relief of the impotent, and setting and keeping to work the said sturdy vagabonds." During the next hundred years bequests for Public Charities became common. Of late years people have begun to learn that it is better to distribute their possessions with their own hand whilst they live, than to leave them to be distributed by others when they are gone.

The following are the Charities belonging to Coggeshall:—

I.—Paycocke's Charity.

This was left by Thomas Paycocke, son of Robert Paycocke, and nephew of Thomas, the founder of the chantry. He was a staunch protestant (pp. 105, 127). He lived in a house in West Street, where there remain his initials carved in wood, and an ancient gateway (which admitted to Vincent's close and an old chapel) with two carved figures. By his will, dated 20th Dec., 1580, he devised £200 for the purpose of purchasing free lands and tenements, to be conveyed to ten of the headboroughs of Coggeshall upon trust—

"That the whole revenues and yearly profits of the said lands, shall from time to time be given and distributed to and amongst the poor people dwelling in Much and Little Coggeshall, by the consent of the Collectors of the Poor and the Churchwardens of the same parish, for the time being, in manner and form following, that is, that with one-half of the said yearly rents and profits, shall be bought as much *wood* as it shall amount to, *and to be given and distributed yearly indifferently to the poor people of the same parishes*, always betwixt Easter and the first day of August; and with the other half of all the revenues and profits aforesaid, that there shall be bought by the persons aforesaid, always one month before Lent, as many *white herrings* and red as the same one-half of the rents and profits aforesaid will amount unto, and so to see it given and distributed equally to and amongst the said poor people, always in the beginning of Lent, so long as this uncertain world shall endure."

The sum of £156 was accordingly laid out by Richard Benyon, of Little Coggeshall, one of the executors, in the purchase of 23 acres of land near Halstead, which were granted (24 Eliz. June 20) to Wm. Fuller, Robert Litherland, Cyprian Warner, Thomas Dammet, Thomas Till, Robert Aylett, Henry Purcas, Robert Brittle, George Laurence, Thomas Hopper, Peter Ryse, and Edward Warner. Some dispute having arisen about the appropriation of the rents between Great and Little Coggeshall, it was determined by a Decree of Sir John Samms and others, dated 30th May, 1613, that the yearly rent of three pounds should be paid to—

" the Overseers and Collectors for the poor in Little Coggeshall, at the two feasts and terms of the year most usual, that is the feast of St. Michael the Archangel, and the Feast of the Annunciation of our Blessed Lady St. Mary the Virgin, for and towards the relief of the poor in Little Coggeshall."

The whole rental amounted to little more than £50 until lately, when six acres were sold for £1500, which has of course increased the annual amount for distribution considerably. Herrings for Lent are no longer needed, and the circumstances of this "uncertain world" otherwise altered since the times of the founder of this charity; and the trustees now wisely distribute it to the poor in money or clothing.

The present trustees are—Mr. Appleford, Rev. W. J. Dampier, Mr. Dennis, Mr. Doubleday, Mr. M. Gardner, Mr. Giles, Mr. Hanbury, Mr. Kirkham, Mr. Pattisson, Mr. Sach, Mr. W. Swinborne.

II.—Hitcham Charity.

SIR ROBERT HITCHAM was born of poor parents at Levington, in 1572, and was educated at the Free School, Ipswich, and at Pembroke Hall, Cambridge. He was student of Gray's Inn, and attorney to Queen Anne of Denmark. In 1596 he was M.P. for West Looe, and knighted 25th June, 1614 by James I. who called him, 4th January, 1616, to be his senior sergeant-at-law.* He was Recorder of Hadleigh, 22 Jas. I.

* " Hoskins, an eminent lawyer, used to calle Sergeant Hitcham his ape, because of his writhen face and sneering look. Some say, the lawyers being merry together, one asked his brother Hitcham when he would

and died 15th August, 1636, aged 64 years, a few days after making his will (8th August). He had purchased Framlingham Castle for £14,000, and spent considerable time and money in clearing his perplexed title to the estate.

"In the name of the Glorious and Incomprehensible Trinity, I, Sir Robert Hitcham, of Ipswich in the county of Suffolk, knight, the King's Majesty's serjeant-at-law, this present Monday, being the 8th day of August, 1636, in the 12th year of King Charles, do make this my last will and testament in writing as followeth. . . . . For my Castle and Manors of Framlingham and Saxtead, and all other the lands, tenements, and hereditaments which I and my feoffees purchased of my lord of Suffolk and his feoffees, I will that my feoffees and their heirs, and the survivors of them, after my debts paid, do presently stand seized, as in trust to the use of the Master and Fellows of Pembroke Hall in Cambridge, and their successors. . . . . . First, I will that the said College do presently after my death erect and build at Framlingham one house to set the poor on work, the poor and most needy and impotent of Framlingham, Debenham and Coxall in Essex, first, (and after them of other towns if they see cause,) and to provide a substantial stock to set them to work, and to allow to such needy persons of them so much as they shall further think fit. And likewise I will that they do build one or two alms-houses, consisting of twelve persons, namely, six a piece for twelve of the poorest and decrepited people there, which I will shall have two shillings a week during their lives, and also forty shillings a year for a gown and firing every year, the said two shillings to be paid weekly, and the

---

marry. 'Never,' says he, 'I had rather lead apes in hell.' 'Nay, faith,' says Hoskins, 'if it come to that once, I am sure thou wilt pose them all there: for there will be such gaping and inquiring which is the man and which is the ape; and they never can distinguish, unless thou goest thither in thy sergeant's robes."—Quoted in *Davy MSS.* Brit. Mus.

other yearly. Item, I will that a school house be built there at Framlingham, and a master appointed, whom I will shall have £40 by the year during his life, to teach thirty or forty or more of the poorest and neediest children of the said towns of Framlingham, Debenham and Coxall, to write, read, and cast accounts, as the said College shall think fit, then to give them £10 a piece to bind them forth apprentices, at the discretion of the four senior Fellows of the said College, and the said schoolmaster not to take in any other, upon penalty of losing his place and stipend. Item, I will that there be presently built after my decease one alms house at Levington for six female persons of poorest and impotent of Levington and Nacton, and they to have the like allowance in all things as the poor of Framlingham are appointed to have. To begin first with the poor at Levington, and so successively. Item, I will that there shall be for ever one that shall read prayers in the Church of Framlingham daily, at the hours of 8 in the forenoon and at 4 in the afternoon, unto whom I give £20 by the year, and to the sexton £5 yearly, and such of the poor people aforesaid, and the schoolmaster or scholars there, as shall make default in coming to hear prayers there, I will that their allowance shall be proportionably abated for the same neglect, except their excuse be allowed by the minister of the parish of Framlingham for the time being."

Francis Bacon, Esq., J. R. Butts, R. Butts, and their heirs, were trustees. Disputes arose upon this will; and the property does not appear to have been devoted to the purposes intended until an Ordinance of Oliver Cromwell was issued:—

"After reciting the will, and that the great distance hindered the people of Coxall from sending their children to Framlingham, and suits did arise among the said parties, upon which it was ordered by his Highness the Lord Protector and his Council, that an Ordinance should forthwith be printed, Monday, Mar. 20,

1658, wherein it was ordered that the said College should pay £150 per annum to Coxall. The trustees appointed to receive it were—Robert Crane the elder, Thomas Guyon, William Tanner, John Sparhawke, R. Shortland, W. Cox, Isaac Hubbard, W. Gladwyn, W. Guyon, Samuel Crane, and George Guyon. The sum aforesaid to be paid at the Cow Cross in Framlingham, on the first Tuesday in March and first Tuesday in September, and employed for a Workhouse at Coxall, for a school-house there for teaching 20 or 30 poor children, grammar, reading and writing, for binding them out apprentices, and for sending some of the grammar-scholars to Cambridge, to the said College, as the said trustees shall think fit. The Master of the said free-school to be chosen by the said Master and Fellows of Pembroke Hall, and paid £40 per annum."[*]

By indenture, 14th August, 1666, new trustees were appointed to receive the same amount for Coggeshall. This arrangement was altered in 1722. A deed of partition between the inhabitants of Coggeshall and Debenham, with the consent of the Master and Fellows of Pembroke Hall, was prepared (18th September) and the rents of the estates called Oldfrith Wood, Bradley Wood, and Newhall Wood, amounting to £178 per annum, were allotted to Coggeshall, subject to the payment of annuities of £21. 12s. to Levington and Nacton, and £9 to Debenham. These estates consist of about 290 acres of land, and their rental in 1862 is about £400. Some £800 have been laid out in repairs.

Since the above deed of partition the proceeds of the estates have been variously administered by the

[*] Collection of Statutes during the Protectorship of Oliver Cromwell, by Henry Scobell, Esq.

Hitcham's School, Coggeshall, Essex.

Master and Fellows of Pembroke Hall and the local trustees. An annual amount has been distributed among the poor of Coggeshall. There has been a school in the town, and a master has also been paid £80 per annum. Formerly the school was held in one of the buildings on Market Hill, and until lately in a room belonging to Crane's Charity. New school-premises have been recently erected in the town, at a cost of upwards of £1200. It has been questioned whether this was a legal appropriation of the monies arising from the Charity. The Charity Commissioners are devising a new scheme of management, by which £200 per annum may be devoted to pay the existing debt; the rest to sustain the school, &c. Although this deprives the poor of the amount hitherto distributed amongst them, a good free-school, constituted on more liberal principles, and better adapted to the present exigencies than this has been, would be of great service to the parish generally.

The local trustees are—Mr. Appleford, Rev. W. J. Dampier, Osgood Hanbury, Esq., F. U. Pattisson, Esq.,

Mr. Sadler, Rev. C. G. Townsend, Mr. W. Swinborne, Mr. Westmacott.

Mr. Duddell, curate of Mr. Du Cane, was formerly master; afterwards Henry Emery for many years.* The present master is Mr. T. J. Hyde.

III.—Guyon's Bread Money.

This consists of two annuities. The first was given by the will of THOMAS GUYON, a clothier in Coggeshall,† dated 21st November, 1664, "charged upon the messuage, farm lands, grounds and premises anciently called Windmill fields," amounting to £10. 8s.

"for the use and benefit *of the most honest aged poor people* of Great Coggeshall, to be bestowed in bread for their relief weekly, upon every Lord's day after the sermon in the forenoon, and that the trustees shall lay out the sum of 4s. weekly in three-penny bread, to be given to 16 of the most honest aged poor people of Great Coggeshall aforesaid."

"NOTES of ye sermon preached at ye funeral of old Mr. Thomas Guyon, the great clothier, upon Satterday, in the evening, by candlelight, Nov. 26, 1664, by Mr. Jessop. I Cor. xv. 26.

"I now come to the occasion. My worthy friend, as when he was alive he was above your censures, so now he is deceased he is not concerned in your commendations. He was a person of great wisdom and judgment; of sober conversation; diligent in his employment. He was surpassingly compassionate to the poore. I fear now this great man is fallen among you, many

---

* There have been also several private schools established in the town from time to time. One of these was kept by Thomas Harris, who wrote a *farce* in ridicule of the 'Volunteer' movement, in 1803, which displeased certain persons and got him into trouble. He had his joke, but lost his pupils.

† "Tho. Guyon. The tenement called *Vincent's* close, with the Dovehouse sometime in the tenure of John Gray."—*Inquis.* 1664.

mourners among the poore will go about the stoeets. He was of a peaceable disposition to the neighbourhood, and I persuade myself he was a religious attender on God in his ordinances, and had a respect to the ministry, which is a rare virtue in these days. So I take my farewell of my friend and neighbour, in his bed of earth, in which I myself must shortly lie, and you that hear must shortly follow me."—*Bufton.*

The second annuity was given by deed of gift of SIR MARK GUYON, son of the above, dated 1st of May, 1678, amounting to £13, and charged upon the messuage, farm and lands, called High fields and Windmill fields, to be distributed to—

" 20 of the *most aged and necessitous persons inhabiting within the* parish of Great Coggeshall aforesaid, to each of them a three-penny loaf, the said bread to be placed on a shelf, to be set up for that purpose over or near the seat of the said Sir Mark Guyon, then standing in the chancel of the church of Great Coggeshall aforesaid."

The trustees were Matthew Guyon, Isaac Hubbard, Jos. Drywood, R. Shortland, R. Sheppard, A. Sutton, W. Cox, T. Buxton, T. Keeble, Geo. Nichols, Simon Richold, and Jacob Cox.

Sir Mark lived in a house now demolished, in the Warren, near the poplars in West Street, not far from which are the remains of two ponds. He afterwards purchased and resided at Dynes' Hall, Great Maplestead. He was high-sheriff in 1676, and knighted; and died 1690.

" 1678, July.—Sir Mark Guyon was made Justice of the Peace.

"1679, June 19.—The Lady Abdy of Kelvedon died. June 24.—The Lady Guyon, Sir Mark's second wife, daughter of Sir Thomas Abdy, died, and was buried on 26th, late in the evening, by torches, without a sermon.

"1682, Dec. 14.—Sir Mark Guyon was married to Mrs. Augurs, his waiting maid, and kinswoman of Mrs. Andrews of Feering.

"1690.—Squire [Edward] Bullock married Sir Mark's eldest daughter [Elizabeth]. 1691.—Mr. Thomas Guyon married Sir Mark's second daughter. 1693.—Mr. T. Guyon was brought down from London and buried here. Mr. *John* Bullock [brother of Edward] married to Mr. T. Guyon's widow. [Went to reside at Dynes hall, M.P. for Maldon 1700, died at Clapham.]

"1690, Nov. 1.—S^r· M. Guyon was buried about 10 o'clock in ye evening, by torches, without a sermon; there was about half a score coaches, and about 30 or 40 men had black gowns and caps: they carried the torches to light the coaches. There was one breadth of black cloth hung round the chancill, and ye pulpit was covered with black, and the great Bible.

"1691, Aug. 21.—Wm. Guyon, Esq., S^r· Mark's son, [by his first wife, Elizabeth Fancourt], died at London, being 21 years old, and was brought down to Coxall with great pomp, nigh 200 horsemen riding before, about 40 of them with black cloaks, and about 10 coaches following, about 9 o'clock at night, by torches, and abundance of people."*

---

* "1676, June 13.—*Mr. George* [brother of Sir Mark] *Guyon's* wife, who lived at Hovells, daughter of Mr. Plumb of Yeldham, was buried. Her name was Rachel, and Mr. Jessop preached from the text, 'And Rachel died.' Oct.—Mr. George Guyon of Hovills, who was captain of the trained bands. 1673.—Thomas, eldest son of George Guyon [pp. 87, 109].

"1678.—Died *Matthew Guyon* [p. 104], clothier, a rich man, leaving 7 sons and 2 daughters.

"1686.—Martha, eldest daughter of Matthew Guyon, married to a lawyer at Braintree."—*Bufton.*

IV.—Smith's Charity. (Tilbury Bread Money.)

This is an annuity of £15, left by the will of JOHAN SMITH, formerly of London, widow, dated 21st April, 1601. This lady left £400—

"therewith to provide and purchase the sum of forty marks yearly, to be bestowed and employed for the relief of the poor in Coxall and Bocking in Essex, the same to continue and be as her free gift for ever. Twenty marks whereof *to be bestowed upon the poor of Coxall yearly, by 5s. in Bread every Sunday*, and the distributors'thereof to take for their pains yearly, six shillings and eightpence."

In consideration of this £400, Sir William Smith, her son, granted to trustees (Thomas Fuller, T. Aylett, H. Warner, G. Cockerell, Tho. Bridges, T. Shortland, N. Richold, Thomas Gray, John Gray the younger, T. Guyon, W. Gladwin, Thomas Allistone, R. Fuller the younger, W. Bufton, C. Gymlett, W. Clarke the younger, John Clemance, W. Fuller, T. Shortland, jun., and R. Crane) an annuity of £15, issuing from the Rectory and Church of East Tilbury, reserved to him by letters of James I. with the same conditions as those above mentioned. A part of this annuity has been for many years given away at the door of the Parish Church; but this is not directed by the trust. The present trustees (appointed by Mr. Stephen Unwin and the late Mr. Fisher Unwin) consist of upwards of twenty of the principal inhabitants of the parish of Great Coggeshall.

V.—Gooday's Charity. (Clothing Money.)

Jane Gooday, of Feering, widow, by will left £30 to be laid out in the purchase of house or land, to be estated to some of the parishioners of Great Coggeshall, to the intent that the profits thereof should for the time being be laid out at the discretion of the vicar and overseers of the poor, *to buy needful clothing for the aged poor of Great Coggeshall for ever.* John Gooday, her son, did with this sum, and £20 more of his own money, purchase on 8th April, 1618, a messuage and garden in Church Street, called *Pagett's*, which he granted upon the above trust to John Dodd, vicar, and others; and on 15th April, 1654, Robert Crane, only surviving trustee, granted the same to John Sames, vicar, and others. In 1714 the trustees granted the said messuage to Daniel Cooke, who pulled it down, and laid the ground to the Swan Inn yard, and granted them an annuity of 32*s.* issuing out of the King's Arms in East Street.

VI.—Crane's Bread Money.

Samuel Crane's will was proved 10th August, 1670. It contains the following gift:—

"I give the rents and profitts of my messuage or tenement, with the appurtenances, situate in Stoneham Street, in Great Coggeshall aforesaid, and now in the occupation of Elizabeth Starling, widow, to the use of the poor of Great Coggeshall for ever. . . . . . And I constitute and appoint my very loving friends, Mr. William Cox, clothier, and Mr. Isaac Hubbard, executors."

On one corner of these premises a turret was built in 1795; and in 1787 a room was leased to the Hitcham trustees who recently released it to the remaining trustees, of whom Mr. S. Unwin alone survives.

VII.—Hibben's Cottages.

These are three cottages in Church Street which were devised by ANTHONY HIBBEN *alias* WEAVER, "for the benefit of the poor of Great Coggeshall." The original will is no longer to be found. The last trustee was the late OSGOOD HANBURY, Esq. It is understood that the rents of these cottages have been appropriated of late to certain repairs of the buildings.

VIII.—Market Hill.

The Fullers and Weavers of Coggeshall, by deed dated 7th October, 1588, purchased the messuage or old Chapel, (from which probably the name of the inn, which at present exists opposite the spot, is derived,) and the ground thereto adjoining, lying in the then market place of the said town, for the purpose of building a store house, and also a clock tower for the better ordering of apprentices * The property was

---

* "1686, Sept. 30.—A new clock was set up at the market house, made at London, said to cost £23."—*Bufton.*

put in trust for the use of the Company of Fullers and Weavers of Coggeshall. Changes having come about amongst them, it was decreed by a Charitable Commission of the 11th year of James I. that the premises should be let by the trustees to any person who was willing to take them at an annual rent, the preference being given to a fuller or weaver, *and the proceeds paid over to the overseers for the relief of the poor.* From that time the trustees let the upper rooms, and appointed a poor weaver or comber to clean the market-house underneath, who received a fee from every one who came to sell his goods there. The buildings were at length found useless, and in 1795 were pulled down by the trustees, and with the money arising from the sale of the materials they erected on a corner of the property belonging to Crane's Charity, a turret for the reception of the clock and watch-bell, which had occupied part of the then removed tenement. The trustees also built two alms-houses. The site of the above buildings has never since been built upon, but has been relinquished to the public. A claim has been made to any proceeds which might arise from its use, on behalf of the oldest fuller and weaver, and has been allowed by prescriptive right: but according to the above decree, it appears that any benefit arising from the place should be for the poor generally. The last trustee was the late OSGOOD HANBURY, Esq., appointed 3rd August, 1795.

IX.—Alms Houses.

These are situated near the church-yard on a part of the Butts field. There was formerly in the church-yard an alms-house appropriated to the oldest horseman in the parish, in lieu of which two of the present houses were built. The other four were erected partly by the trustees of the Wool-hall on Market Hill, and partly by public subscription, on ground given by Joseph Greenwood, (who possessed the field just mentioned,) by deed of gift, 11th December, 1795.

X.—Spot of Ground in West Street.

Holman says " there are (in addition to *three* almes houses without endowment) :—

" Two Almes Houses more at the upper end of West Street, going to Braintree, given by Sir Marke Guyon to this parish, in lieu of 2 Almes Houses y^t were pulled down neare his House."*

These houses have also now disappeared, and there is only a piece of land near the Gelatine Factory with a rental of 10*s.* a year, which the churchwardens have been accustomed to take and distribute.†

The seven last-named charities are now about to be put, by the Charity Commissioners, into the hands of new trustees, under a new scheme of management.

* " 11 Henry VIII.—The lord granted to John Seman one tenement and a garden, lying in West Strete, near the Almeshouse, at the yearly rent of 2*s.*"—*Manor Roll.*
" John Bullock, Esq., in right of his wife, for a strake of Copyhold next Almehouse, 1*d.*"—*Manor Rental,* 1695.

† The above is reprinted with slight alterations from " An Account of the Public Charities of Coggeshall," which the writer printed in 1861.

XI.—Richardson's Charity. (LITTLE COGGESHALL.)

ANN RICHARDSON gave by will to the poor of Little Coggeshall, a rent charge or annuity of £8 payable out of certain lands in that parish. The Master of the Court of Chancery ordered, 14th March, 1842:—

"That the overseers and churchwardens of Little Coggeshall shall keep a list in each year of All the most deserving poor Husbandmen and poor widows inhabiting or belonging to that parish not receiving parochial relief; from which list they shall select the persons who are to receive the charity, (the preference to be given to the most aged and infirm); but such persons shall be removed from such list when and as they shall see occasion, who are to distribute rateably and in rotation to and amongst such persons, so that all on such list may in their turn partake of the advantage of the charity.—That there shall be five trustees appointed of the charity who shall receive the said rent charge and lay it out in bread weekly by 3s. at a time, except in Christmas week, when there shall be expended 7s. to be distributed as aforesaid.—That if at any time there shall be no Trustees of the Charity the officiating minister for the time being, and the churchwardens and overseers, shall be considered and taken to be Trustees of the charity until Trustees shall be duly appointed."

There is this inscription in the church-yard:—

"Here lyeth the Body of Mr. John Richardson, who departed this life upon the 20th day of November, and in the 33rd year of his age, 1693. Here also lyeth the Body of his only daughter, Mrs. Anne Richardson, by Anne his wife, Daughter of Mr. John Willsher, who departed this life at Scrip's Farm, in Little Coggeshall, aged 18 years, 4 months and 21 dayes, upon the 13th day of September, 1712."

In addition to the above endowed Charities, there are others sustained by voluntary contributions, of which one of the most useful is the

Coggeshall Benevolent Society.

"This society was established in February, 1808, and was greatly promoted by the efforts of Dr. Mant, who soon afterwards became vicar of this parish. Its design is to afford relief in cases of accident, sudden illness, or other special distress, to poor persons of every religious denomination. Committee for 1862— Mr. Doubleday, Mr. Giles, Mr. Pattisson, Rev. Bryan Dale, Mr. W. Gardner, Mr. C. Smith, Mr. Jacob Unwin, Mr. Appleford (secretary), Mr. Isaac Beard (treasurer.)"

XIII.

BUFTON'S DIARY.

NUMEROUS extracts have been made in the preceding pages from Diaries written by Joseph Bufton, about 200 years ago. He was the son of John and Elizabeth Bufton, who held a respectable position in Coggeshall, where he was born October 26, 1651. He had a brother named John, and three sisters, Mary, married to John Cox; Elizabeth, who died in 1666; and Rebekah, all older than himself. He appears to have been apprenticed to the wool-combing trade, and was at one time in the employ of Mr. Hedgthorne. On the death of his parents, his sister 'Beck' kept his house until she was married to Samuel Sparhauke, Dec. 20, 1699, about which time he left the town, and went to reside at Colchester. From very early life he amused himself by taking notes of sermons, which he afterwards transcribed: most of them were preached at the Parish Church, but some by Nonconformist ministers. He was also accustomed to note down, in the intervals of business, passing events, and make extracts from printed volumes. Sometimes he applied himself to rhyming; but it is plain that he was not born a poet. Had he lived two or three centuries before he would have been a monk, and left behind him a more minute and interesting chronicle than that of Abbot Ralph. His notes are as follows:—

1. A Register of Births, Marriages and Deaths, from 1677 to 1696 (written in an old Almanack entitled *Rider's British Merlin* for 1677.)
2. An Account of Funeral Sermons (in an old *Goldsmith*, 1672.)
3. Notes of Funeral Sermons from 1662 to 1681.
4. Notes of Mr. Boys' Sermons on Relative Duties, from 1680 to 1690.
5. Notes of Sermons, from 1693 to 1698.
6. Business Accounts (in *Brit. Merlin*, 1668.)
7. Ordinances of Clothiers, names of Wardens, &c. (in *Goldsmith*, 1686.)
8. Verses, &c. (in *Compleat Tradesman*, 1684.)
9. Extracts from printed Books (in *Brit. Merlin*, 1680.)
10. Extracts.
11. Extracts.*

From these some additional extracts will not be wholly uninteresting.

Private.

"1675, June 27. Burial of my dear mother, upon Sunday. Mr. Jessop preached from Job xiv. 14.

1678, July 16. My brother John and his wife both took ship at London to go into Ireland. After wch we heard not of them

---

* These little books belonged to the late J. N. Hunt, (who was connected with the Bufton and Sparhauke family), and most of them are now in the possession of Mr. Kirkham. *Eleven* others of a similar kind, referred to in one of these, are lost.

till the 10th day of September, on which day Goodman Lay received a letter from his daughter, wch I saw and read, whereby we understood they were *six weeks* upon the water.

My cousin, Mr. Christopher Sheriffe, who was called Captain Sheriffe, died.

1680-1,* Feb. 25. My sister Rebekah swooned suddenly, and fell down and broke her forehead.

1681, June 25. There was a waggon went over my father's leg, and bruised him on the back.

1684, Aug. 2:—
> Now two and thirty years and more
>   Of my short life are past,
> And in that time how many men
>   Have breathed out their last.
>
> . . . . .
>
> Lord, grant I may more prudent be,
>   Lord, make me truly wise,
> Before the means of grace are gone,
>   Or hidden from mine eyes.

1687, May 13. My cousin Samuel Sparhauke's second wife was buried. She was Dr. Harrison's daughter.

1690, Oct. 2. My cousin Mary Sturges was married to Robert White.

1692, Aug. 23. My father was taken sick in the night, and so continued for a fortnight. Yet blessed be God he recovered again.

1694, Jan. 7. The funeral of my dear father, John Bufton, aged 86. Upon Monday. Sermon preached by Mr. Boys. His text was in Luke ii. 29.

---

* It will be observed that for some centuries previous to 1753, the *legal* and *ecclesiastical* year was reckoned as beginning on 25th March: the *historical* on 1st January, as at present. In order to prevent mistake, dates in January, February and March, were set down in this manner.

		£		d.
[Paid] For my Father's burial:				
For gloves		1	11	0
For 4 gallons of *sack*			1	
For a Coffin				
For a *Sermon*				
For a Burying Sute [woolen]			1	
For 27 gallds of beer			1	
Henry Cooper				
John Taylor				
Nurses				
For bran				
For affidavit [of burial in woolen]				
[Gloves.] 10 pr of Corderant:—		£7	8	0

Six pair to ye Bearers,
One pair to Mr. Boys,
One pair to Thos. Pool,
One pair to Wm. Cox,
One pair to Cousin Jno. Bufton.

Two pair of sheep to Matt Fenn and Henry Ireland,

Three pair of kid to Sister Cox and Sister Rebekah and Cousin Wm. Coxe's wife,

Three pair of lamb to Hen Greland's wife and Mary Warren, the nurses, and to Goody Knowles.

Mr. Hedgthorne had about 8 combers and 60 weavers when he died. About 23 weavers were taken in when I lived with Mr. Hedgthorne. In 1697 one hundred and six pieces were brought in in one week.

I paid my sister Beck a quarter's wages. I have given her bond for £46. 1700, April 1. I paid the rest of my money, and took in my bond.

1716, Aug. 8. I reckon I have here 22 Almanacks, 13 Rider's, one of which I keep on my board and write in dayly, 6 Goldsmith, 1 Partridge, 1 Raven's, 1 Tanner.

> Time swiftly runs away and never stays
> Until death puts a period to our days."

Sermons, &c.

Funeral sermons preached by Mr. Jessop (p. 177):—

"1663, Apl. 1. John Sudbury, clothier. 1664. Old Edmund Cox, clothier and tanner. Old Widow Hills of West Mill.

1667. Wm. Gardner, lawyer, of Kelvedon, he died a Batchelor at his mother's, Mrs. Merrills.

Dec. 13. Richard Shortland, clothier. This sermon was finished by candlelight. . . . . . 'Now for the occasion. I was in great dispute in my thoughts, whether to speak or to hold my peace of this my worthy friend. Considering ye techyness and censoriousness of ye place we live in, I thought at first to omit it; but considering death hath placed my friend above your censures, I shall offer somewhat to it. His parents were persons of substance and repute among ye. His father intended him for learning, and sent him to the University of Cambridge, where he was brought up at the feet of Gamaliel, and his Tutor was Mr. Joseph Mede; but for want of health he was incapacitated for a further progress in study, wherefore he was sent for home, to succeed his father in yt sometime beneficial trade of clothing. This 5 year I have had the happiness to be acquainted with him. I am confident there be sundry here that can protest his abilities in ye public business of ye towne. And he was firme for government, both in church and state. He was orthodox in his opinions, and a constant attender on God's public worship, which I knew he did out of conscience. Many people enter into public worship as ye high priest into the holy of holies, but once a year, if they do that. But above all this, I looked upon as ye flower of all his virtues, that he had a great esteem of our Lord and Master Jesus Christ. The 'last words I heard him speak were—'Ah! what are we? we have nothing without Jesus Christ.'

1668. Mrs. Brockwell, first wife of Mr. John Brockwell, physician, daughter of old W. Gladwin. 1677. Old Mr. W. Gladwin, clothier, aged 93. Robert Todd, of Little Coggeshall, who there held a great brewing office—Buried by candlelight.

Robert Sach, farmer. 1670. M. Richold, clothier. Robert Merrills, of Little Coggeshall.

1674, Oct. 15. Young John Wildbore. 'We have lived to see strange sicknesses and mortalities in the neighbourhood. The arrow that flieth by day hath cut off thousands at Colchester, and hundreds at Braintry.'

Dec. 11. Charles Binion, brother of Mr. Henry Binion. He died at Mr. Tho. Stafford's, of Inworth.

1675. Ambrose Armond of the *White Hart*.

1678. R. Shortland's first wife, daughter of *Major Grimes*. John Cox, clothier, *Mount*, but died at another house. Francis Lay, at the *Swan*."

Funeral sermons preached by Mr. Boys (p. 178):—

"1680, July 24. Goodman Willsher, Farmer of Little Coggeshall. 'We are fallen into an age that have got the knack of dissembling both with God and man. But if you dissemble with God, death will strip you of all your disguises. If death be to be provided for, then set about the work with all speed. Do not deceive yourselves with false signs of grace. No name does become us but Christian, and no actions will be accepted but Christian ones. Remember the days of darkness, and prepare for them; and come to the house of God before you are brought upon a herse. Hearken to him that is your servant, and the minister of Christ. Let me persuade you as you love your souls, to walk as Christians, and perform your service to God. Do you perform your duties, and I shall endeavour to perform mine, that when we shall all descend into darkness, we may give up our accounts with joy to the great Judge of the whole world.'

1681. R. Rayment, who had been an exciseman, but of late a maultster in ye Hamlet. Young Edmund Atkinson, barber, called the young Gold, because his father was called the Gold. Old Mr. Ambrose Sutton, clothier. He had no child. He was I think above 60 years of age. Old Mr. Robert Merrill's widow, wife of Thomas Levitt, butcher. Robert Groome, a young man that dyed at Mr. John Digby's: he was his nephew. First wife of W. Cox, son of *Mr. Tho. Cox, minister:* she was Dr. Harrison's daughter. 1696. Mr. W. Cox dyed at his daughter Mullings'.

1684. Mr. Tho. Stafford, lawyer, son of old Tho. Stafford, glover. 1688. Wife of old Thomas Stafford: she was a very ancient woman: it is said had lived 60 years with her husband. Wife of Mr. D. Battery, at the White Hart, sister of Mr. *Jeremy Aylett's* wife. Wife of John Wood, tanner. She was daughter of *Mr. Glasscock,* schoolmaster of Felstead.

Wife of Mr. John White, apothecary. She was Dr. Harrison's daughter.

Old Mrs. Mount, widdow. She kept scholars. Her husband lived at Tollesbury.

1686. Old Mr. John Digby, a lame man, who had formerly been a shopkeeper.

Young Mr. Andrews, a kinsman of Mr. Andrews's of Feering, who dyed and was buried at Feering, but his funeral sermon was preached at Coxall.

Mrs. Judith Shortland, an ancient maid.

1692, Sep. 28. Second wife of John Cox, Esquire. She was

Major Haines' daughter. 1693, Aug. 28. Old Major Haines was carried to Cockford to be buried.

1696. Goldin Mullings, butcher, a young man, upon Satterday, Sept. 12, by candlelight. But from the same text he preached on at my father's funeral, because Goldin Mullings chose that text before he dyed. The first wife of Mr. W. Armond. She was Counsellor Coxe's sister.

1698-9, Feb. 1. Old Mrs. Peirson, a very ancient gentlewoman. She was Mrs. Livermore's mother. It was preached at Markshall Church. And Mr. Boys preached the same sermon at Coxall Church on Sunday in ye afternoon. Rob. Cornill, a farmer at *Griggs,* and had lain lame and sick about 4 or 5 yeares.

1699, Apl. 21. Anthony Blackbourne, farmer, who lived in the hamlet. It was preached at Bradwell Church, but ye sermon was ye same which he preached on Sunday in ye afternoon, except 3 heads added at last, suitable to the occasion.

There were 40 funeral sermons; 37 new texts, 3 old ones; 1 old sermon with a new text; 21 males, 19 females. Of ye males I reckon 5 widdowers, 9 married men, 7 single men. Of ye females, 8 widdows, 10 married women, 1 single woman.

I left Coxall, Jan. 1, 1699 [1700], and so kept no further account of funeral sermons."

Other ministers are also alluded to:—

"*Mr. Ralph Joslin*, of Earls' Colne, preached funeral sermon for old Mrs. Porter, Nov. 11, 1669. [He was presented 1640 by Harlackenden. "He complied with the Bartholomew Act; but was uneasy in his conscience. In his *Diary* he speaks of his often seeking the Lord at Lady Honywood's, at Markshall." He married Jane, daughter of Mr. Constable, the rector of that parish.] 1683, Aug. Old Mr. Joslin, minister of Earl's Colne, was buried.

Mr. Livermore preached at Markshall funeral sermon of old James Linnet, 20 Sept. 1679. [Mr. L. was rector of Markshall. He preached at Coggeshall nearly every Sunday in 1696, and afterwards.]

Mr. Thomas Shortland preached June 16, 1695, in the fore noon, from I Sam. xii. 24.; but his sermon I found was the same with *Mr. Gulliver's,** preached from the text Dec. 28, 1679.

Mr. Wadkinson preached Oct. 6, 1695, from Eccl. ix. 1. Also June 7, 1696.

Mr. Sanford, minister, married Mrs. Sutton, Sept. 25, 1683.

Old *Mr. Sparhawke*, minister, was buried Sept. 7, 1678. He lived within 5 miles of Colchester. [Ejected from Black Notley.]

1680, Sep. 12. I first heard *Mr. Stockton* the minister was lately dead. [Ejected from Colchester.]

Mr. Gouge [p. 201] preached on Monday, May 13, 1695, at the funeral of John Bowyer, from Ps. xxxiv. 19. 'Here then is the state of the righteous in this life. Their sighs and groans are many, and through much tribulation they enter into the Kingdom. Though much beloved of God they are severely handled. And this is done that he may have full possession of their hearts; and that he may show forth in them the glory of his grace. There are many martyrs we should never have heard of, had it not been for their prisons and flames.

But here is the blessed end and issue of them. The Lord delivers them out of them all. Although their afflictions be

---

* "1681, Sept. 11.—Mr. Gulliver was married to Anne Todd. 1686, April 30.—Mr. Gulliver's mother was buried" [p. 180].

sometimes of their own procuring, yet none but the Lord can deliver them. The righteous shall have an end of their sorrows: the time is short, therefore their sorrows cannot be long. They shall get safe through the red sea of troubles; but the unrighteous shall be swallowed up in it. The troubles of the righteous are going off; but the troubles of the wicked are coming on. The righteous are almost at home; but the wicked are setting forth for Hell.'

Social.

1678, Feb. 12. Being Shrove Tuesday, Abram Emming roasted a small bullock whole on *Church Green.* 1679. Ab. Emming, comber, alehouse keeper, drummer, was buried soldier-like. Moses Love, weaver, cryer, *clerk of the market*, was buried.

1678, Sep. 11. The *Bishop of London* came to Coxall, and walked on foot to Church, where Mr. Jessop read divine service; then he came down again and rode to Markshall to dinner.

1679, Feb. 4. A *watch-house* was set up in Mr. Hubbard's corn-field. Oct. 21. Robert Giggins came from Colchester in the road, backwards.

1680, Sep. 22. Mr. W. Gladwin being drunk, fell from his horse and died soon after. 1681, Feb. 1. There was a man, a stranger, whipt up Church Street at the cart's tail. 1682, Dec. Y[e] widow Mootone paid £15 because she had had a bastard. £10 of it was given to the poore. July 26. John Ilger, weaver, was married to widow Ringer, she was his *sixth* wife, she was Nich. Browning's sister. In April, 1682, there was y[e] floore of a chamber fell downe at y[e] White Hart at Bocking, where y[e] Justices sat and about 200 people in y[e] roome, and one man broke his leg.

1684. In Dec. it was said 7 butchers were robbed by 4 thieves of above 500 pounds, above 200 of it of Nicholas Foster's, and above 40 of Roger Mullings.

1685, March 5. The poore that take collection had badges given them to weare, which was a P & C cut out in blew cloth. In the latter end of May, 1693, the poor had badges given them to wear, which 'tis said were made of pewter, and 'Coggeshall poor, 1693,' set upon them. 1686, Feb. 25. The roof of the back part of the *shambles* fell in. About March, the *meal men* first began to come to Coxall *market*, and had their meal cryed 15 pounds for a shilling, and the bran was taken out and 14 pounds of fine flour for 14d. 1686, Nov. 9. Mary Taylor, a low wench, was buried. 1687, Dec. 16. Old widdow Cowell was buried, said to be above 100 years old. 1688, Aug. 13. The old widow York was buried; she was called upright York. 1689, July 2. Philip Parker of the Abbey, miller, was buried.

1687. In the latter part of the summer there was a great talke of a little boy at Brinkley within 6 miles of Haverhill, that was the 7th son and did great cures upon those that were bursten, lame, deaf, had the evill, &c.; and several went out of this town to him, but it did not prove true, for they were not cured.

1688, Jan. 15. *Sir W. Wiseman* was buried in the night. [of Rivenhall, married daughter of J. Lamotte Honywood.] 1689. Mr. Honywood, being high sheriff, went through Coxall with his men to the assizes. 1692, Feb. 15. There was a bonfire made at the Crown, for joy that Squire Honywood got the day of Sir Eliab Harvey, and was not cast out of Parliament; and when he came home from Chelmsford the night after he was chosen, abundance of candles were lighted up for joy. 1693, Jan. 23. John Lamott Honywood was brought downe from London to be buried at Markshall [buried by Richard Tillesley, curate of St. Sepulchre's in London: he dying there.] 1696, April 2. Mr. Robert Honeywood came to live at Markshall.

1688, March 1. There was a *guard house* set up for the soldiers at the market house. 13. The soldiers went away. There was a great fire at the kilne at Hovell's, so that a man was forced to run through the fire to save himself, and burnt his face and hands. 1689. In June, the *church pond* was cast: it cost 50s. [now filled up and enclosed from Church Street by a brick wall.] 1696, Sept. *Peter's well* was very well repaired by the constables.

1690, July 27. Two companies of the Trainbands which lay here, were marched up to the Church in the forenoon, being Sunday, with their arms and drums beating and flags flying.

1691, June 5. A maid, daughter of the widow Chilton, was buried, and a garland carried before her. 25. The widdow of Matt. Waters was buried. She had been drunk, and fell down stairs and died. July 24. Old Moses Richardson at the *gate-house*, was buried.

1692, Sep. 8, being Thursday, and the same day that Jacob Cox dyed, about 2 o'clock there was an *earthquake* at Coxall, and many towns beside hereabouts, and at London, and severall other countries we heard, and the news-letter said it was at the same time in Holland and ye rest of ye provinces in ye Netherlands. I was in our garret at that time, and heard the house crack and perceived it shake, and was afraid it would fall, and therefore ran down staires.

In 1693, Mr. Mayhew sold Coxall lordship to Mr. Nehemiah Lyde. May 11. He first came for his rent, and June 5th, being Whitsun Monday, kept court, and counsellor Cox was his steward. 1st Sept. Old Mr Augustine Mayhew was carried through Coxall to be buried at Passwick.

May 1. The soldiers set up a May-pole at the *Woolpack* door. May 18. The poor did rise because the bakers would not bake, because some of the bread was cut out the day before for being too light. 1695, Oct. 8. The poor did rise at Coxall in ye evening to hinder ye carrying away of corne, and Jonathan Cable beat a drum to gather them together, for which he was carried before a Justice but not sent to Jaile. The poor did rise at Colchester and other places about the same time, and it was said, burnt several waggons.—The combers broke up their purse. It was occasioned by Jonathan Cable being so unreasonable. It was thought if he might, he would have had all the money belonging to the purse.

1694, March 8. Mr. H. Ennew's house was robbed of above £100. 1697, June 15. Old Mr. *Buxton* was robbed on the London road. 1696, May 4. Richard Pemberton set out to go to Bath, and came home again in June, and had little or no good. 1698, Oct. 26. I received a letter from my brother John (in Ireland) by *Lieut. Grimes* [see p. 112]. My brother John's part of Mr. Diodate's *composition* money was £3. 14s. 4d., so I have 13s. 4d. in my hands for him still, and this I sent him by Lieut. Grimes.

1697, March 29. There were a great many fighting cocks carried through Coxall on horseback, in linen bags or clothes.

April 18. There was brave singing in Coxall church: it was said to be by youths that came from Bocking and Braintree.

1695, Nov. 6. The widow Comon was married to one Pudney in ye hamlet. 1699, July 13. The widow Comon was put into the river to see if she would sink, because she was suspected to be a witch, and she did not sink, but swim. And she was tryed again July 19, and then she swam again, and did not sink. July 24. The widow Comon was tryed a third time by putting her into the river, and she swam, and did not sink. Dec. 27. The widow Comon, that was counted a witch, was buried.

Public.

1683, Sept. 9. Being Sunday it was kept as a day of *thanksgiving* for the discovery of a *plott* [Rye House], about 3 months before, against the king's life; and there was much ringing of bells, and beating of drums, and shooting off muskets, and yᵉ drakes [small pieces of artillery], and making of bonfires. 1684, June 19. Our two great guns were fetched away from the church. 1687, Jan. 29. Prayers were read in the church for Queen Mary, upon the account of her being with child. June 10. King James had a son borne. Prayers were read in the church to give thanks for the birth of the prince.

In 1688, about Sept. 28, *King James 2nd* set out a proclamatian yᵗ yᵉ Dutch would speedily invade England, and the PRINCE OF ORANGE came with an army, and began to land in yᵉ west of England, about Dartmouth, about yᵉ 5th Nov., and took the city of Exeter soon after. It was said the King went out from London to meet him as far as Salisbury, but he came toward London again, and on Dec. 11 went away and left Whitehall. Dec. 12, we were in a fright at Coxall in yᵉ night, and in many places, by reason of lies yᵗ were raised about some Irish soldiers yᵗ were coming, they said. Dec. 16. The King came to Whitehall again, and on the 18th went down into Kent, on the same day that the Prince of Orange came to Westminster, to the palace of St. James. King James, 'after several days' continuance at Rochester, withdrew himself with a slender train about 12 o'clock in the night, 22nd Dec., with great secrecy, to the seaport, where he embarked, and was afterwards known to be landed in France.' He stayed sometime, and then went to Ireland, where he called a parliament, which, as was said, began May 7, 1689.

The Prince of Orange being at Westminster, by the advice of some lords and others that had lately been parliament men, sent out letters over all England for an election of knights and burgesses, as is usual for a parliament, and this convention met 22nd Jan., where, after several debates, they voted King James had abdicated y^e government, and y^e throne was vacant. Feb. 12. The Princess of Orange landed; y^e next day the House of Lords and House of Commons prayed the Prince to accept of the crown, and so he did, and y$_e$ same day the Prince and Princess were proclaimed, in London and Westminster, King and Queen of England. Feb. 14. There was a day of thanksgiving kept over all the nation, by order of the convention, (as there was in London 14 days before), for our great *deliverance from Popery and Slavery* by y^e coming of the Prince of Orange; and the same day at Coxall they made a shift to ring ye bells after a fashion, and after sermon the effigies of a Pope was carried about ye town, and at night burnt in a bonfire; and, Feb. 21, King William and Mary were proclaimed at Coxall (it being Thursday). The coroner came, and it was a bailiff read the proclamation, and a great many guns were shot off here that day, and bonfires made at night.

Apl. 11, being Monday, King William and Queen Mary were crowned at Westminster. On ye same day at Coxall a garland was made, and *oranges* hung on it, and carried about ye town, and a drum beat before it, and ye bells were rung as well as they could ring them then, and a great many bonfires were made at night.

> Many deliverances we, in this land,
> Have had vouchsaf'd us by God's mighty hand,
> But if in wickedness we still remain,
> Can we expect deliverance again?
>   Our sins for vengeance call,
>   And on us it may fall.

In May, 1689, King William proclaimed war with France, and June 5 was kept at London, and 19th in the country, as a fast to pray for success in that war.

The Parliament (wch of a convention was made so not long after King William was proclaimed) made an act for *Toleration of Dissenters*, whereby the penall laws against them were taken off.

This Parliament gave King William 6 months' assessment, which came to 400,000 pound; and this year poll money was paid to reduce Ireland; also a subsidy was paid.

In the latter part of summer, 1689, the Duke of Schomberg went over with an army to Ireland, as generall for King William, some relief having been sent before by Maj. Gen. Kirk. In 1689-90 King William assembled another Parliament, wch met March 20, and this year it was ordered that a fast should be kept every month, to pray for success in the war. A subsidy was paid; also in this year was a review of ye poll, whereby those were rated who were left out before, and every one was to be rated 20s. yt was worth 300£, 40 was rated on yt account in Coxall, but many of them got off againe. In May, 1690, another rate was made here for poll money, and men thereby were rated 10s. for a 100£ stock. But that was taken off againe, because it was said men were not rated for stocks in other Townes.

In 1691 a great tax was given to ye King in the nature of an assessment—there was above six score pound a quarter paid in Coxall.

In June, 1690, King William went into Ireland, and there, about ye first of July, he routed King James his army, and gained Dublin, wch was presently yielded without fighting; afterwards he besieged Athloan and Limerick, but did not take them; but in Sept. came into England againe, and set over a fresh army, who quickly took Cork, and not long after Kinsale. July 12. Here were bonfires for King Wm.'s victory in Ireland; and Sept. 9, bonfires and ringing of bells for King Wm.'s arrival in England. On ye 19th of October, 1690, was a thanksgiving for King William's success in Ireland, and safe returne to England.

1690-1. In January King William went over into Holland, and stayed till April before he came to England againe.

1691, May 1. King William came down from London, and went *through Kelvedon* to Harwich, and so went to Holland againe, and stayed there all ye summer, and then came home againe; but the French would not fight, and so there was little done: but this summer Ireland was wholly reduced to King William, for which a general day of thanksgiving was kept, Nov. 26. Againe he went through Kelvedon, March 4. In May the French were beat at sea. This year also a general fast was kept and Nov. 10 general thanksgiving for the victory at sea, and King William's preservation and safe returne.

1692, May 23. There were bonfires at Coxall for a victory over the French at sea. June 21. I saw a ship launched at Wivenhoe. 1692, Oct. 20. King William went through Kelvedon, and then he stayed and dined at the Angel. In 1692 King William did fight with ye French once in Flanders, and many were killed on both sides.

King William went againe through Kelvedon, Mar. 24, 1693, and went to Harwich, and when he came there, the wind lying contrary, he came back the 28th, and soon afterwards went over to Holland. And he went through againe, Oct. 30, 1693. (There was six times King William went through Kelvedon; but I find no more that I recorded. But in 1700 he was at Colchester, I think it was in October, and then he went through Kelvedon as he went to London, and that makes seven times.)

In 1693 was a great fight in Flanders, wherein the French 'tis said lost most men, and yet won ye field.

Nov. 26, Sunday forenoon, being general thanksgiving for ye King's preservation and safe returne, Mr. Boys preached from Ps. cxxxvi. 33. 'We were in a low and mean condition, we had fasted in dissimulation and returned to our sins, and provoked God, and he scourged us by his providence, so that part of our trading fleets miscarried at sea, and we partook of the merchants' loss and disappointment in the deadness of trade. We laboured and had no profit, and our enemies increased in strength and overpowered our armies, and at the same time we had scarcity of bread. Our sins deserved we should be brought much lower, but God has remembered us in mercy. Though he discouraged our army, he did not destroy it. We are in a fair way, under Providence, of recovering our former state. Our counsels are at present united, and if we will repent, God will still pity and help us.'

In 1694, in May, King William went over to Flanders againe. A great assessment was paid againe of 4s. in ye pound, and another poll-tax was paid of 12d. a quarter for a head. Besides several other taxes were laid on salt. And a general fast was kept.

1694, June 13. On Wednesday, being a general fast to pray for the success of the war, Mr. Boys preached from Is. liv. 4. Also Sept. 19, being a general fast. King William came home in November, and on Sunday, Dec. 16, was kept a general thanksgiving in ye country, for King William's preservation and safe return, and y^t measure of success that God gave this summer to ye forces of our King and his confederates by sea and land, so far as to put a stop to ye proceedings of ye French. Mr. Boys preached from Ps. xcii. 11. 'Though our enemies have less truth than we, yet if they be more virtuous than we, God may give them commission to scourge us, for not living up to the truth we profess. And if we would see our desires accomplished on our enemies, we must ascribe all the glory and praise of it to God. We must praise him that we can live peaceably in our habitations, and that our enemies are impoverished, and their courage fails, their counsells are nonplussed, and their fame and honour diminished; and that our soldiers and fleets are in heart and vigorous, and in a capacity to defend us.'

It was said we gat ground of the French this yeare, and burnt two townes in France, and took some part of Flanders from them that they had conquered before. But Dec. 28 Queen Mary dyed of ye small-pox, and was buried on Tuesday, Mar. 5 following, on wch day our great Bell was tould for 2 or 3 hours at severall times in y^t day.

In 1695 King William went over to Flanders againe in May, and there was a tax paid this year also of 4s. in ye pound, and another tax laid upon births and burialls, and marriages, and widdowers and batchelors.

June 19. On Wednesday, being a general fast to pray for success in the war, Mr. Boys preached from Is. lviii. 4. 'Before we undertake to fast, we may be sure our enemies fast and pray as well as we, and are more strict in keeping fasts than we, and more earnest in their prayers. They call much upon the Virgin Mary and all the angels and saints. But one nation must be in a wrong cause. Now our enemies seem to aim only at empire and dominion. They have invaded and conquered part of the neighbouring countries, and driven many of the Reformed religion out of their land, and tortured many more to death; but we stand up only in our own defence, that we may enjoy our peace and liberty in the country God hath given to our forefathers. Our enemies have been great oppressors in this part of Europe, and have threatened us, and on occasion endeavoured to ruin us; but we would live in peace. . . . . Then as we contend with them by the sword, let us contend with them by prayer; and if we can prevail that way, it will be most noble.'

This summer King William besieged and took the citty and castle of Namur; and some other townes were bombarded in France. In October King William came home againe, and dissolved his parliament and called a new one, and the 18th Dec. was kept as a generall fast, to pray for a blessing on the proceedings of the parliament. About the latter end of February, 1695-6, a great plot was discovered against ye King's life, and for ye invasion of ye realme, for which severall were tryed and executed, some of which were knights; and the 16th of April following was kept as a thanksgiving for ye discovery of ye plot, on which day Mr. Boys preached the same sermon which he did in the afternoon on Sunday, Oct. 19, 1690, which was a thanksgiving day also. Then the King went over to Flanders againe. The year '96 a great assessment was paid as before, and a tax was laid on windows, to make good ye deficiency of ye clipped money, which was called in and new coined.

1697, April 28, Mr. Boys, which was a general fast, preached the same sermon, or much like it, from Is. x. 21, which he did from Ezra ix. 14. on Aug. 9, 1693.

This year was much talk of peace, which was concluded at last, and certain news of it came first in Sept., for which there was great rejoicing severall times. The King came home in November, and Dec. 2 was kept as a general thanksgiving for the peace.

1698. This year was the latest harvest that was ever knowne almost, and there was great scarcity of corn in all countries, but blessed be God we had good crops hereabouts; yet it held up at a great price, because they said a great deal was carried away.

1701-2. King William died 8th March, and on 18th March following, Princess Anne of Denmark was proclaimed Queen at Colchester.

1703, Nov. 26 and 27. There was an extraordinary great wind, which did more hurt by sea and land than ever was known to be done by one wind, by any person now living. *Besides* some persons were killed, many houses blown down or much damaged, many trees blown down, and many ships and seamen lost, which occasioned besides, a prayer read every Sunday for sometime, and a general fast to be kept on the 19th Feb. following.

1714, Aug. 1. Queen Anne died, and the same day George, Elector of Brunswick, was proclaimed. Sept. 18. King George landed at Greenwich.

1715, April 22. Was a great eclipse of ye sun, the middle of it was about half an hour after 9 o'clock, when it was a totall eclipse and very dark for some minutes, so that people could not see to work, and severall stars were plainly seen in ye sky.

1715-16, Mar. 6. Was seen a meteor (as it was called). It was a great light in ye aire. It was seen first soon after candle-lighting, and continued great part of the night, more or ess; some said it was a sign of *drought*.

> The more of worldly wealth we do possess,
> The harder 'tis to Heaven to have access."

APPENDIX.

Local and Family Name of Coggeshall.

IN Cheshire there is a hamlet in the Bucklow Hundred named *Cogshull;* also in the Broxton Hundred the township of *Cogshall* or Coghull, sometimes spelt in the same manner as Coggeshall in Essex; likewise in the Duchy of Lancaster, but without any connection. There is also in Essex a manor named Coksales (Hoohall, Martell's) in Rivenhall, and another of the same name, otherwise Wigghepet, in Arkesden; but these were once the possessions of the Coggeshall *family*, mentioned on pages 51 and 81. Sir *Ralph* de Coggeshall held, in addition to Little Coggeshall Hall and Codham Hall the manors of North Benfleet, East Fall and South Hall, Pakelsham, &c. He had a brother named *Roger*, and left a son* *John* his heir, who held Coksales in conjunction with John Martell; lands ih Messing and Inworth, of John de Kelvedon; and Shernehall in Shalford, near which there was a free chapel in the gift of the lord of the manor. He married the sister and heir of Philip, son of Jordan de Peu.

Sir John his son was knighted by Edward the Black Prince, and was a man of note in his day. He had

---

* Perhaps his grandson; for in one place Morant (from Holman) says his son died three years before him.

free warren (2 Ed. III.) in the above-named manors, and Dodenho and Rogworth-marsh. He was one of the Commissioners for *laborers*, for Essex.* He also held Alresford, Hawkswell Hall, and Sturmere. From his younger brother descended the Coggeshalls of Hundon, Fornham, St. Genovese, and other places in Suffolk and Norfolk.

Sir John left a son, *Sir Henry*, who was buried at Coggeshall. He married Joane, daughter of William de Welle, and in her right had Great Samford: he had also the manor of East Tilbury and the gift of that living; and, in conjunction with his brother Thomas, the manor of Newhall (Chelmsford), and its appurtenances in Boreham, Springefeld, Little Badewe, Little Waltham, Bromfield, and Hatfield Peverel, in exchange for Bradeker in Shropham, and Holkham.

" King Richard II. reg. 16. granted license to Rob. Rykdon, N. Fitz-Richard, and Henry Franke, clerke, to give one messuage, 40 a. of arable, 8 of meadow, 2 of pasture, and 4s. 9d. rent, in Great Badewe and Sandon, to a certain priest, to celebrate divine service for the good estate of Tho. Coggeshale every day in this church."—*Inquis.* 16 *Ric. II. fol.* 73. [See also ante, p. 54.]

Thomas Coggeshall was sheriff, 17 Richd. II. He held Newhall, Reeshams in Little Baddow, and sold the lordship called Barentyne's Fee, in Hinckford Hundred, (21 Richd. II.) to Sir John de Bourchier. In 1422 he held the manor of Sandon of the King *in*

---

* The Sheriffs' Accounts contain several of Sir John de Coggeshall, who was sheriff of Essex for a considerable period during the reign of Edward III., among which is a subsidy of 'cloth works,' &c.

cap. of his castle at Dover, by the service of one knight's fee, and a yearly rent of 10*s.* for castle guard. He died 10 Hen. V. His son Richard died young, and his daughter Elizabeth, wife of Thomas Philip, became his heir.

Among the names of those who were of the King's Privy Council, are:—1 Hen. IV., John Coggeshall; 2 Hen. IV., Thomas Cogsale and William Cogshale; 5 Hen. IV., William Coggeshale and John Doreward (son-in-law).* Sir William Coggeshall, married Antiochia, daughter of Sir John Hawkwood (son of Sir John Hawkwood, the renowned warrior, who died at Florence) of Sible Hedingham, who, after his death, was married to Sir John Tyrrell, of East Horndon.

One likewise of this family was owner of the manor of Leadenhall Hall in London, and patron of St. Peter's, Cornhill; and some eminent citizens of this name were buried in the church of St. Nicholas, Cole Abbey, and St Margaret's, Old Fish Street. *Weever* has several inscriptions of the name.

In the time of Ed. VI., a John Coggeshall held the capital messuage near Coggeshall bridge in Halstead, (Munchensies, Collups or Elue Bridge), and there is a tablet to his daughter in Halstead Church. In 1626, John Coggeshall, one of King Charles' musicians, received a pension of £40. In 1677, Henry Coggeshall published a work, entitled, "Timber measure by a line

---

* Morant gives as 'Representatives of the County'—Sir John de Coggeshall, Ed. III., 7-10, 13, 17, 31, 32; Henry, 37, 47; Thomas, Ric. II. 11, 18, Hen. IV. 1: William, Ric. II. 15, 20, Hen. IV. 2, 3, 4, 6, 9, Hen. V. 2, 9, Hen: VI. 1.

of more ease and exactness than any other." He was the inventor of "*Coggeshall's* Sliding Rule." George Coggeshall and William Turner Coggeshall have published several works in America.

Holman's and other Collections for Essex.

A few particulars in the preceding pages are derived from an account of Coggeshall written by William Holman. He was Independent minister at Halstead, where also he was buried, and his tombstone had this inscription:—

"Near this stone lieth the body of the Rev. William Holman, who was near 30 years pastor of the Protestant Dissenters in this town; and was near 20 years in writing the Antiquities of Essex. He died Nov. 4, 1730, aged 60 years."

His death is said to have occurred in the porch of Colne Engaine Church. The materials used by him were largely collected by Thomas Jekyll, Esq., who was the first person who laid the foundation of the History of Essex; and communicated partly by Nicholas Jekyll of Castle Hedingham, grandson of the last named, and partly by the Rev. Antony Holbrook, son-in-law of the Rev. John Ouseley, who had obtained a portion of the Jekyll Collection, and made valuable additions to it. Holman visited every parish, and filled above 400 volumes with his own handwriting. He was much assisted by Samuel Dale, apothecary of Braintree, (whose patron was John Ray of Black Notley) who died in 1739 at the age of 80, and was buried at the Independent Meeting-house at Bocking, where his tombstone formerly had a latin inscription, no part of which now remains. Some of the manuscript collections of Jekyll and Holman found their way into various hands; but the most valuable portion came into the possession of the Rev. Philip Morant, and was used by him in his History.*

There still exists an agreement between Mr. Holman's son, of Sudbury, and the Rev. Nicholas Tindal, vicar of Great Waltham, dated 2nd February, 1731-2, by which the latter was to prepare Holman's papers for the press, and the profits of publication to be divided between them; but Mr. Tindal published only two numbers of the History of Essex. The papers of Morant, who was one of the witnesses to this agreement, are now in the possession of Robert Hills, Esq., of Colne Park.

Since Morant's time many have laboured in the same field, and several valuable collections are in the library of the British Museum; but there is nothing relating to Coggeshall, except in a collection of the Rev. D. T. Powell, two or three sketches, and an interesting account of a visit paid some years ago to the remains of Coggeshall Abbey. (Add. MSS. 17,460, 17,461.)

Among the *Leake* MSS. (at the end of a volume of Salmon's History of Essex) in the Museum at Colchester Castle, is a copy of a seal of the Monastery of

* See *Nichols' Literary Anecdotes*, vol. ii. p. 705; *Notes and Queries* (1855), vol. xii. pp. 362, 454.

Coggeshall, temp. Henry IV., which differs somewhat from that given on p. 63. It is round: the Virgin *standing* under a canopy with the child in her arms, (*without* the females praying and the double shield,) with an olive branch on each side and two cocks at her feet. Legend — SIGILL . COVENTUS . MONASTERII . DE . COGGESHALE.

Records of the Abbey.

When Bruce and Baliol appealed to Edward I. in support of their respective claims to the crown of Scotland, and the King desired to prove the supremacy of the English crown, he addressed circular writs to the monasteries, commanding them to search their archives for particulars relating to Scotland. From Coggeshall, "although it once possessed an historian of much diligence, only one short extract was obtained, relating to the transactions with the Confessor and the Conqueror," viz.—

"In the year of our Lord 1042 St. Edward the Confessor being King . . . . Siward was sent by command of the King to meet Macbeth the King of the Scots in Northumberland, whom the same Siward despoiled of life and kingdom, and there ordained Malcolm King. . . . ."—*Palgrave, Documents illustrating the History of Scotland,* p. 108.

The above extract does not occur in Ralph's Chronicles,[*] which are of a later period.

[*] These Chronicles have never, I believe, been printed in England, except by Mr. Dunkin. More than once it has been proposed to publish them. See Nichols' Lit. Anec. vol. i. p. 82 (1714), vol. i. 256 (1728). The *Caxton Society* has published "Additiones Monachi de Coggeshale"

Unfortunately the *Chartulary* of the Abbey is not to be found; nor can a complete list of the Abbots be obtained.* The copy of the Register mentioned in note to p. 63 contains particulars concerning Childerditch, Toleshunt, Springfield, &c.; but little can be extracted from it of any interest. There is reference in *Tanner* to an "Apographum cartarum de fundatione donationibus et privilegiis hujus Abbatiæ ex archivis Ducatus Lancastriæ: viginti schedis, penes Nic. Tekyll de Castro Hedingham in com. Essex. arm. MS.;" and from this Holman probably obtained his copy of King Stephen's Charter, &c. (For list of letters patent, &c., see Dugdale's Monasticon.)

Charter of King Stephen, p. 24.

"**Stephanus,** Rex Angliæ, Archiepiscopis Episcopis Abbatibus Comitibus Baronibus Justiciariis Vice-Comitibus et omnibus ministris et fidelibus suis Francis et Anglis totius Angliæ salutem. Sciatis quia prece et requisitione Matildæ Reginæ uxoris meæ et Eustacii filii mei dedi et concessi et in perpetuam elemosinam confirmavi Deo et Ecclesiæ beatæ Mariæ de Coggeshala et Abbati et monachis ibidem servientibus Deo manerium de Coggeshall totum cum omnibus pertinentiis suis. Quare volo et firmiter precipio quod ecclesia predicta et monachi teneant et habeant totam terram predictam bene et in pace et libere et quiete

---

at the end of Ralph Niger. The Editor refers to another Museum MS. [King's 13 A xii.] containing the whole of Ralph Coggeshale's Chronicle. Dugdale gives the date of the foundation of the Abbey as 1142 from Nero D. 2. An edition of Ralph is in preparation by the Rev. J. Stevenson.

* Symonds mentions a *Fine*.—"A 2 Ed. II. inter John de Bousser, Quer. and *William*, Abbot of the Convent of Mary of Coggeshall, Defor. de Childerditch."

et honorifice in bosco et plano et pratis et pasturis et omnibus aliis aquis et stagnis et molendinis et viis et semitis et soca et sacca et toll et team et infangtheif et omnibus aliis rebus et liberatibus et liberis consuetudinis quæ ad terram illam pertinent cum quibus ego tenui illam in manu et dominio meo, sicut aliæ ecclesiæ Angliæ melius vel liberius teneant alias elemosinas meas. Et ut hæc donatio mea et confirmatio perdurent presentis sigilli mei impressione confirmo et subscriptorum attestatione corroboro. Testibus Matilda Regina et Eustachio comite Willielmo de Ipre Willielmo de Warrenne et Ricardo et Roberto de Valenco—*apud Coggeshall.*"

King John at Coggeshall, (p. 39.)

The *Itinerary* of King John speaks of his being often at Colchester and the neighbourhood. It is probable that he paid several visits to Coggeshall Abbey, but only one is definitely mentioned. He appears to have been there on Sunday, Oct. 15, 1205: and from thence he went to Hedingham.

"The King to John the son of Hugh, &c. We command you that without delay you restore to the Abbot of Westminster the manor of Perforford, which was seized into our hands by our command on account of our palfreys being badly kept, and if anything shall have been removed thereout except what was necessary for the palfreys and their keepers, that you cause the whole to be restored to him without delay. Witness, William, Earl of Essex, *at Coggeshall,* the 16th day of October."—*Rot. Lit. Claus.* p. 55.

Among the references to Coggeshall in the *Public Records* are the following:—

" 10*th Richard I.*—Hundred of Edwinestre.

"The jurors say that in a grange of the monks of Cogeshal at Torinden two mendicants there entertained, killed a third, and it is not known who they were. Judgment, murder."—*Palgrave. Rot. Cur. Regis.* vol. 1. p. 160.

"*Amerciaments*, &c. Of Alexander of Coggeshall, half a mark because he had not any plea. Of the frankpledge of Roger de Stratford near Coggeshall, half a mark, by flight of Roger.

"*Presentments*, pleas, &c., of the Hund. of Tendring.

"A certain woman (found in the house of Leuegar) the friend of Walter de Bumestede, was delivered to Alexander of Coggeshall, and the frankpledge of Roger de Stratford, by the liberty of the monks of Coggeshall; who escaped. Judgment: Alexander, in mercy; and the frankpledge of Roger de Stratford."

"24 *Edward I.*—Taxation in the Borough of Colchester.

"Adam of Coggeshal has on the day aforesaid one quarter of barley, price 4s. 3 quar. oats, price per quar. 2s. Coreum et fortular', price 1 marc. 2 pigs, price 3s. Sum, 26s. 4d. Out of that the seventh, 3s. 9¼d.

"*John, the Vicar of Coggeshall*, has on the day aforesaid 3 quarters and a half of oats, price per quar. 2s. Sum, 7s. Out of that the seventh, 12d."—*Rot. Parl.* vol. 1, p. 228.

"Hund. de Berdestapel. Westorenden. Also the abbot of Coggeshall holds in the same vill, 50 acres, which were wont to be of the King's fee."—*Rot. Hund.* p. 137.

"Hund. de Lexeden. Holonde parva. Moreover it is presented that the abbot of Coggeshall in Coggeshall has capital jurisdiction,[*] holding view of frank-pledge without the bailiff of the lord the King, and receives the amend of assize of broken bread and beer, but it is unknown by what warranty, and from what duration of time." [p. 139.]

"Chafford. They say that the abbot of Coggeshall has with-

[*] *Furca* = Jurisdiction of punishing felons, i. e. men with hanging and women with drowning.

drawn two services [sectas] at the tourn* of the sheriff, per annum, of the tenement he holds, which formerly belonged to the lord Robert Hovel, in the vill of Chiltenditch; and two services of the tenement which formerly belonged to the lord Simon, son of Richard, in the same vill, and withdrawn from the said 2 tenements 8 wardpennies per annum, by what warranty they are ignorant." [pp. 149, 148, 156.]

"10 *Ed. III.*—John de Kelvedon and others gave to the abbot of Coggeshal three messuages and 2 tofts, in Coggeshal."—*Cal. Inquis. ad quod Damnum.*

"28 Ed. III.—Galfridus de Stocton gave to the abb. of Coggeshal one messuage, and certain lands, &c., in Coggeshal, Stisted, Fering and Pateswyk."

"34 Ed. III.—Matilda, wife of John Cachpol, gave to the abbot and convent of Coggeshal one messuage and half an acre of land, with appurtenances, in the aforesaid vill."

John Sewale, Sheriff.

John Sewale, of Coggeshall, Esquire, was sheriff of Essex and Herts, 4 Richard II. (1381).† This was the year in which the exaction of the poll-tax led to the insurrection of the peasantry (p. 55). The sheriff was a friend of Walworth, and probably took a prominent part in putting down the insurrection. An allusion to him occurs in the following year:—

"The King to the Treasurer and his Barons of the Exchequer

---

* Sheriff's court held twice a year. *Secta regalis* was a suit by which all persons were bound twice in a year to attend the sheriff's tourn, that they might be informed in things relating to the peace of the public.

† See p. 121, note. Robert Sewale of Coggeshall had in 1354 from John, Earl of Oxford, the custody of all lands in Little Yeldham: in 1374 he purchased a water-mill of the manor of Jenkins (sold to Stephen Fabian in 1404) and in 1397 the manor itself.

greeting. For that by assent of our council in our parliament at Gloucester, held in the second year of our reign, we exonerated the sheriffs of Essex and Herts for the year then last past of one hundred, and to each sheriff of the said counties of one hundred marcs per annum, for three years then next to come only—We command you that *John Sewale* of Coggeshall, the last sheriff of the said counties, be exonerated of 100 marcs in his account at the Exchequer aforesaid, for the past year, and that you cause him to have due allowance therein. Witness, the King at Westminster, the 30th day of Jan."—*Rot. Claus.* 5 *Ric. II,* m. 19. In *Rolls of Parl.* vol. iii. p. 390.

The name was retained in Coggeshall to a late period (p. 226). His arms were sable, a chevron between three gad-flies, argent.

Great numbers of the Essex men who had taken part in the above outbreak were executed. Among those who were "excepted and altogether excluded from every grace made and conceded by the King to his people," were the following persons, who were "ringleaders, abettors, procurers, and notoriously the beginners" in the late insurrections:—

"Adam Michel.
Robert Cardemaker.
John Taillour, Chaplain.
John Smith.
Henry Ive.
John Turnour, Herde, Boclerplaier, of Stistede.
John Wynterflode of Cokeshale.
Richard Coventre, Labourer.
John Poyntol.
John Adam, servant of Richard Wright of Branketre.
Gregory Skynner of Branketre."—*Ibid,* p. 111.

Chief Stewards of Coggeshall Abbey, (p. 54.)

"To all the faithful of Christ to whom this present writing shall come, *William*, by divine permission, abbot of the monastery of the blessed virgin Mary of Coggeshall, in the county of Essex, and the convent of the same place, salutation in the Saviour of all.

"Whereas lord John Sampford, late abbot of the monastery aforesaid, and the convent there, gave and granted to lord HENRY, *Earl of Essex*, the office of chief seneschal* of all and singular the manors, demesnes, lands, territories and possessions of men, and whatever else in the kingdom of England belonged to the same late abbot and convent in the right of the aforesaid monastery, to have and to hold that office to the same earl of Essex by himself or his sufficient deputy or by his sufficient deputies, to be occupied and exercised for the term of the life of the said Earl, with the dues and payments to the same office belonging and appertaining, as by a certain writing sealed with the great seal of the convent more fully appears. Know ye therefore, that we the before mentioned, now the abbot and convent of the monastery aforesaid, have given and granted, and by these presents give and grant to the illustrious lord JOHN DE VEER, earl of Oxford, high-chamberlain of England, the office aforesaid, to have, hold and occupy that office by himself or by his sufficient deputy, or by his sufficient deputies for the term of the life of the Earl of Oxford, immediately after the death of the said Earl of Essex. We also give and grant by these presents to the same Earl of Oxford, for the execution and occupation of the office aforesaid, one annuity or annual payment of *three pounds* per annum issuing from and in all our manors and lands in the county of Essex aforesaid, and all other dues, payments, proceeds and emoluments to the same office in any way belonging or appertaining."

* His office was to hold the courts, to do the abbot's business with the King, &c., for which he had certain very valuable fees and privileges in hospitality and other respects.

APPENDIX. 289

Reversion was granted after the death of John de Vere to his son and heir apparent John de Vere, and to his second son Alberic. Dat. 23rd October, 19th Henry VIII.*

Ecclesiastical Surveys.

The Pope once claimed the "first-fruits" or first year's whole profits, and the "tenths" or tenth part of the annual profits of all ecclesiastical benefits. Pope Nicholas IV. granted the tenths to Edward I. for six years, to defray the expenses of an expedition to the Holy Land; and a taxation was made for the purpose of collecting them at their full value in 1291. In this taxation (see p. 52) the rents of Abbey lands are set down thus:—

	£	s.	d.
In Berkeweye de redd.		0	0
In Alflamestion de redd.		8	6
In Northon		4	0
In Springesfeud.		0	0
In Lega Magna.	1		0
In Chelmersford.			0
In Parva Waltham.			0
In Borham			0
In Mulesham		1	0
In Esthorp			8
In Birithe Magna			0
In Messing		1	6
In Inneworth		6 13	4
In Coggishale		67 11	10

* Penes C. Gray arm. Copy among papers of Mr. Morant.

		£	s.	d.
In Markishale		1	1	11
In Ferringge		3	5	4
In Goldhangre		5	9	0
In Tholishunte Mangers		14	3	2
In Tholishunt Tregoz		3	3	4
In Bracsted Magna		0	4	0
In Colcestris		1	3	2

Taxes were afterwards regulated by the above taxation, as in p. 230, until the time of Henry VIII., when the first-fruits and tenths were transferred to the King, "for more augmentation and maintenance of the royal estate of his imperial crown and dignity of supreme head of 'the Church of England;" and a general Survey of ecclesiastical benefices was made, known as the *Liber Regis* or *Valor Ecclesiasticus*, and from this a compilation entitled *Liber Valorum*. In the Val. Eccl. proper there is no return for Coggeshall, and only a single line from the Liber Valorum giving the amount (see ante, p. 61). But among documents recently discovered at the Augmentation Office and the Chapter House was a fragment (the earlier portions being lost) of the return for the monastery of Coggeshall, which has been printed as an Appendix to the Valor:—

DIOCESE OF LONDON.—MONASTERY OF COGGESHALL.

Temporalities in the County:—

		£	s.	d.
Tillingham. Value in rents there per annum		61	10	0
Spryngfeld. Value in rents and farms there per annum		25	0	0

APPENDIX. 291

	s.	d.
Inworth. Value in farms and assize of rents there per annum	13 6	8
Canewden. Value in farms of one marsh there, with lands called Coggeshey, per annum	2 0	0
Tolleshunt Major. Value in farm of the manor there, called Tolleshunt Grange, per annum	34 13	4
Wyston. Value in farm of the manor there, called Hauyly Graunge, per annum	3 6	8

Temporalities in the city of London:—

Value in rents and farms at Towerhill there, with farm of a tenement called Spyghtes house, per annum	10 13	4
Sum of the aforesaid	£280 18	6

Thence in reprisals as follows. Per me, John Talcarne, in the absence of Thomas Argall, Deputy.

Reprisals:—

	£	s
By repayment of rent to our lady the Queen of England, for her manor of Filolhall	0 5	0
To the Abbot of Westminster, for his manor of Feryngbury	0 12	0
To John Fabyan, for lands called Smythfeld	0 8	0
To the Prior of the Church of Canterbury, for his manor of Stysted	0 2	0
To the Prior of Saint John, Jerusalem, in England, issuing out of the manor of Coggeshall	0 0	6
To John Mordaunt, for his manor of Thornedon Hall	0 1	4
To William Bowde, for his manor of Coryngham	1 3	6
To John Tirrell, knight, for his manor of Warley	0 8	0
To the Rectory of Westgilby	0 4	4
To Thomas Poyntz, for his manor of Northkyngton	0 6	8
To the lord the King, for view of court, and for pipe-silver [roll-payment]	0 1	0

	£	s.	d.
To the Bailiff of the hundred of Barstable. .	0	4	0
To the Bishop of London, for the manor of Orsett .	0	1	0
To Thomas Thressher, for the land called Crokedcrofte, issuing out of the manor of Tillingham and Childerdiche	0	0	8
To Henry, Earl of Essex, for his manor of Burchiers, issuing out of the manor of Chedyngsell in Inworthe	0	2	0
To Anthony Dany, for the manor of Tolleshunt Darcy	0	6	0
To William Sharpley, for the chantry called Kebill's chantry, issuing out of the tenement called Spightes House, per ann..	8	0	0
	£12	6	0
Paid for Pensions paid to the Dean of Stoke	0	6	8
To the Vicar of Childerdiche.	4	0	0
To the Rectory of Warley, issuing out of the manor of Tillingham	0	10	0
To the Vicar of Coggeshall, issuing out of the Rectory there	0	4	0
To Richard Pygott, for a certain Corrody,* issuing out of the said Monastery by writ of our Lord the King founded there	3	0	0
	£8	0	8
Fees of John, Earl of Oxford, and Henry, Earl of Essex, chief steward of the county . .	6	0	0
Of George Ermyn, Receiver	3	0	0
Of Thomas Mildemey, Auditor	3	0	0

* A payment due to the King, and granted by him towards the sustenance of a person residing in the abbey. "1512, 12th April.—3127, Privy seal. For Hen. Stephenson, gent. of the Chapel Royal. Corrody in the monastery of Cokkeshall, lately held by *Edward Johnes*, deceased. Westm. 23rd March, 3 Hen. VIII. *Del.* Knoll, 12th April."—*Brewer's Letters and Papers of Hen. VIII*, p. 345.

		£	s.	d.
Of Richard Duke, Under-Steward of the Court .		1	6	8
Of Richard Tanner, Bailiff			0	
Of Thomas, the Bailiff of Childerdich and Stoke			0	
Of the Bailiff of Tolleshunt			6	
		£20	13	4

Alms given and distributed to the poor for the three anniversaries for ever to be made for the souls of Hugh de Badowe, Margaret his wife, and Thomas Coggeshall, 102s., viz.—at every obit 34s. to be distributed, and for the soul of Stephen, formerly King of England, as by ordinance for them shewn £5 8 8

There remains clear . . £251. 2s. 0d.
Tenths therefrom . . . . . . £25. 2s. 2½d.

By me, John Talcarne, in the absence of Thomas Argall, Deputy.

Will of John Fabyan. (1477.)

"**In the name of God, Amen,** the vij day of Maye, the yere of our Lorde God MCCCCLXXVIJ, and the xvij yere of the reigne of Kyng Edward the iiij, JOHN FABYAN, citezein and draper of London, in his gode and hole mynde, being made and ordeigned this mv present testament nuncupatif in the presencez of Henr: Sharp, clerke, Henry Chacombe, Roberte Henley, William Nynge, drapers, John Nicholl, grocer, and Robert Spayn, scryvaner, citezeins of London, in manner and fourme hereafter folowyng, that is to witt: First, he bequathed and re-comaunded his soule to Almighty God his Creatoure and Maker, and to his blissud moder Mary the Virgin, and to all saintes, and his body to be buried in the parrish chirch of Saint Michell, in Croked Lane of London. Item, he bequathed to *Johanne his wife* in the name of her parte and pupart of all his goodes to her of righte belongyng, V^C *li* sterling. Item, he bequathed to *John his sonne,* to him to be delivered whanne he comyth to the age of xxi yeres, m^l marc sterling. Item he bequathed to *Johanne his doughter,* to her to be delivered whanne she comyth to the age of xxi yeres, or sonner whanne she is maried c c c marc sterling. Item, he bequathed to *Agnes his doughter* in lyke fourme c c c marc sterling. . .   . And if all his saide children dye before they com to the saide age, or before they be maried, thanne he willed and ordeined bi this his present testament that of parcell of the same sommes of money his saide executours shuld susteigne and fynde on honest preest to syng and pray for his soule, and for the soules of his fader and moder, and all his children and gode doers, and all xpen soules, in the parrish church of COGGESHALE, *wherein his fader lieth now buried,* in the countie of Essex, by the space of x x yeres next suying after the dethe of that childe of his of the saide children that last deceaseth. And the residue of the said sommes of money to his children as is aforesaide bequathed, he willed that it be evenly departed betwene and among the children of his *brethren, Stephen Fabyan and Robert Fabyan.* Item, he bequathed C more sterling, therewth to ordeigne, susteigne and fynde an honest preest to syng and pray for his soule and for the soules aforesaide in the foresaide parish church of *Coggeshall* by x yeres next suying after his decesse. Item, he bequathed to William Heysand his servant, for to pray for his soule, XX *li.* sterling, or elles he willed that he should have a tenement with the appurtenances in the towne of *Coggeshall* aforesaide in which — *Sterling,* widow, now dwellyth, to have to him his heires and assignes for evir more. Item, he biquathed to John Ramsey, servant of Stephen Fabyan his brother, XL *s.*

"The residue of all his goodes, catalles and dettes what soever they be after his dettes paied, the costes of his burieng doon and this his present testament in all thinges fulfilled holy, he yave and biquethed to Stephen Fabyan his brother, therewth to do, ordeigne and dispose for his soule and for the soules aforesaide in charitable dedes and other goode uses as he wold he shold doo for him in caas lyke which saide Stephyn of this his present testament he made and ordeined his executoure and his overseere he made and ordeyned Fenkyll, citizein and draper of London, and he biquethed to the same John Fenkell for his laboure, XX li. Yoven the day and yere abovesaide."

[On same day.]

"As to the disposicion and ordenaunce of all *his landes and tenementes* with all their appertenaunces that he hath or of right to him in any wise belongen in the parrish of *Coggeshall*, in the Countee of Essex. Except a tenement with the appertenaunces in which — Sterlyng widowe nowe dwellith. First he willed and ordeined that John Fabyan his sonne aftir his decesse have to him and to the heires of his body lauffully bigoten all his said landes and tenementes with all their appertenaunces. [In default, to his daughters: then to his brothers.] Yoven the day and yere abovesaide." Probate, 4th Feb., 1478.

A Stephen Fabian is mentioned as early as 1404. (See p. 57, note.) Morant says, under Stisted, "This Stephen Fabian was a cordwainer at Coggeshall, but undoubtedly a man of substance. John was the son of Stephen, and succeeded by his son, John Fabyan, Gent., whose son, Edw. Fabian, Esq. died 4th February, 1561."*

William Grouthouse, of Coggeshall, granted a mes-

* His son William sold the manor of Jenkins in 1569. One of the name is mentioned in Archd. Hall's Precedents. "1596, 14th Jan.— Master John Fabian, Rector of the Church of the Parish of *Warley Magna*. Notatur publica fama, that on Sunday, at night, the second of January last, he did, to the scandall of his calling and offence of good Christians, behave himself very dissolutely and wantonly in the parish of Kelvedon, in taking upon him to be a *lord of misrule* or Christmas lorde, &c., among certain yongelinges, &c. [Suspended.]"

suage in 1425 to Stephen, Robert and John Fabyan, John Starlyng, and others. (Harl. Charter, 51 A 9.) Robert Fabyan, the Chronicler, in his will (later than the above) speaks of *John* and Agnes Fabyan, his parents; of his four sons, John, Robert, Thomas and Anthony; of Nicholas *Sharp;* and John Fabyan, his brother. The exact relation between the above-named testator and the Chronicler is thus somewhat uncertain.

*Subsidies** (4 Chas. I.)

"THIS Extract and Certificate indented made the 19th daie of December, in the 4th yere of the raigne of our Sovereign Lord Charles, &c.—

"**Witnesseth** that Sir Thomas Wiseman and Sir Wm. Maxey, Knt., Wm. Towse, serj^t at lawe, Wm. Smith, and Robt. Sandford, Esq., Commissioners for the taxing and assessing of all persones to and for the paiment of the fourth subsidy of the five entire subsidies graunted unto his Matie in the parliament holden at Westm. in the 4th yere of his Matie's raign, of England, &c., to be levied in the said countie of Essex, and by division allotted to the hundreds of Lexden and Tendringe, and to the half-hund. of Thurstable, Winstry, and Wytham, doe certifie unto the Rt. Hon. the Ld. High Treasurer of England, the Treasurer and Barones of his highnes court of Exchequer, that we have done in all things for the taxing, assessing and collecting of the s^d 4th subsidie, as by the s^d commission and act of subsidie we are charged, and we have appointed Thomas San-

---

* A subsidy was a tax on persons in respect of their reputed estates, after the nominal rate of 4*s*. in the pound for lands, and 2*s*. 8*d*. for goods. The above subsidy was granted by the third parliament of Charles I. on his assent to the *Petition of Rights.* The King dissolved it not long afterwards, put aside his engagements, and entered on the arbitrary course which led to his ruin.

ford of Great Coxhall, in the s^d countie, gent., to be collector thereof for the aforesaid division, and the same to collect and gather, and thereof to make payment to his Maties use, into his highnes s^d court of Exchequer, at or before the 10th day of January next ensuing. In witness, &c.

* * * *

Coggeshall Magna *Lands.*

	s.	s.
Marg. Purkas, widd.	xxij	iiij
Ambrose Till	xl	viij
William Clark, sen.	xx	iiij
Edw. Beckwith	xl	viij
Nicholas Noreby	xx	iiij
Widdow Damatt	xx	iiij
Clement Gymblett	xx	iiij
W. Raven	xx	iiij
John Starling	xx	iiij

Goods.

	£	s.	d.
John Foakes	iij	viij	
William Tanner	iiij		viij
Thomas Coxe	iij	viij	
Widdoe Buxtone and Thomas Buxtone	iij	viij	
William Clarke, jun.	iij	viij	
Thomas Nicholles, sennior	iiij	x	viij
John London	iij	viij	
John Gray	iij	viij	
Thomas Guyon, sen^r.	iij	viij	
Nicholas Gladwyn	iij	viij	
John Thedam	iij	viij	
Robart Fuller	iiij		viij
John Sparhawke	iiij		viij
Thomas Guyon, jun^r.		xiij	iiij
William Enowe	iiij		viij
William Digby	iiij		viij
Symond Richold	iij	viij	
Samuell Finch	iij	viij	
Thomas Somersone	iij	viij	

		£		s.	d.
Henry Johnson	... ...	iij	...	viij	
Nathaniell Sparhawke	... ...	iii		viii	
William Gladwyn	... ...	iiii			viii
Robert Shortland	... ...	iii		viii	
Thomas Samphford, gent.		v	...	xiii	iiii
Thomas Aylett	... ...	vii	...	xviii	viii
Thomas Shortlandes	... ...	vii	...	xviii	viii
Nicholas Richallde	... ...	vi		xvi	
Henry Innowe	... ...	vi		xvi	
Robert Crane	... ...	vi		xvi	
George Cockrell	... ...	iii		viii	
Sum	... ...	xvii	...	xviii	viii

Plus in proxim' shedis de Chapple parish.

Manor of Coggeshall, &c.

In the calendars of the proceedings in the Chancery of the *Duchy of Lancaster* are numerous allusions to suits concerning lands at Coggeshall; in which the following occur:—

"10 Eliz. (Pltf.) Thomas Peycock, claiming under Wm. Tusser, lessee of Philip and Mary. (Deft.) Rob. Gyrdon, lessee of the parsonage, and Richard Warner and Hen. Lilley his tenants—of Darye House and barns, lands and tenements, with kyne or cattle with the straw of the tithe corn for their fodder. Coggeshall Rectory and parsonage."

"20 Eliz. Hy. Warner—Thos. Peycocke, Jno. Mott and Jno. Coleman—mansion house called Coggeshall Grange, &c., part of Coggeshall Monastery."

"22.—Duchy Surveyor—Richard Abberforde, farmer of the woods—destruction of timber—Coggeshall Manor."

"23.—Rob. Coleman, the lessee of the Duchy—Thomas Tyll as representative of Thos. Peacocke—Robin's land—Coggeshall Manor."

In the *Manor Rentals* also of a later period are a few entries worth recording:—

"1695. I. Potter paid 3s. 1d. for house late *Lady Ventris'*—abutting on the highway leading to the church—little Constantine's—[widow of Sir Peyton Ventris of Ipswich, who died April 1691: connected with a family named *Thorn*, some of the members of which lived at Coggeshall.]

"Matthew Guyon for Correction House, Market End, and gravel, 5s."

"*Robert Gouge*, for 3 tenements in occupation of himself in Stoneham Street."*

[Later date.] "Lands next Colchester road belonging to Lady Cotton, occupied by John Wright."

Markshall.

The manor and parish of Markshall is so closely connected with Coggeshall, as to demand a brief notice. It contains 804 acres, and has only 8 houses and 42 inhabitants.

Its name appears in Domesday Book:—

"Lands of HUGO DE MONTFORT. Hund. de Lexendan. NIGEL holds of HUGO MERCHESHALA which Godmund held in the time of King Edward for one manor, half a hide and xxx acres. Always ii villeins. Then vii borderers, lately viii. Always v slaves. Then ii carucates in demesne, lately one and half. Always one carucate and half belonging to the men. Wood for 200 hogs. 1 acre of meadow. Then ii beasts, lately x. Then xxx sheep, lately lxxx. Always xii hogs. Lately iii stocks of bees. Then worth xls., lately lx."

---

* "Mr. Tho. Brown, who lived at Hovells, bought for Mr. Gouge, a parson, the farm in Stock Street now in the possession of Robert Cornell."—*Old MS.*

Hugo de Montfort, son of Hugh with the Beard, held 16 lordships in this county, which he left to his son and grandson, the latter of whom died in a pilgrimage to Jerusalem. Markshall was afterwards possessed by *Henry of Essex*, who was standard-bearer to Henry II., and in cowardice flung down the standard in a war with the Welsh, for which he was charged with treason by Robert de Montfort, and vanquished in solemn trial of battle: he became a monk in the Abbey of Reading, and his lands were seized by the King.

The following account is given of the contest:—

" And it came to pass while Robert de Montfort thundered on him manfully with hard and frequent strokes, and a valiant beginning promised the fruit of victory, Henry of Essex rather giving way, glanced round on all sides; and lo, at the rim of the horizon, on the confines of the river and land, he discerned the glorious king and martyr in shining armour, and as if hovering in the air, looking towards him with severe countenance, nodding his head with a mien and motion of austere anger. At St. Edmund's hand there stood also another knight, Gilbert de Cereville, whose armour was not so splendid, whose stature was less gigantic, casting vengeful looks at him. This he seeing with his eyes, remembered that old crime brings new shame. And now wholly desperate and changing reason into violence, he took the part of one blindly attacking, not skilfully defending. Who while he struck fiercely was more fiercely struck; and so in short fell down vanquished and it was thought slain. As he lay there for dead, his kinsmen magnates of England, besought the king that the monks of *Reading* might have leave to bury him. However he proved not to be dead, but got well again among them; and now with recovered health, assuming the Regular Habit, he strove to wipe out the stain of his former life, to cleanse the long week of his dissolute history by at least a purifying sabbath, and cultivate the studies of Virtue into fruits of eternal Felicity."*

Markshall was then granted by the King in fee to the family of the before-named Nigel, which had long held it as tenants under the chief lords, and taken their name from the place. In this family it continued nearly 500 years, and John Markshall sold it in 1561 to John Cole, whose son sold it to Edward Deraugh, by whose son it was sold to Robert Honywood, Esq. (p. 143). He left behind him several sons, among whom were Robert of Charing, and Thomas of Markshall, both knighted. Sir *Robert* married Frances, daughter of Sir Henry Vane the elder, sided with the Parliament, and was one of the Council of State in 1659: his son succeeded to Markshall, on the death of John Lamotte Honywood, Esq. A fine series of family portraits exists in the mansion.

The Church, dedicated to *St. Margaret*, is a rectory appendant to the manor. In the west window of the old Church was the portrait of an armed knight, kneeling; on his surcoat the arms of Markeshall;† in a label from his mouth, "*Erasme int'cede pro me.*"

The rector first named in *Newcourt* was Walter de Gosefeld, pr. 4 non. Feb. 1330: patron, Alicia la Hunt. The patronage was in the *Markshall* family for several centuries. On 23rd June, 1553, Thomas Francis, clerk, (ante, p. 118) was admitted on the death of Robert

---

* "Chronica Jocelini de Brakelonda." See Carlyle's Past and Present, p. 155.

† Argent, a bend dexter cotised sable, charged with a nebule, or unde of the last; in the sinister quarter, an etoile sable, pierced argent.

ap Rice, at the presentation of John Spooner, Gent. by an advowson granted for that turn by John Markshall. On the death of Francis, James Caterall, cl. 29th November, 1591, was presented by Ed. Deraugh, and on his death, Robert Lewis, John Greene, and William Daniell, successively.* Sir Thomas Honywood presented Gamaliel Carr, 20th April, 1642; also Chr. Chirch; William Clopton, M.A. (1653); and Rob. Constable, cl., 2nd Feb., 1662 (on the death of Chirch). Lady Honywood presented George Barnesley, cl., 2nd September, 1670, and John Livermore, A.M. 21st November, 1674. Henry Wastell, M.A., 14th January, 1718, was presented on Livermore's death: afterwards William Sisson, M.A., 23rd September, 1723, by whom a mural tablet was erected in the Church, with an elegant latin inscription to the memory of Catherine

---

* "Mr. Wm. Daniel, preacher of the word of God, and minister of this parish, March 25, 1642."—*Markshall Register of Burials, &c.* This Register was transcribed from an older one, from 1585 to 1737, by William Sisson, rector. It contains the following entries:—

"1641, Nov. 6.—Buried *Mr. Jno. Crakenthorpe*, preacher of the word.

"1658-4, Feb. 17.—Baptized. Margaret, daughter of William Clopton, rector of this parish, and Elizabeth his wife. [W. Clopton, M.A., of Eman. Coll., Camb., ejected from *Rettenden*. He was half-brother to Philologus Sacheverell of Eastwood. 'They were both ill at the same time, but Mr. Clopton died first. Mr. S. overhearing some in his room talking of it, said, *then there is a good man gone to heaven;* and laying himself down again, died immediately, and they were both buried in the same grave.']

"1658, Oct. 20.—Married. Sir *Robert* Cotton, knight and baronet, [probably a mistake in transcription. Sir Robert died 1631, leaving his library to his only son Sir Thomas, from whom it descended to his son Sir John Cotton], and Elizabeth Honywood of this parish.

"1705, Nov. 18.—Married. Mr. John Harrison, vicar of Burnham, and Mrs. Mary Cox of Coggeshall. 1743, April 3.—Buried. Sir R. Sandford, baronet, of Howgill Castle in Westmoreland, and brother to Mrs. Honywood, wife to Robert Honywood, Esq., of Markshall." For these extracts I am indebted to the courtesy of the Rev. P. J. Honywood, B.A., the present rector of Markshall.

his wife, who died 7th December, 1741. There are also tablets to John Shepherd, A.M., rector, who died 6th April, 1773; and to John Cott, B.D., rector, who died Oct. 13, 1781.

The present Church was built by Gen. Honywood (p. 158, note) in 1763, and contains other tablets and inscriptions:—

PHILIP HONYWOOD, of Markshall, Esq., Gen. of his Majesty's Forces, Governor of the town and citadel of Kingston-upon-Hull, Col. of the 3rd Regiment of Dragoon Guards. He married the eldest daughter of John Wastell, Esq., of Anderby in the county of York, by whom he had one son, who lies buried near him in the chancel of this Church. He served conscientiously 31 years in parliament for the borough of Appleby, and quitted when no longer able to discharge his duty there. To the world his character as a soldier was known: to his friends his private virtues. He lived an honest man, and died universally regretted Feb. 20, 1785, aged 75 years.

In this Churchyard are deposited the remains of FILMER HONYWOOD, Esq., who died June 2, 1809, aged 64 years. He succeeded to the estates in Essex and Kent by the will of Gen. Honywood in 1785. . .

Sacred to the memory of WILLIAM HONYWOOD, Esq.; of Markshall in this county, and of Libton in Kent . . . who died Feb. 9, 1818, in the 59th year of his age.

A mural tablet to the memory of the late W. P. Honywood, Esq. (son of W. P. Honywood, d. 1831) who died 20th February, 1859, aged 35 years, has been erected by his widow, Mrs. Honywood, in whose possession this estate continues.

ERRATA.

Page 25, note, for "Tekyll" read "Jekyll"
,, 58, for "38 H. VIII." read "28 H. VIII."
,, 77, at bottom of page omit "M.P."
,, 81, 82, for "Hereford" read "Hertford"
,, 100, insert "Christ and" (the Apostles)
,, 124, for "cumburendo" read "comburendo"
,, 143, omit "O." (R. H. O.) copied from Morant
,, 144, read "pientissimæ;" also "1587-8"
,, 178, for "gentlemen" read "gentlewomen"

The gold coin mentioned on p. 13 is really of Honorius. Several other coins have lately been found.